T0330143

Building National and Regional Innovation Systems

Building National and Regional Innovation Systems

Institutions for Economic Development

Jorge Niosi

Professor, Department of Management and Technology, Université du Québec à Montreal, Canada and Research Chair on the Management of Technology, Canada

Edward Elgar
Cheltenham, UK • Northampton, MA, USA

Published by
Edward Elgar Publishing Limited
The Lypiatts
15 Lansdown Road
Cheltenham
Glos GL50 2JA
UK

Edward Elgar Publishing, Inc.
William Pratt House
9 Dewey Court
Northampton
Massachusetts 01060
USA

A catalogue record for this book
is available from the British Library

Library of Congress Control Number: 2009941409

Mixed Sources
Product group from well-managed
forests and other controlled sources
www.fsc.org Cert no. SA-COC-1565
© 1996 Forest Stewardship Council

ISBN 978 1 84980 254 3 (cased)

Printed and bound by MPG Books Group, UK

Contents

v

Preface

This book was written out of my own discomfort about what is going on in developing countries. The 1990s were the period of the Washington consensus. All that developing countries had to do was to open their economies, adopt free trade, reduce the size of the state, and let the markets take care of their problems. We know now that this consensus was built on false premises. Latin America, Russia and other developing countries are heading leftward. Nationalizations are again on the rise in several countries, such as Argentina, Bolivia, Ecuador, Russia and Venezuela. But the key issues, how to promote science, technology and innovation for development and catching up are not discussed, or if they are discussed they are not taken seriously. This is particularly worrisome because most resource-rich developing countries have experienced an affluent decade due to the high prices of oil, minerals and foodstuffs. It is also probable that the resource bonanza will come back in the near future. The question is: is it possible to draw most developing countries out of the vicious circle of poverty and inequality on the basis of industrial and technology policies? I am not advocating planned economies, but just the type of innovation policies and other institutions that Canada, Japan, the European Union, and the United States have implemented for decades, and South Korea, Singapore or Taiwan (province of China), and now mainland China, are so successfully applying. These policies, that include building human capital and related institutions for science, technology and innovation in order to absorb foreign science and technology, and later to grow their own, have also the advantage of promoting equity and reducing social unrest. These policies include applying incentives for industrial research and development (R&D). They represent the only way towards economic growth.

Even if a country decides to skip economic planning, its R&D environment (Industrial and Science, technology and innovation (STI) policy, domestic companies and academic research) may attract foreign direct investment (FDI), particularly high-quality one. The adoption of a whole set of STI policies (or the building of a national system of innovation) is required for economic development to occur. Those policies have at the same time to promote the supply of human capital, and the demand for it, particularly in the private sector. Keynes has rejected Say's law (that supply creates its own demand) in its explanation of economic slumps.

Say's law is equally useless to explain the production and absorption of human capital during the process of economic development. The creation of skilled labour and its introduction in the economy is nothing spontaneous, but instead the result of deliberated efforts by the national authorities. Information asymmetries and bounded rational agents will play havoc with any self-organized process of market building for human capital in less developed countries. In sum, building the absorptive capacity of nations, in both technology and institutions, requires active policy making from national and often regional governments. I believe thus that only an evolutionary framework, and the abandonment of most of what is called neoclassical economics, with its rational expectations, complete market hypothesis, instantaneous adjustments, and similar currents, can allow us to understand economic development. Also, evolutionary concepts bring a plethora of new methodologies and model tools to the social sciences, such as system dynamics, Markov chains and game theory.

This book is based on the work of many previous social scientists; most of them may conveniently be regrouped under the label of evolutionary and institutional economics. Among the deceased social scientists, I am particularly indebted towards Moises Abramovitz, Alfred Chandler, John M. Keynes, Sanjaya Lall, Gunnar Myrdal, Raul Prebisch, Joseph Schumpeter, Herbert Simon, Thorstein Veblen and Raymond Vernon. Among the modern ones, I must acknowledge W. Brian Arthur, Paul A. David, Christopher Freeman, Paul Krugman, Bengt-A. Lundvall, Franco Malerba, Richard R. Nelson, Erik Reinert, Nathan Rosenberg and Joe Stiglitz. In management, I am indebted to the ideas of Wesley M. Cohen, David A. Levinthal, David C. Mowery, and John Sterman.

Acronyms

BERD	business expenditures on R&D
BRIC	Brazil, China, India and Russia
CMA	census metropolitan area (Canada)
CNRS	Conseil National de la Recherche Scientifique (France)
DBF	dedicated biotechnology firms
DTI	Department of Trade and Industry (DTI)
EAP	Economically active population
EU	European Union
FDI	foreign direct investment
FTE	Full-time equivalent
GDP	gross domestic product
GERD	gross expenditure on R&D
HERD	higher-education expenditure on R&D
ICT	information and communication technology
ILC	industry life cycle
IMF	International Monetary Fund
INTA	Instituto Nacional de Tecnología Agropecuaria (Argentina)
INTI	Instituto Nacional de Tecnología Industrial (Argentina)
IRAP	Industrial Research Assistance Program (Canada)
ISI	import-substitution industrialization
MITI	Ministry of International Trade and Industry (Japan)
MNC	multinational corporation
NAFTA	North American Free Trade Agreement
NRC	National Research Council
NSF	National Science Foundation (USA)
NSI	national system of innovation
OECD	Organization for Economic Cooperation and Development
PLF	product life cycle
PPP	purchasing parity power
PRO	public research organization
R&D	research and development
RSI	regional system of innovation
SBIR	Small Business Innovation Research program (USA and Japan)
SI	system of innovation

SIS	sectoral innovation system
SME	small and medium-sized enterprise
S&T	science and technology
STI	science, technology, and innovation
STPF	Science and Technology Promotion Fund (Finland)
TEDCO	Technology Development Corporation (USA)
TFP	total factor productivity
UNIDO	United Nations Industrial Development Organization
USPTO	United States Patent and Trademark Office

1. Convergence, catching up, institutions, and growth

Convergence of productivity among countries in the international economy has been one of the most standard predictions of neoclassical theory. Rich nations would experience declining growth rates as the return on investment in these nations would be lower; conversely, poor countries would attract capital because they offer higher rates of return. During the last twenty years, the issue of convergence and divergence in the international economy has produced a large and multifarious literature (Islam, 2003). Scholars study convergence and divergence in terms of both productivity and income. Evidence shows that global convergence across economies does not occur, but some 'club convergence' does, particularly among members of the Organization for Economic Cooperation and Development (OECD). Yet most nations do not converge towards the rich countries' OECD club, most conspicuously poor ones in Africa, Asia, and Latin America. The gulf between the richest and the poorest countries has increased, even if some major South East Asian nations – first South Korea, then China, and more recently India – have started to converge towards the rich club. Twentieth-century history tended more to periods of catching up for groups of nations, such as western Europe, South East Asia or Latin America, some of which later fell behind. In the last hundred years, few countries (mainly Japan and main nations in western Europe) have consistently caught up with the leader (first the United Kingdom, then the United States), and these are today's major OECD countries. Behind the hypothesis of convergence, one finds in neoclassical theory the usual assumptions of easily diffused knowledge moving freely across regions, countries, and organizations, and rational agents, which effortlessly capture the signals of the environment. The neoclassical policy prescriptions are based on the idea that if prices are right markets will provide adequate solutions. More recently the debate has moved from 'putting the prices' right to crafting appropriately the crucial institutions – intellectual property, democracy, and constitutional rights.

Evolutionary economics looks at development very differently. In its perspective, countries need to build absorptive capacity before they can master foreign science and technology. This capacity depends on learning, which occurs in institutions relating to science, technology, and innovation (STI). Economic development and catching up are collective learning processes that take place only within an adequate framework of policy for STI and related organizations. STI policies should aim to increase the absorptive capacity of private firms, government bureaucracies, institutions of higher education, and public laboratories. In this approach, there is no guarantee that convergence and economic development will flow from public and private investments in science, human capital, technology, or innovation. Neither are there 'one-size-fits-all' formulae for all countries, large and small, at any level of economic development, to apply. Each society needs to find its own combination of sectors, technologies, institutions, and human capital that will suit its situation when it begins to catch up. Economic development, in this perspective, involves the addition of new and more advanced sectors, as a country moves from dependence on natural resources towards creation and expansion of manufacturing and high-technology services (Nelson, 2005b; Saviotti and Pyka, 2004; Reinert, 2007).

In neoclassical theories, convergence would occur because 'backward' countries experience faster economic growth than more advanced countries. Such societies would catch up and converge by adopting more advanced technology. They could pick and choose from a large backlog of technologies (Knack, 1996). Because such a catching-up process seems often to be patchy, we should investigate why many nations seem unable to draw effectively from that backlog and adopt advanced technology.

In a thorough empirical analysis of the conditions relating to catching up, Fagerberg and Godinho (2003) and Fagerberg and Srholec (2005) have shown that knowledge appears to be the variable that best explains how some nations began catching up in the 1990s. Knowledge is a composite variable including human capital (particularly tertiary education in science and engineering), cumulative expenditures on research and development (R&D) as a percentage of gross domestic product (GDP), patents and articles per capita, and openness to existing outside knowledge. The authors relate their findings to Cohen and Levinthal (1990) and their concept of the firm's absorptive capacity and extend it to the nation: by speeding up formation of human capital and undertaking more R&D, countries (like firms) increase their absorptive capacity. Knowledge so defined is close to Abramovitz's idea of 'social capability.' The second most useful variable explaining catching up was 'governance,' which consists of policies, governments, and institutions and is close to Richard Nelson's concept of 'social technologies.'

Fagerberg and his co-authors conclude that 'innovation' (technological as well as organizational) is the key to catching up. Technological innovation in most cases consisted in the creation of new and industrial sectors that became the most dynamic in the world (chemicals and electrical equipment in Germany, information technology and automobiles in Japan and South Korea, and telecommunication equipment in Canada, Finland, and Sweden). Organizational innovation was both macro-economic (in most countries, new planning roles for government departments and new public research laboratories and universities) and micro-economic (e.g., investment banks in France, Germany, and Switzerland, just-in-time systems and kaizen, keiretzu, and saibatzu in Japan, and chaebols in South Korea).

Social technologies (organizations, policies, and institutions) have thus become the most promising factors for explaining divergence and convergence, catching up and falling behind (Abramovitz, 1986; Lazonick, 1994; North, 1990; Nelson, 2003). By social capabilities, Abramovitz understands human capital (years of education), but he also points to institutions – political, commercial, and financial – even though he admits that we have only qualitative indicators of such capabilities. Other authors have emphasized social organizations, particularly managerial forms of organization (Lazonick, 1994). In this view, Britain declined because of its early adoption of and continuous adherence to personal capitalism, which was less efficient than U.S. managerial capitalism. Douglass North (1990), a notable proponent of institutional explanations of growth, includes public policies and formal rules of the game, as well as informal culture, beliefs, and religion. North and his followers have stressed such institutional variables as rules to enforce contracts and property rights, acceptance of rent-seeking activities, and political stability.

Our view adopts the institutional explanation of catching up but focuses on institutions that foster adoption, creation, and diffusion of new science and technology. This approach is the theory of the system-of-innovation school (see Chapter 2), and more generally within the evolutionary perspective in economics. This chapter presents (section 1) a more detailed review of convergence literatures, then introduces one of the first evolutionary accounts of growth, the one based on product and industry life cycles (section 2), then brings the evolutionary perspective on growth (section 3), linking convergence and economic growth, and pinpointing the evolutionary and institutional perspectives on economic development, and (section 4) proposes that technology policies are key for convergence and growth and suggests a new typology of the key institutions (section 5).

1.1 ECONOMIC GROWTH, EXOGENOUS AND ENDOGENOUS

Since the pioneering work of Robert Solow (1956), most scholars have agreed that technical progress is the main determinant of economic growth. However, capital accumulation still provides the principal explanation for the rate of growth, with technical progress not the main target of research but only a residual category – total factor productivity (TFP) – comprising everything that the additions of capital and labour do not explain. Second, in Solow's model the economy converges towards a steady state, because of the diminishing returns to capital investment. Finally, economic growth is only productivity growth; no novel product enters the economy, and the models simply assume process innovation. Solow does not include institutions or study technical change as something different from capital accumulation. His theory is exogenous because non-economic factors explain both the saving rate and technical progress. He studied technical change indirectly via the size of the residual.

In the 1980s, new growth theory relaxed some of the assumptions of the Solow models, allowing for R&D, R&D subsidies, education, and externalities to increase the rate of growth, over and above what it saw as the main determinant, the rate of savings (Romer, 1986, 1990). This new series of 'endogenous growth models' represents an advance over the first group of exogenous models, yet suffers from similar, fatal difficulties: they draw the same conclusion of convergence – namely, increasingly similar levels of productivity and income among nations. Also, Romer's work, like most endogenous growth models, preserves perfect competition. However, this family of endogenous models was closer to reality than the early exogenous models, as growth could continue indefinitely, even if countries converged. Knowledge – now a determinant of economic growth – could expand without limits and generate increasing returns. It could thus overcome the diminishing returns of capital and produce endless growth, because it produced everlasting spillovers while maintaining perfect competition. Knowledge led to greater returns in the economy, without altering competition.

Convergence among nations is accordingly a main corollary of the neoclassical view of economic growth, whether exogenous or endogenous. This group of models retains perfectly or quasi-perfectly rational economic agents, which display maximizing behaviour, can obtain free and easily accessible information, and experience perfect (or quasi-perfect) competition and a unique equilibrium. Theories usually take institutions and organizations for granted and omit them from the analysis. They recommend public policy for speeding convergence that harnesses market virtues: eliminating all barriers to the free mobility of capital. The standard economic recipe for convergence and economic development in developing countries is simple: governments need only open the economy and let international capital flow in and invest, bringing technical progress with it. According to Aghion and Howitt (2005), in this view 'thrift and capital accumulation are the keys, not novelty and innovation.'

In the 1990s, however, developing countries that based policy on the standard, neoclassical textbook found more problems than solutions, as Joe Stiglitz (2002) has shown. Also, the fast-growing South East Asian countries ignored the neoclassical corollary of opening their economies unilaterally to foreign direct investment (FDI). On the contrary, they protected their financial markets, regulated FDI to ensure that it brought technology, and nurtured local firms and new industries through R&D incentives, new government laboratories in selected industries, and export promotion (Kim and Nelson, 2000). In the 1990s, application of orthodox ideas increased international divergence, as countries that followed neoclassical prescriptions faced slow growth, experienced outright recession, or defaulted on their debts.

Economic historians (such as Abramovitz, Landes, and Reinert) empirically refuted neoclassical growth theory and its corollary of convergence. They showed forcefully that countries, far from converging, differed radically in their trajectories of growth, with some advancing towards the technological frontier, most continuously falling behind, and some catching up during some periods and falling back in others (Abramovitz, 1986, 1989; Landes, 1969, 1999; Reinert, 2007). Each country, as evolutionary economics predicted, seemed to follow its own path.

1.2 PRODUCT AND INDUSTRY LIFE CYCLE AND ECONOMIC GROWTH

The product life cycle (PLC) and the industry life cycle (ILC) are popular models in administrative science. Deriving from the path-breaking work of Raymond Vernon (1966), they outline a four-phase life for products and industries. In the first phase, the new product emerges from a major technical novelty, and unspecialized machinery manufactures it; production volume is low, product design is still fuzzy, and market uncertainty is high. Yet imitators appear; entry to the market is easy, and companies compete, trying to impose their own design. The second phase involves rapid growth in sales and a shakeout, which lessens the number of competitors. Product innovation increases and then declines, as a dominant design emerges, while process innovation increases. In the third phase, that of maturity, innovation in both product and process dwindles, returns soar because of incumbents' R&D and marketing power, and economic concentration increases in the innovator country. Process technology standardizes, and technological diversity disappears. Firms know their markets, and larger companies dominate the new industry. Prices fall. In the fourth and final phase – decline – innovation wanes and products become commodities.

Product and process innovation and its diffusion shape international production and trade. New products usually receive their launch in the richest countries, most often the United States. Innovating companies first sell them in their domestic market, then export them to countries with similar or slightly lower revenue levels (e.g., Canada, Japan, and western Europe), and then invest directly in these second-cohort countries to block new competitors. However, imitators emerge there and often invest in less-affluent countries (e.g., in Latin America or South East Asia), where over time a new cohort of imitators also appears, and the geography of production changes, as manufacturing gravitates towards low-wage nations. A new group of multinational corporations appears, with bases in developing countries (Wells Jr., 1983).

PLC-ILC theories provide a fairly accurate description of industrial evolution in several sectors such as automobiles or basic metals. They also help explain delocalization of manufacturing towards low-wages countries such as Japan first, then South Korea, Brazil, China, and India. Rich nations stop producing such goods as textiles, plastic products, and bicycles and develop new products by harnessing their innovative advantages.

Yet there are telling criticisms of this family of models. First, even if the United States remains the most affluent nation, convergence among the richest countries has somewhat levelled innovation in the world, and new products often start out in 'second row' Canada, Japan, and western Europe. FDI is not as unidirectional as it was in the 1960s, and it flows fairly evenly back and forth between the United States and second-row countries.

Second, several industries do not readily fit into the models' four-phase cycle. For instance, PLC does not predict the new wave of product and process innovation that Asian car producers launched in the 1960s (Klepper, 1997). In telecommunication equipment, three waves – not one – mark the industry's history: first, Alexander Graham Bell's invention and patenting of the telephone in 1876 and the emergence of manual switch panels; second, AT&T's introduction of the electric machine switch in 1919; and third, AT&T's launch of the electronic switch in 1970. In this industry, there are few signs of decline in product or process innovation, and new designs continually challenge existing ones. In the meantime, international communication moved from submarine cables to fibre optics to satellites, systems changed from wire to wireless, and semiconductors and optical equipment multiplied.

Third, the PLC-ILC models do not make room for the supporting infrastructure of institutions, organizations, and policies. It assumes that technological change determines market structure, without government or other visible intervention. Supporting institutions, organizations, and policies were less important to theorists at the model's inception, when they were looking at low-skill, labour-intensive, traditional industries, such as textiles and leather products. To attract these industries, developing countries needed to provide only cheap labour, free trade (or at least free trade zones), and suitable taxation rules. However, the supporting infrastructure increases in importance when delocalization affects medium- and high-technology sectors. To enter the computer industry, Japan began in 1957, through the Ministry of International Trade and Industry (MITI), to develop a sophisticated set of technology policies and supporting organizations (Anchordoguy, 1989). Similarly, the Brazilian state has supported development of the country's aerospace industry – the only competitive such industry in the developing world (Cassiolato et al, 2002).

The omission of supporting elements in the PLC-ILC models becomes also more problematic over time, as more industries and countries accelerate R&D and the proportion of workers with tertiary degrees increases. Delocalization becomes less and less a pure market process and comes to depend more on the institutional framework of the host nations.

As well, the traditional theories ignore the increasingly restrictive conditions of sustainable growth, assuming that growth can continue forever without damaging the environment, that new resources will replace those that disappear, and that it is easy to repair environmental damage.

1.3 ECONOMIC GROWTH, EVOLUTIONARY

The evolutionary explanation of economic growth derives from different premises. Unlike in neoclassical models, agents are not perfectly rational but only bounded rational, as Herbert Simon proposed. As such they can arrive only at reasonable, satisfying solutions, not optimal ones. Economies are systems with not one but many possible equilibrium states, and systems move from one state to another, so that economic change is at least as important as equilibrium. Under such conditions, countries would not tend to converge towards any particular state. Adapting biological models, evolutionary economics presents the world as one in perpetual change, with no end of evolution in sight. Innovators and entrepreneurs regularly destroy equilibrium and launch new periods of economic change.

Unlike in PLC-ILC models, growth determinants include supporting institutions, organizations, and policies, or what Richard Nelson has called social technologies.

Any evolutionary analysis of economic growth starts with the contribution of Joseph Schumpeter (Rosenberg, 2000). His work emphasizes the evolutionary character of capitalism, the central role of innovation in growth, and the endogeneity of technology as corporations conduct R&D as a routine activity (Schumpeter, 1934, 1950). Also, Schumpeter saw the capitalist market economy as a system where cascades of technical novelties regularly interrupted equilibrium. Economic growth occurs through creative destruction: new products and processes destroy previous technologies, usually increasing the scale of production and demanding ever-expanding markets. Technological innovation is thus at the centre of economic growth, and technical progress is different – and should be a separate focus of study – from capital accumulation. Innovation is not exogenous to the economic system, but a specific activity of entrepreneurs.

Once scholars begin to study technical progress on its own merit and consider it a regular activity of firms and other organizations, then the nature of the innovative firm becomes important and the trajectory of technical change requires closer attention. Nelson and Winter (1982) advance some of the key concepts about innovative activities or the lack thereof. Routines (or 'practices,' as we call them in management science) constitute the core of the firm's STI organization. Firms adopt not optimizing routines, but satisfying ones, that fulfill not the condition of perfect rationality but the less stringent requirements of bounded rationality. Firms' capabilities are some of those routines – for example, for hiring personnel, for searching for new technologies or markets, and for producing and selling better goods and services. Firms, but also other organizations (government departments, universities, and public laboratories), decide strategies with less-than-perfect information, and then markets decide, with equally bounded rationality, which technologies, strategies, business models, and final products and services they adopt, and they discard the others. Technological and organizational innovation is thus a dynamic process and does not necessarily achieve any equilibrium in the firm or in the macro-economy. There may be one or several equilibria or none, particularly in periods of rapid technical change. Equilibrium tends to be short-lived; change – particularly technical change – destroys any type of static equilibrium.

Many major consequences flow from such an evolutionary framework that assumes bounded rationality. If knowledge is not free and costless but in fact requires substantial investments to acquire, then firms and other economic agents will tend to search close to the knowledge they already possess – 'path dependence in knowledge acquisition.' This dependence includes a 'selection bias,' as people and firms select only some of the available data, and an 'interpretation bias,' as they recombine pieces of knowledge on the basis of the knowledge they already have (Noteboom, 1997). But path dependence encompasses more than knowledge. It occurs both at the micro-and the macro- levels. It affects technological progress and the economic organization of firms, markets, and countries.

David (2000) defines path dependence as a dynamic property of allocation processes that are limited by their past states. In path-dependent processes, initial conditions matter. Individual economic agents, companies, markets, and entire national economies are the product in part of their origins. Many conditions help to rigidify the original path. Original knowledge, sunken costs, initial technical choices, contracts, laws, and regulations are often difficult to abandon, necessitating writing off of previous investments in equipment, learning, or training. If path dependence is widespread, then evolutionary economics becomes a historical science.

Organizations, even entire regional or national economies, often show characteristics unsuitable to their environments. In addition, path dependence brings economics closer to biology: living organisms also exhibit traits that reflect their biological past, many of which are not suitable for their current environments. Firms and national or regional economies reveal their origins through specific technical choices, organizational forms, and routines. Some of them, as Dorothy Leonard (1996) observes, may be core capabilities in a specific environment and then become core rigidities in a subsequent one, without firms or nations being easily able to dispose of them. Organizations, as well as regions and countries, may lock themselves into inferior technologies, routines, or other institutions either by lack of knowledge or by the weight of past investments. The result can be economic and organizational inertia.

Yet change occurs, and evolutionary economics postulates that innovative technical change, bringing new processes and products, is at the juncture point of many path-breaking new trajectories. Scientific research is as well a disrupter of technological trajectories (Rosenberg, 1994). For instance, new biotechnology is altering the conduct of pharmaceutical research. But technical change emerging from R&D departments of innovative firms can produce similar results, as the history of AT&T and IBM repeatedly show (Chandler, 2001).

Economic development is thus not simply the result of technical change's making existing industries and firms more productive. It is often qualitative change – the creation of new products and industries through technological innovation that is radical enough, or lucky enough, to differentiate itself from similar products and start a new technical trajectory

(Saviotti and Pyka, 2004). This view explicitly differentiates itself from endogenous-growth approaches such as those of Romer, which postulate but do not explain increasing variety, and Aghion and Howitt, who find creative destruction but no increase in variety. Saviotti and Pyka thus expand Nelson and Winter's (1982) theory of economic change.

However, nurturing new economic sectors in developing countries is not easy. First, intellectual property rights exist to protect the incumbents from new entrants. In most electronic industries, as well as in pharmaceuticals, newcomers will face a barrage of claims from existing producers. Second, new industries require new skills that the local population does not possess. Institutional training will be essential. Third, innovation needs money. Existing financial institutions will require either a new regulatory environment to allow them to take on risk investment or backing from government. Fourth, incumbents already serve existing markets. New entrants must either look for new markets (e.g., new countries, new segments of consumers) or fight with incumbents for a share of current markets. Fifth and finally, retraining, the search for new markets, improvement of financial institutions or creation of new ones, and development of new products must take place quickly.

Evolutionary Economics Represents Economies as Complex Adaptive Systems

Gunnar Myrdal (1957) advances the idea of economic underdevelopment as a dynamic system, feeding back on itself: poverty produces bad health and creates obstacles to education, and illiteracy in turn reduces income and markets, which increases poverty. Under these conditions, some economic activity will emerge, but only that which employs low-skilled, low-income workers. Economic underdevelopment, like chronic unemployment and poverty, is thus not a temporary malfunctioning of otherwise-perfect markets, but the normal functioning of markets trapped in low-equilibrium situations. In the last twenty years, the idea of economies as complex systems has gained ground, and such a theoretical framework can help explain economic development (Anderson et al, 1988; Arthur, 1994; Arthur et al, 1997; Axelrod and Cohen, 2000; Barkley Rosser, 2003; Beinhocker, 2006; Sterman, 2000). What are the properties of such systems? Definitions range from the simplest to more demanding: 'A system is complex when there are strong interactions among its elements, so that current events heavily influence the probabilities of many kinds of events' (Axelrod and Cohen, 2000: 7). Arthur et al (1997: 3–4) offer a more sophisticated definition, outlining several characteristics:

- dispersed interaction of heterogeneous agents acting in parallel;
- no global controller, no single agent, able to exploit all the opportunities in the economy;
- cross-cutting hierarchical organization, with units at several levels: individuals, organizations, industries, regions, nations;
- continual adaptation: behaviour and strategies adjusting to experience;
- perpetual novelty: niches emerging from new markets, new technologies, and new institutions;
- out-of-equilibrium dynamics, with the economy operating far from any optimum or global equilibrium, improvements always possible and regular.

The micro-foundations of the complexity approach in economics exclude rational expectations and perfect knowledge. Agents live in a world that changes continuously and is difficult to interpret. Also, rules and institutions (some explicit, some implicit) frame the way agents interact with each other. Finally, the system is difficult to decompose; it has emergent properties, and simple cause-and-effect relationships are not sufficient to explain it.

1.4 TECHNOLOGY POLICIES AND OTHER INSTITUTIONS FOR CONVERGENCE AND GROWTH

When one moves from the micro- to the macro-economy, organizations, routines, and policy become central issues. Policy implications of neoclassical models of growth include more than removing barriers to free trade and liberalizing markets. New concepts are necessary, including market failures and externalities. Market failures are circumstances 'where the private pursuit of private interest does not lead to an efficient use of society's resources or a fair distribution of society's goods' (Weimer and Vining, 1992: 30). There are many types of market failures, but the most useful in explaining STI policies are failures of financial markets. Innovation is difficult to monitor, subject to adverse selection, long-term, risky, and uncertain. Under such conditions, financiers fund them inadequately.

Kenneth Arrow (1962) portrays technical knowledge as non-rival (two or more agents can use it at the same time) and partially appropriable (agents can sometimes prevent others from using it by secrecy or legal techniques such as patents). But because knowledge always leaks out from the original inventor, the agent who has invested in it never can recover the entire investment; thus the problem of externalities. Externalities are effects of one agent's activity that other agents bear (or take advantage of) without using the market mechanism. Externalities by definition operate outside the market mechanism. Knowledge most often produces positive externalities, and technical knowledge promotes adoption of new technologies across the economy. Externalities (or spillovers) are a particular type of market failure, and the only one that all brands of economics and management recognize. Economic agents, left to themselves, will tend to invest little in knowledge, because they cannot recover all the benefits. Thus science and technology policy will usually subsidize production of scientific activities and R&D that benefits many agents, including consumers as well as other producers. In these neoclassical models, new knowledge diffuses freely and instantaneously without any transaction cost. Governments will also promote investment in technical knowledge by means of a legal system that delays diffusion or use of the new knowledge and allows the inventor to collect more returns on the invention; thus all developed countries have legislation on trade secrets, patents, copyrights, trademarks, and industrial designs.

Such technology policies are 'horizontal': they do not discriminate among producers, industrial sectors, or geographical regions. 'Vertical' policies promote specific sectors, such as aerospace, biotechnology, and computers. R&D subsidies that promote a particular industry are also vertical. Alternatively, governments can produce new knowledge in specialized public laboratories (e.g., agricultural and industrial research institutes) and diffuse that information free of charge or below cost to producers in a particular industry. Governments may also subsidize scientific activities in higher education in targeted fields, such as bio-pharmaceuticals, which may later benefit local industrial producers.

Market failure, as an economic concept, does not lack critics. First, it supposes that free markets are basically efficient and that such failures are few. Government policy thus could take care of (to prevent) those failures. But if their numbers are without limit, and they are difficult to identify, why should governments care for some of these failures and not for other ones. For instance, rich countries have had mass poverty and depressed economic regions for decades despite public policy to address them. Why do governments not eliminate these market failures? Second, as Romer suggests, some of the most conspicuous market failures – technological externalities – may have positive characteristics; for instance, externalities allow diffusion of knowledge, and the way that governments deal with them is in itself a major issue. Patents, for example, which societies use to reduce such market failures, appear to hinder development, and many industrializing countries do not allow patents on computer software, pharmaceutical products, or living animals. Many experts (such as Richard Nelson) see these patents as a hindrance to widespread health or an obstacle to development of certain types of knowledge. Third, in many cases, private arrangements between producers have eliminated market failures without government intervention; co-operation among innovators may be more widespread than proponents of market failure imagine. Fourth, government activity in some STI areas may result not from market failures, but from public values, such as the improvement of universal health care in Japan, western Europe, and Canada and defence in such countries as France, the United Kingdom, and the United States. Fifth, in technology, governments provide not only funds, but also guidance of the entire system, including a portfolio of large technical projects (Nelson, 1983). Sixth, governments are also prone to failures, which they may find as hard to deal with as the market failures they sought to correct or avoid (Cowen, 1988; Nelson, 2005). Ultimately, as Coase has underlined, we can learn little from the study of theoretically optimal systems, and market failure is a concept that derives from the supposed best-possible operation of free markets (Zerbe and McCurdy, 1999). Evolutionary economics, like evolutionary biology, prefers to examine what happens in the real world, instead of modelling imaginary situations.

The evolutionary approach proposes fairly different policy implications and rationales for government intervention than those deriving from perfect market theoretical landscapes. Why do governments implement science and technology policy? Teubal (1998), among others, suggests adding the concept of system failure to evolutionary economics. Authors (including Nelson, and Teubal) argue that what most often fails is not simply one market under particular adverse conditions (e.g., the market for technical knowledge), but the whole institutional system that frames the market or the industry. A particular sector may not grow because of the society's lack of academic programs to form human capital, as well as public laboratories to conduct advanced research, venture-capital policies, and the like. Technology policy thus requires not simply punctual intervention by the state to solve one or a few market deficiencies, but a whole set of institutions, ranging from regulations to policy incentives, as well as provision of specialized human capital, that structure such a market. When this infrastructure for science and technology does not exist, or is inefficient, the system cannot provide adequate goods and services in science and technology. Similarly, the obstacles that some countries face to providing universal health care consist of more than a market failure, and what they need is a set of institutions, incentives, and regulations.[1]

The concept of system failure is preferable to market failure for several reasons, and it may be better to abandon altogether the notion of market failure. First, for markets to behave in a socially desirable way most frequently requires a set of institutions. Second, institutions frame markets, as both the new institutional economics deriving from the work of Coase and Williamson, and evolutionary economics, have shown. Markets and institutions are both constituents of the same systems and deserve joint study. Third, as North (1993) argues, in a world of perfect information and rational agents, institutions are not necessary; but if humans possess limited capacity to process information, then institutions and organizations reduce uncertainty, although we cannot take for granted their efficiency, or that of markets. In sum, if market failure grounds neoclassical analysis of public policy, system failure underlies the evolutionary and institutional approach to technology policy. The difference between the two concepts (market versus system failures) is the notion, from this second approach, that markets are not perfect and that system failure carries the idea that we should study failures within the appropriate institutional and organizational structures.

In the evolutionary approach, public policy may break national or regional inefficient path dependencies. How does it break the hold of inferior technologies or industries? How does it promote variety and emergence of new sectors? If unilateral free trade is not the policy formula, what can we deduce from evolutionary economics? Sanjaya Lall writes, 'industrial success depends essentially on how enterprises manage the process of mastering, adapting and improving upon existing technologies' (Lall, 2004: 11). According to him, the process is often difficult because firms in developing countries do not have full information about technical options or about how to build the necessary capabilities; firms learn as they incorporate technology, but they would probably be risk averse in relation to new and difficult technologies, long learning periods, and major externalities (which incidentally are those of the new science-based industries). Because learning processes are specific to each industry and technology, governments have to tailor incentives for each case. Lall proposes promotion of competition and increasing technical, scientific, and engineering skills in order to reduce firms' and national learning costs as key policy elements for an evolutionary policy. In addition, he recommends that governments subsidize or create organizations and institutions relating to technical change, such as higher education, research institutes, venture-capital industries, and mechanisms to disseminate technical and export information. Lall (2004) insists that there is no one universal South East Asian model and that each country adopted its own policy mix. The most interventionist governments, those of South Korea and Taiwan (province of China), offered very different sets of incentives. Also, as government policy is prone to government failure, the rapid rise of these countries reveals inefficient interventions and new departures. Protection of infant industries, Lall argues, is ineffective if domestic firms do not have to compete in world markets and if public officials do not consider factor markets (e.g., skilled personnel, financial investments, machinery, infrastructure, and support institutions). Protection by itself does not assure any type of learning process in the protected industry, as decades of protectionism in Latin America since 1945 have shown clearly.

Evolutionary technology policy should jointly support capital investment and technological change (Lipsey, 2002). At the basis of such a policy, Lipsey sees several key facts. First, innovative activities are endogenous to the economic system because firms must regularly introduce new products and processes in order to survive. Second, uncertainty, not just risk, pervades decisions about R&D and innovation; economic agents know the results of such investments only after the fact. Trial and error are part of any technical choice by private firms. Third, therefore agents do not maximize: if firms in the same industry look for different solutions they do so because they do not know the correct answer in advance. Variety is thus another major consequence of bounded rationality. Fourth, asymmetric knowledge is not a hindrance to the performance of a market, but rather is often the source of profits and technological breakthroughs and hence the source of economic growth: some agents know technologies and related opportunities that others do not, and they create new products or processes that create destruction (and profits) to the innovators. Fifth, externalities may represent market failures[2] but also lead to economic growth, as knowledge leaks out of the original innovator and creates benefits for consumers and competitors. Finally, perfect competition may not be desirable in markets: almost all modern inventions have come either from monopolistic and oligopolistic markets or from universities and government or non-profit laboratories. On the basis of such theoretical premises, Lipsey arrives at the same policy implications that Lall reached on the basis of South East Asia's rapid catching up: there are no ready-made, one-size-fits-all policy sets for technological change or human capital. Each country must devise its own policies on the basis of its specific endowment of natural resources, human capital, internal market, and government capabilities. One of the goals of this book, however, is to try to discover major regularities in the implementation of such policies.

The systems perspective requires a systems approach to inefficiency and failure. If, as I argue in later chapters, economies are complex adaptive systems, then it is appropriate to study markets in the context of the institutions and policy incentives that create, nurture, and legitimize them, and market failure often results from failure of those institutions and incentives, and hence of the system. But such systemic failure can also arise because of inefficiencies in firms or support organizations. Contrary to neoclassical theory, bounded rational economic agents do not run perfectly efficient firms and other organizations, but only x-efficient ones with several degrees of adaptation to their environments.

Also, public policy is less about applying one optimal policy to adjust markets than about creating resources to produce new goods and services, creating new sectors, and developing new markets. This evolutionary perspective requires a delicate balance between catching up in existing sectors and competing for entry into new sectors, which have not yet stabilized. Theorists have proposed two distinctive approaches. In one, new sectors represent windows of opportunity for developing countries, entering as soon as the scientific and technological frontier reveals new opportunities; in this view, the best way to harness such openings is by creating independent national R&D capabilities (Perez and Soete, 1988). In the other, Lee and Lim (2001) reject this independent way of learning and catching up. They discover three ways of catching up: creating paths, skipping paths, and following paths. In addition, they find that South Korean firms tended to learn through collaboration with multinational corporations rather than by acting on their own. Entry into new sectors resulted not from domestic creation of new knowledge, but more often from 'following the path.' The economists also note few exclusively public capabilities participating but most often public–private collaboration. Also, entry barriers depend on the appropriability of technology – the way that a society produces and diffuses it. Textile technology may be easier to appropriate, master, and modify than automobile technology, and both are more appropriable than aerospace technology. Biotechnology and nanotechnology, even if they are new technologies and should represent windows of opportunity, seem to be out of reach except for the largest and more affluent developing countries, because of their complexity, their fast-moving scientific frontier, and the need for major public and private investments, which require long periods to pay back (Niosi and Reid, 2007).

Evolutionary economics and its sector approach to economic development illuminate the processes of catching up and growth: most developed countries have specialized technologically on a few sectors, and the smaller their domestic economy, the more they have done so (Archibugi and Pianta, 1992). Thus, except in very large nations, such as China and the United States, governments need to choose a few sectors, in order to avoid scattering investments too widely. Thus some of a catching-up country's crucial initial decisions in technology policy involve the number, sequence, and nature of the sectors it plans to expand. In doing so it needs to take into account human capital, technological capabilities and other domestic resources, and possible external sources of technology. It will have to create economic institutions and resources to nurture such sectors. Once again, as both theoretical considerations and South East Asian experience show, each country needs to develop its own set of priorities and policies, and no one-size-fits-all approach would work. Yet, as the following chapters explain, there are constant patterns in the sequence of public policy that appear in all developed countries.

1.5 INSTITUTIONS, ORGANIZATIONS, AND POLICIES

In this book, I discuss four types of institutions – customs, organizations, routines, and policies. Institutions exist and evolve in the context of bounded rationality: they exist to be deposits and fountains of knowledge. Under perfect rationality they are unnecessary, because rational actors always guess right what other actors will do. Or institutions are simply the result of 'stability that can arise from mutually understood preferences and optimizing behaviour' (Crawford and Ostrom, 1995). But, if their knowledge is limited, and the environment is uncertain, then institutions and organizations help to reduce such limitations: the knowledge that a large group possesses is necessarily more extensive than that of an individual; organizations and institutions create routines that reduce uncertainty and risk and thereby diminish the chance of intra- and inter-organizational conflict (Loasby, 1999; Nelson and Winter, 1982).

(a) Customs are rules of the game that shape human interaction; they are informal practices, internalized norms, even if they oppose rational behaviour (North, 1990). Similarly, Hodgson defines them as 'the commonly held patterns of behaviour and habits of thought, of a routine and durable nature, that are associated with people interacting in groups or larger collectives' (Hodgson, 1993: 253). These institutions help frame human behaviour and cognition and reduce uncertainty. Culture and policies, whether socially optimal or not, influence them (Nelson and Sampat, 2001). Such institutions may change when new technologies require new rules of the game, in which case we speak of 'co-evolution' of technology and organization; but sometimes institutions may remain static for long periods, and institutional inertia may prevail because of the vested interests or the uncertainty surrounding the outcomes of any type of institutional change (Valderrama-Ferrando, 2006). Economic historian Timur Kuran (1997, 2004), for instance, suggests that communalism – systematic discouragement of individual entrepreneurship and innovation – as well as the Islamic law of inheritance, hindered economic development in Muslim countries. In other words, institutions may be neither optimal nor reflective of any kind of optimality. They are more often the result of political power and pressure from various groups and the outcome of the relationship of different political forces (Nelson, 1995).

(b) Organizations (e.g., firms, universities, public laboratories, and departments) are social groups that involve a definite set of authority relations and act on the basis of some common activity, interest, or purpose. They are social units that people construct deliberately to pursue specific goals (Aldrich, 1999). An organization possesses a formal set of rules, usually has a limited membership, and is often hierarchical, with a well-defined division of labour. Organizations often change under the stimulus of new technology and environmental disruption, but they may suffer from inertia, or resistance to change, because of age, uncertainty, routine, size, or conflict (Kelly and Amburgey, 1991). The British automobile, cotton, and shipbuilding industries suffered from inertia since the nineteenth century and only imperfectly and slowly adopted modern bureaucratic methods of administration; several factors were at work: inefficient decision-making procedures in industrial associations, uncertainty about the results of the new routines, and adversarial relationships between labour and management (Lorenz, 1994).

Firms are specific types of organizations, producing goods and services. They exist not to reduce transaction costs, as Coase and Williamson suggest, but to earn rents and reduce uncertainty, a premise that is consistent with economic agents' bounded rationality and myopic behaviour. This book presents firms as bundles not of contracts but of strategies and routines, some of which contain their competencies or capabilities, their specific ways to solve the problems of producing and selling goods and services in the marketplace. Firms differ because of initial conditions, strategies and routines, environments, and resources. This heterogeneity is visible also in any other type of organization (universities, government departments, or public laboratories). On the basis of different initial conditions, organizations evolve under the dual pressure of environmental change – including external technological change – and internal capabilities – including in-house R&D and other innovative activities (Carroll, 1994; Nelson, 1994b; Williams, 1994).

(c) Routines are a specific subset of institutions, those that rule the games within organizations. They consist of repetitive patterns of action (Cohen et al, 1996). Routines allow organizational learning, adaptation, and production, as well as enrolment of new organizational members. Organizational competencies, but also organizational rigidities, are based on routines. Members must comply with routines. Routines also change slowly in organizations, as they carry enormous inertia. Routines are the smallest building blocks of organizations.

(d) Public policy, whether socially optimal or not, is a course of action that a public authority chooses to address a problem. Public policy takes expression in a body of law, regulations, decisions, and actions. The study of public policy is a new and expanding field. In an evolutionary framework, policy is a response to system failures (Smith, 1991; Galli and Teubal, 1997; OECD, 1999b). How do policies change? Evolutionary approaches suggest two transformation patterns: long periods of slow, incremental policy change, and short periods of rapid change ('saltation') (Sabatier, 1999). Yet public policies, like organizations and institutions, are neither optimal nor tending towards optimality or equilibrium. On the contrary, they may experience long periods of policy inertia and implementation of inefficient policy regulations. In addition, the evolutionary approach looks at policy not in terms of its goals of moving the economic system back to an optimal equilibrium, but rather in terms of potential learning and innovation in the public and private sectors, enhancing technology diffusion, and introducing socially responsible routines in public and private organizations. In other words, policy is a process in which policy makers experiment through trial and error and economic agents undertake an interactive process of learning and change.

Economies are social systems and as such contain many types of organizations, institutions, and policy-making organizations. This book portrays social systems as complex economic systems, which exhibit all the characteristics that I mention above, such as heterogeneous agents with adaptive behaviour, perpetual novelty, and cross cutting relationships. In such systems, the elements are multitudinous types of organizations and institutions, including both private firms and policy-making organizations implementing policies to direct the system, and they may vary greatly in their effectiveness and success.

To Conclude

Convergence and catching up are discontinuous events that occur only in countries that emphasize absorption, creation, and diffusion of knowledge, through human capital, new public organizations, and policies; that foster new types of private-sector organizations; and that give incentives to public and private R&D. Empirical evidence reveals no single, homogeneous path for catching up, yet there are patterns, all of which point to domestic nurturing of technological and organizational innovation. There are several dozen countries that have 'caught up' (western Europe with the United Kingdom in the nineteenth and twentieth centuries) and many more that have 'fallen behind.' The former states have built domestic capabilities for absorbing existing knowledge, while preparing to produce new knowledge as they advanced towards the knowledge frontier.

In this book, macro-economic systems do not display optimal states or converge to them. They are complex systems that just evolve, with no end in sight, following specific development laws, and often display inertia, like stasis in ecosystems within the natural world. Many types of organizations compose these economic systems, including firms, government departments, universities, and public laboratories. Institutions and policies structure relations among these units. The rules guiding these interactions include policy incentives that governments implement; others are rules of the game, institutions that derive from traditional social customs and norms.

The nature of complex systems flows from their foundation by bounded rational agents, who include entrepreneurs, inventors, and policy-makers. Bounded rationality (limited knowledge and computation capabilities) explains the emergence of variety in firms' strategies, technologies, and policy-making. It also helps us to understand why institutions and organizations exist: they are basically devices to reduce uncertainty. Bounded rationality also explains why learning is so central in complex thinking.

People construct complex economic systems on the basis of empirical data and induction, not deduce them from pure theory. Therefore complex systems approaches are close to economic history and empirical analysis. Also, complex evolutionary thinking can easily accommodate environmental restrictions and limitations of resources.[3] It can also accommodate models in which institutions, organizations, and policies for innovation and technology play a central role in economic development. And, unlike the exogenous approach, it portrays institutional and organizational innovation as endogenous to economic systems. Evolutionary economics is thus now a major tradition that breaks from the constraints of orthodox analysis; as such it competes, along with other approaches, with the theory of property rights, game theory, the French theory of economic regulation, and neo-Marxian theories of the state (Ruttan, 2001: 121).

Many economic systems have trapped themselves in inferior, low-efficiency situations of economic equilibrium. The goal of institutional economics is to discover the sets of institutions, organizations, and policies that have helped (or may in the future help) them to break the vicious dynamics of underdevelopment. Economic growth is neither an automatic result of the operation of free markets nor the outcome of policy-making by omniscient governments. It is also not the product of endogenous market processes, but more often occurs through interaction of private- and public-sector organizations, which institutions constrict. Yet governments play a key role in the system, because only they can dictate or frame some of the relationships among the component organizations, possess enough resources to create missing organizations in the system, and can direct the whole or part of the system towards creation of new sectors.

This book thus puts institutions (customs, organizations, routines, and policies) at the core of economic systems and studies their evolution or their inertia through time. Quoting Clark and Juma (1987: 165), it characterizes the economic system as one of 'complex evolutionary interrelationships, taking place over long time periods, strongly influenced by events in the science/technology system and involving complicated informal networks which operate in an interactive fashion to a considerable degree independent of economic markets.'

Among these institutions, industrial organizations and policies, as well as science, technology, and innovation organizations and policies, are key. We now turn to these policies and related organizations.

NOTES

1. Teubal recommends redefining market failure as the particular difficulties of an enterprise in restructuring, even in the presence of the necessary institutions and incentives. However, administrative science concentrates on firms' difficulties in adjusting to markets, and, if we are following Simon seriously, no firm is perfectly efficient.
2. Lipsey and Carlaw propose to keep the concept of market failure, but to redefine it: 'Whereas in neoclassical theory the market fails when it does not achieve the unique optimal equilibrium, it fails in the structuralist-evolutionary theory when it does not lead to some desirable and attainable state' (Lipsey and Carlaw, 1998).
3. Jay Forrester, one of the founders of system dynamics, wrote a major book on limits to growth due to resource limitation (Forrester, 1971).

2. Systems of innovation and economic development

The idea that institutions, organizations, and policies are endogenous to the economic system, and thus can help explain economic development as well as economic stagnation, is not new. It appears in the new institutional economics, game theory, systems dynamics, and economic and business history, to name a few currents (Aoki, 2007; Chandler, 1962, 1977; Williamson, 1985). Evolutionary and institutional economics adopted it, from Veblen in the late nineteenth century to such theorists as March and Simon (1993), Nelson and Winter (1982), Hodgson (1993, 1999), Lazonick (1994), Nelson (2005a), and Witt (1993). Within this perspective, the systems-of-innovation approach appeared in the late 1980s and unfolded into a major current. This chapter describes three levels of systems of innovation – national, regional, and sectoral – and traces the history of government intervention in business from industrial policy to technology policy.

2.1 SYSTEMS OF INNOVATION: NATIONAL, REGIONAL, AND SECTORAL

National Systems

In the late 1980s, Christopher Freeman (1987, 1988), Bengt-Ake Lundvall (1988, 1992), and Richard Nelson (1988, 1993) launched the concept of national systems of innovation. They were including in it the central institutions of technology – mores, organizations, policies, and routines – in the economies of advanced industrial nations. Their definitions were not identical, and other definitions emerged later, as we see in Box 2.1.

All these definitions designate institutions as endogenous elements of the system, look at institutions within nation-states, and link the system to the economic and technological performance of the private sector and the entire economy. Nelson (1993), Niosi (2000b, 2002), and others emphasize the formal institutions that constitute the heart of the innovation system – namely, research universities, public laboratories, R&D-active firms, a small set of government departments, and the training system, particularly

BOX 2.1   NATIONAL SYSTEMS OF INNOVATION
DEFINED

'the network of institutions in the public and private sectors whose activities and interactions initiate, import, modify and diffuse new technologies' (Freeman, 1987: 1)

'The narrow definition would include organizations and institutions involved in searching and exploring – such as R&D departments, technological institutes and universities. The broad definition which follows from the theoretical perspective presented above includes all parts and aspects of the economic structure and the institutional set up affecting learning as well as searching and exploring – the production system, the marketing system, and the system of finance present themselves as sub-systems where learning takes place.' (Lundvall, 1992: 12)

'the set of institutions whose interaction determine the innovative performance of national firms' (Nelson and Rosenberg, 1994: 4)

'A national system of innovation is the system of interacting private and public firms (either large or small), universities and government agencies aiming at the production of science and technology within national borders. Interaction among these units may be technical, commercial, legal, social, and financial, inasmuch as the goal of the interaction is the development, protection, financing or regulation of new science and technology.' (Niosi, Bellon, Saviotti, and Crow, 1993: 212)

tertiary education and research. Freeman (1987, 1995) includes the main elements of organizational innovation (macro- and micro-routines) that characterize national systems, as we saw in Chapter 1. This definition usefully focuses on a more manageable group – the core set – of innovative organizations and renders their numbers fairly small: several thousand firms in each OECD country.

Lundvall (1992) proposes a broader approach, centring on interaction between producers and users. As McKelvey (1991) emphasizes, his own definition stresses links among all firms, not only among those active in R&D. This approach may be ideal for micro-innovation and the national surveys in Canada and western Europe that study it. Such research finds most firms innovative, whether or not they conduct R&D. Yet producer–user interactions and innovation regimes may differ widely within the same country. The even broader approach of Edquist (1997), where innovation may be cultural and social, is still less precise for quantifying social and cultural innovations, ranging from religious beliefs to public attitudes towards science, which no doubt affect innovation but are distinct from technological and organizational innovation.

In this book, I use the narrower concept, which is more tractable and economical, even if one should rather model broad sets of all innovative firms' interactions with all their customers. It may be preferable to focus on the core R&D organizations and the central relations among them, as they appear in Nelson (1993), Niosi et al. (1993), and most research papers and public documents on national innovation systems. These core relationships consist of financial, personal, technological, and regulatory flows, inasmuch as they affect production, diffusion, and adoption of new science and technology. This narrower approach also makes it possible to focus the analysis on science, technology, and innovation organizations and to public policy and related organizational routines, including the system's regulatory and incentive elements, which affect core organizations much more than they do marginal ones. As well, most empirical analysis must employ the narrower perspective, as most countries publish national data only on R&D-active organizations.

The concept of national systems of innovation (NSIs) has gained wide acceptance from international organizations (e.g., OECD, 1997a, 1999a), national governments (Finland, 2003), and scholars (Aboites and Cimoli, 2002; Alcorta and Peres, 1998; Amable et al., 1997; Chung, 2002; Correa, 1998; Freeman, 1995; Liu and White, 2001; Motohashi and Yun, 2007; Niosi, 2000a). Much of this vast literature describes the main R&D-intensive sectors and firms, publication and patenting, venture capital, and geographical localization of innovative activity. It is probably the best place to start our analysis of innovation systems and can teach us a great deal.

Some 20–25 industrial OECD countries[1] display fairly dense and complex NSIs, most of them with thousands of R&D-active firms, dozens of research universities and government laboratories, well-established systems of incentives for companies to conduct R&D, and inducements for universities and public institutes to perform research and transfer their results to industry and society. These economies differ in size, technological specialization, the role of civilian versus military R&D, and the institutional and organizational structure within their NSI. Yet in all of them gross expenditure on R&D (GERD) constitutes more than 1 per cent of GDP, and in most of them it keeps growing in absolute, and sometimes relative, terms. Their innovation systems differ substantially and tend to reflect the size of their economies, their natural resource base, and their proportion of civilian and military research (Nelson, 1993).

Members of this group present notable internal differences. Some seem to be pulling ahead, in both innovation and revenue; the United States is clearly regaining its position as technological leader, as well as richest nation in the world. Others are falling behind, such as France and Italy. And still others are catching up, such as South Korea.

Can we distinguish families of models among these countries? Over twenty years ago, Ergas (1987) distinguished between 'mission-oriented countries' – a category that included the United States, the United Kingdom, and France – and 'diffusion-oriented countries' – including Germany, Switzerland, and Sweden. In mission-oriented nations, 'big science was deployed to meet big problems.' This type of country centralizes decision-making in technology policy, and the problems related especially to expenditures on R&D (ibid, p. 53). Diffusion-oriented states possessed much more decentralized systems and stressed education more than large technology programs. This early categorization of national systems would now include Israel in the first group, and all the other advanced countries in the second group. According to Ergas, smaller 'mission-oriented' nations, such as France and the United Kingdom, suffered from resource constraints and the tendency to form 'clubs' of private-sector suppliers and government officers, whereby administrative procedures rather than commercial efficiency lead public decision-making. Nelson (1993) does not clearly decide whether defence R&D hinders or aids civilian technology. Similarly, Peled (2001) suggests the need for an empirical evaluation of the economic effects of defence-related R&D in Israel.

Amable et al. (1997) propose another system of classification – 'market' (especially the Anglo-Saxon countries – the United States, the United Kingdom, Canada, Australia, and New Zealand), socialdemocratic (the Nordic countries), continental Western European (notably France, Germany, Italy, and Spain), and meso-corporatist (Japan and South Korea). A very engaging feature of this classification, which the author did not contemplate, is the geographical and the ethnic proximity of the countries, which may flow from the institutional imitation that occurred at the origins of the innovation systems. Japan inspired South Korea in the 1960s, France has inspired Latin Europe since Napoleonic times and (West) Germany since the Second World War, and Sweden was after 1945 a model for the Nordic countries, which in turn learned from nineteenth-century Germany. If this is the case, this pattern suggests how countries create NSIs: international diffusion of knowledge may occur not only in science, technology, and innovation (STI), but also in organizations that nurture creation and adoption of science, technology and innovation.

A second group of some 15–20 countries tries to catch up with the OECD. It includes above all China and India, which have grown quickly in the last decades and have rapidly increased innovation; several nations of central and eastern Europe, particularly new members of the European Union (mainly the Czech Republic, Slovakia, Slovenia, Hungary, Poland, and Romania); the largest Latin American country (Brazil); and other Asian states such as Iran and Turkey. Within Africa, only South Africa fits in this set. Some southern European countries, such as Greece and Portugal, also belong to this group. In these 20–25 countries, many organizations and other institutions of the NSI are already in place, particularly within the public sector. However, the private sector most often performs comparatively little R&D. In Brazil and South Africa, business expenditure on R&D is a small percentage of GERD. Conversely, in China and Taiwan, business expenditures on R&D (BERD) is large and rapidly growing, and constitutes a major part of GERD; a new model of catching up may be emerging there, with foreign direct investment (FDI) playing a major role and a more decentralized industrial structure and policy-making than Japan or South Korea.

A third group of countries has created only bits and pieces of an NSI. This set includes most of Africa, Asia, and Latin America – over 100 countries. Some may have substantial natural resources – for example, oil-producing nations in the Middle East and most of Latin America – but no NSI to replace these non-renewable resources in the long run (Correa, 1998; Cimoli, 2000).

The concept of NSI has provoked several criticisms. For some authors, increasing internationalization of scientific and technological activities through expatriate R&D, international technology alliances and scientific collaboration, and emergence of European Union STI programs reduces the scope for NSIs. However, empirical research shows that the growing significance of expatriate R&D, international technology transfer, international flows of scientific and technical personnel, and cross-border alliances has not reduced national technological specialization (Archibugi and Pianta, 1992). Also, regional and supranational institutions have not reduced the role of the nation-state (Niosi and Bellon, 1994). In addition, NSIs' characteristics explain the performance of large multinational firms (Pavitt and Patel, 1999). These large enterprises still conduct more than half of their R&D at home, specifically their more strategic and core innovative activities. And there is not that much convergence in countries' institutional, technological, and economic performances. Productivity is converging among several OECD countries, and more so within families, as in Amable et al.'s (1997) models; productivity is sometimes also converging within regions. In economic and technological performance, the market-model Anglo-Saxon countries look increasingly similar, as do the Nordic countries, Japan and South Korea, and western European nations. Yet internationalization seems to lead nations to further technological specialization, not to reduce it. And most STI policies are national in scope.

Other scholars have found that key systems of innovation are more sub-national (regional, metropolitan) than national (de la Mothe and Paquet, 1998; Metcalfe, 1995). They emphasize the 'sticky' character of knowledge, the importance of face-to-face communication in its transmission, and the fact that in any advanced country large metropolitan areas concentrate much or most of the R&D, innovation, and invention. These responses resemble those about internationalization: regional concentration of innovative activity does not contradict the facts that most STI policies are national and that most regional innovation is the product of national firms and other national institutions such as public laboratories and universities. As we see below in this chapter, regional innovation is a major element of the system-of-innovation approach (Howells, 1999; Niosi and Bellon, 1994).

Regional Systems

In the 1990s, the NSI approach received a shot in the arm when such experts as Cooke (1992, 1996), Cooke et al. (1997), de la Mothe and Paquet (1998), and Howells (1999) added a regional component. Later, dozens of authors did likewise (Asheim and Gertler, 2005; Niosi, 2005; Sigurdson, 2004) and public policy-makers and international organizations placed the concept in their agenda (UK DTI, 1999a and 1999b; OECD, 2007a and 2007b; UNIDO, 2003).

The basic ideas resembled those of the NSI: innovation is not an isolated act but the result of interactive and systemic learning, organizations and institutions are the best encapsulation of knowledge, and policy-makers heavily influence such bodies. These elements form systems, whether at the national or the regional level. Understanding such elements and links is essential for regional economic development to occur, as it is for national economic growth. Some elements are new: the literature on the regional system of innovation (RSI) highlighted the importance of tacit knowledge and hence geographical proximity, and borrowed learning by interacting from the NSI literature. Also, increasing returns benefit regions: if for any reason a region starts early in a new industry, it may attract entrepreneurs, scientists, engineers, and other relevant factors from other regions; new

---

BOX 2.2   REGIONAL INNOVATION SYSTEMS DEFINED

'Regions which possess the full panoply of innovation organizations set in an institutional milieu, where systemic linkage and interactive communication among the innovation actors is normal, approach the designation of regional innovation systems.' (Cooke and Morgan, 1998: 71)

'The regional innovation system can be thought of as the institutional infrastructure supporting innovation within the productive system of a region.' (Asheim and Gertler, 2005: 299)

'Regional systems of innovation are sets of institutions (innovating firms, research universities, research funding agencies, venture capital firms and government laboratories and other appropriate public bodies) and the flows of knowledge, personnel, research monies, regulation and embodied technology that occur within a region (metropolitan area, sub-national unit or other).' (Niosi, 2005: 16)

---

companies will emerge as spin-offs of existing ones. Feedback processes will attract more skilled labour, which will bring in new companies and lead to new supporting industries and institutions (Arthur, 1994). Such path-dependent processes explain the incredible resilience of regional systems of innovation (RSIs) and the difficulties that new regions have in challenging incumbent agglomerations.

The RSI's definition is still mutable, as Doloreux and Parto (2005) emphasize. Asheim and Gertler (2005: 299) concentrate on institutions (universities, government laboratories, and the like), along the lines of the 'narrow' definition that Niosi also adopts (2005). But Asheim and Gertler, quoting Lundvall, also include 'all parts and aspects of the economic structure and the institutional set up affecting learning as well as searching and exploring' (ibid) (Box 2.2). Niosi (2005) sticks to the 'narrow definition' for the same reasons as before: it is more tractable, the only one that allows manageable quantification, and thus the one that most of the economic literature uses.

The concept of NSI stirred conceptual debate: it presented nations as nation-states, innovation as introduction in the market of new or improved products and process, and systems as sets of elements within relationships (while Lundvall and Nelson still differed over the key elements and relationships). The RSI required more elaboration. What are its geographical delimitations – cities, metropolitan areas, provinces, German-style Länder, regions (such as the Basque country and Catalonia in Spain), or even such agglomerations as Silicon Valley and Route 128? Also, nation-states usually jealously guard key responsibilities regarding research, education, and major technology projects. What policy-making capabilities do regional agglomerations have? Cooke et al. (1997) define these geographical regions as 'territories smaller than their state possessing significant supra-local governance capacity and cohesiveness differentiating them from their state and other regions' (Cooke et al., 1997: 480). This definition would apply to most regional groupings that can collect taxes and implement policy, such as American states and metropolitan areas, Canadian provinces and metropolitan areas, German Länder, Spanish communities, and British regions such as Scotland and Wales. It does not apply to agglomerations such as Silicon Valley and Route 128. Elements of such an RSI are firms; knowledge centres, such as universities and research institutes; contract research organizations; and governance structures, both public (departments, economic development agencies) and private (regional chambers of commerce, industrial associations). Mechanisms for collective learning through monitoring, evaluating, and absorbing existing knowledge, as well as creating new knowledge, are crucial. They include participation in local associations, links to local universities and government laboratories, and imitation of and differentiation from regional competitors.

One could argue that the rise of NSIs in the late nineteenth and the twentieth centuries revealed the geographical localization of both industry and innovation, which Marshall first identified as 'industrial districts.' The more that other countries caught up with the leaders, the more this regional agglomeration became critical. In time, the literature on RSIs merged with regional and geographical economics, and 'clusters,' 'learning regions,' 'industrial districts,' 'innovative milieux,' and other concepts became popular. These authors themselves borrowed hypotheses and data from one another and competed, as they do today, in science and public policy.

Policy motivations involving the RSI concept resemble those that made the NSI attractive: backward and declining regions want to catch up – to replicate the evolution and performance of more successful agglomerations. National governments encourage more regionally balanced development through cluster or regional policies. The emphasis on innovation – technological and organizational – derives from its wider acceptance as the lever of economic growth. Every industrial country, as well as the European Union (through, among other initiatives, the Regional Program for Innovative Actions of the European Fund for Regional Development), has put in place some kind of regional-innovation policy. Market processes tend to amplify regional differences through the feedback of increasing returns; in addition, markets do not necessarily create the links, organizations, and institutions necessary for efficient development of such regional spaces. Yet observers have emphasized that effective regional policy requires a clear understanding of the initial conditions, the region's size, and the sectors they hope to expand. As with national systems, one-size-fits-all policy recipes for regional ones do not produce the expected results (Tödling and Trippl, 2005).

Sectoral Systems

The concept of sectoral systems of innovation arrived in the late 1990s and has spread rapidly (Breschi and Malerba, 1997). Its main underlying assumption is that innovation happens not only at the regional or national, but also at the global, level. 'More accurately, a Sectoral Innovation System (SIS) can be defined as that system (group) of firms active in developing and making a sector's products and in generating and utilizing a sector's technologies: such a system of firms is related in two ways: through processes of interaction and cooperation in artifact technology development and through processes of competition and selection in innovation and market activities' (ibid., p. 131). The key economic agents in SISs are private firms, but only those that are active in the same sector, excluding suppliers, clients, and other private-sector organizations related to the sector. Supporting institutions, organizations, and policies lie at the boundaries of the SIS. Thus the concept is slightly larger than 'global industries.' The economic literatures dealing with innovation received and integrated this new idea, and the OECD has published a series of sectoral studies using this notion (e.g., OECD, 2006a, 2006b).

The new concept comes also with a theory about change in SISs. The dynamics of an SIS, including its spatial boundaries, derives from its technological regime. Such a regime consists of the opportunity and appropriability conditions, the nature and cumulativeness of technical knowledge, and the means of transmitting and communicating knowledge.

Two major technological regimes appear in the literature, and they emerge from Schumpeter's writings. The young Schumpeter of *The Theory of Economic Development* (1911) describes the first version. Many innovators compete under technical conditions of low appropriability, high opportunity, and limited cumulativeness, and this technical dynamics generates markets with high entry rates, high instability, and low concentration. Schumpeter's later writings inspired technological regimes that

Table 2.1   Five types of SIS

Name	Characteristics	Technological regime	Cases
Traditional sectors	Many innovators Geographical dispersion No specific knowledge spatial boundaries	Low appropriability Low opportunity Low cumulativeness Relevant knowledge simple and generic	Agriculture Garment Textiles Wood products
Mechanical industries	Many innovators Spatial concentrations in clusters Local knowledge boundaries	Medium opportunity Low appropriability High cumulativeness Knowledge mostly tacit and specific	Metal products industries
Automobile industry	Few innovators Geographical concentration Firm knowledge boundaries	Medium opportunity High appropriability High cumulativeness	Automobiles
Computer mainframe	Few large innovators High geographical concentration Global system of core areas	High opportunity High appropriability High cumulativeness	Computer mainframe industry
Software	Many innovators Geographical concentration Local and global knowledge boundaries	High opportunity High appropriability High cumulativeness	Computer software

emphasized high opportunity, high appropriability, and cumulativeness. This technological regime generates industries with low rates of entry, high concentration, and a stable number of innovators. On the basis of this classification, Breschi and Malerba recognize five types of SIS, as we see in Table 2.1. Some of the types are just the summary description of a specific industry.

I elsewhere discussed this dichotomy and the five types (Niosi, 2000b). First, Schumpeter's dichotomy does not exhaust all possible technological regimes. Industries or sectors recognize more than two technical dynamics. Some industries, for instance, start their life cycle being dispersed (e.g., the pharmaceutical industry), and then they concentrate. Others begin with concentration in one or two innovators and then disperse through product variety. Second, technological opportunity, appropriability, and cumulativeness do not keep constant. They also change over time. The software industry was the archetypal easy-entry low appropriability sector. It is now becoming more difficult to enter, and patents rise barriers to appropriability. Third, entry, exit, spatial concentration, and other characteristics are not the products only of technological regimes. Barriers to entry are not just technological but also economic – obtaining initial capital and exclusive mineral or legal rights – market uncertainty is therefore high in the early stages of an industry and then declines as dominant designs emerge. Finally, institutions play a key role in the entrance of new competitors. Witness the role of the Brazilian, Chinese, Japanese, and Soviet/Russian states in their entry or re-entry into aircraft manufacturing. After all, there is a massive literature on product and industry life cycles showing that industrial, institutional, and technological conditions within an industry change over time.

Thus a few industries emerge under Schumpeter's early-version conditions of low barriers to entry, low appropriability, and low cumulativeness and remain that way for decades. A prime example is the industry that manufactures professional and medical equipment (Mitchell, 1991). Also, some sectors emerge concentrated and remain so, as in Schumpeter's second version; their appropriability conditions are high, as are their opportunity and cumulativeness. Entry barriers are high, as is spatial agglomeration. Such sectors include petrochemical production and manufacture of satellites, space launchers, and helicopters (Spitz, 1988; Beaudry, 2006).

However, this dichotomy does not represent the whole picture. Other industries come into being under first-version conditions; Kaldor-David-Arthur increasing returns follow, and over time dominant designs appear, large corporations emerge, process technology standardizes, appropriability conditions change, cumulativeness increases, and the resemblance to Mark II conditions grows. Klepper (1997) recalls that hundreds of firms entered the automobile industry between its inception and the 1950s. The industry concentrated later. Breschi and Malerba (1997) only depict the industry as it is today. Similarly, pharmaceuticals registered hundreds of entries and concentrated during the twentieth century; in the meantime, appropriability, cumulativeness, and opportunity changed. Increasing returns in the field derive from increasingly high appropriability and the cumulativeness of the technology. At the start of the nineteenth century, academic research played a vital role in the design of new drugs; by late in that century, industry had taken the lead (Achiladellis and Antonakis, 2001). Other barriers to entry, such as marketing and R&D costs, also usually affect the industry's stability.

In other industries, niches and designs multiply, and technological variety becomes a key characteristic (Saviotti, 1996). Computers constitute a case in point. They started in the early 1950s with IBM and the mainframe. Next followed Control Data and the first supercomputer (1960), and then came the minicomputer with Digital Equipment (1960), the personal computer (Altair, 1975), general-purpose mainframes (NEC, 1976), the super-minicomputers (Perkin-Elmers, 1976), the pocket computer (Radio Shack, 1980), the personal computer (IBM, 1981), the portable computer from Osborne (1981), the workstation (Sun Microsystems, 1987), Cray's supercomputer (Cray Corporation, 1988), and the notebook computer (Compaq, 1989); the list goes on towards wearable computers and other, increasingly small and powerful machines. Thus the computer mainframe niche that Breschi and Malerba present (1997) is just one in which high opportunity and appropriability remained constant through time; other niches experienced different evolutions. Similarly, the first semiconductors of the early 1950s, invented by Shockley, evolved through many families of semiconductors that appeared in telecommunication equipment, numerically controlled machines, robots, watches, cars, aircraft, hearing aids, and hundreds of other products (Schot and Geels, 2007). The technological dynamics involved is one of sequential innovation: firms compete by launching new variations of existing products, which produce an evolutionary branching similar to biological variation. Rapid sequences of innovation, under a regime of low appropriability and high cumulativeness, blur the sector's frontier. Table 2.2 summarizes the new classification of technological regimes I suggest.

SISs have connections to national systems and hold promise for further empirical research. Most countries have only a few industrial sectors. In Finland, electronics represents over half of industrial R&D. In Canada, five sectors dominate industrial research, and the decline of the largest, telecommunications equipment, explains the stagnation of Canadian BERD after 2000. In France, four sectors (automobile, information and communication technologies, pharmaceuticals, and aircraft) represent over half of business R&D expenditures. At country level, the rise or decline of a single sector may help to explain the processes of 'falling behind,' 'forging ahead,' and 'catching up,' which a purely macro-economic approach cannot explain.

2.2 FROM EVOLUTIONARY ECONOMICS TO SYSTEMS OF INNOVATION

Theories about systems of innovation (SIs) had a base in evolutionary economics, most notably in Nelson and Winter (Nelson and Winter, 1982;

Table 2.2   A new classification of technological dynamics

	Initial conditions		
Development over time		Dispersed	Concentrated
	Dispersed	Schumpeter Mark I: Professional and medical equipment (see Breschi and Malerba 1997)	Variation intensive industries: Continuous creation of new niches, opportunity, appropriability, and cumulativeness variables according to niche Computers, computer software, semiconductors
	Concentrated	Increasing return sectors Appropriability, cumulativeness, and opportunity increase. E.g.: aircraft, automobiles, pharmaceuticals	Schumpeter Mark II Heavy chemicals, satellites, space launchers (see Breschi and Malerba 1997)

Nelson, 1993), but they also related to system dynamics (Lundvall, 1992: 2). However, with both fields the links were tenuous and needed development, which occurred in several articles and papers (Niosi et al, 1993; Saviotti, 1996 and 1997; McKelvey, 1997; Balzat and Hanusch, 2004). This section aims at strengthening those links.

Evolutionary Economics and SIs

A brief summary of the main themes of the evolutionary approach may help us grasp the foundations of SI in evolutionary economics.

●   Evolutionary economics starts with economic agents who possess *bounded rationality* and expand their knowledge of the world through trial and error. We may hypothesize that SIs are economic systems that develop in the same way, with agents (policy-makers, entrepreneurs, inventors, and innovators) developing strategies and then modifying them in view of the results. SIs are social systems that emerge through the long and complex interactions of many agents – individual and organizational – within an institutional environment. There is no general controller or planning agency able to construct such complex systems. Bounded rationality is in the economic world the micro-behavioural foundation of *variety*.

- *Initial conditions are key*: They include productive resources available in the country or region, the institutional frameworks (customary and policy-made), the size of the market, organizational heritages, and the like. What triggers the development of a national or regional innovation system? In several countries, wars – or the possibility of war – have certainly played a role. Japan's industrial revolution followed the Meiji restoration of 1868 and flowed from the understanding that Japan was vulnerable to foreign aggression. Italy created many of its heavy industries and research organizations under the Fascist regime of the 1920s and 1930s. The United States and Canada multiplied their initiatives in science and technology during and after the Second World War. South Korea was in ruins after the Korean War when it launched its industrialization program in the early 1960s.
- *Cumulative patterns*: Once industrialization had started, it could – or might not – include creation of an innovation system. In Latin America, twentieth-century industrialization through import substitution took place with little concern for innovation; hence the shaky basis of that process because of its use of foreign technology. In western Europe, the United States, Japan, Canada, and later South Korea, industrialization went hand in hand with efforts to master imported technology and eventually to create new technology. The process led to new organizations (universities, public laboratories), new industrial and technology policies, and new industries, which in turn required more skilled labour and developed new areas of technical expertise. Virtuous circles of technological development, industrial growth, and organizational building followed. Increasing returns are pervasive in evolutionary models.
- *Multi-stability*: In response to their own distinctive resource endowments, institutional heritage, market size, knowledge base, and close cultural neighbours to imitate, nations and regions launch different economic and technological trajectories. Variety again sets in from the start. Innovation systems do not converge but follow their own paths of economic development, at times arriving at periods of stability, with occasional interruptions due to the creation of new industries or the decline of existing sectors.
- *Chance*: As happens in the biological world, chance plays a role, with either positive or negative effects, reinforcing or balancing

existing paths, launching or forbidding new trajectories. In the early 1960s, IBM could not gain permission to build a central software laboratory in Cambridge, England, and accordingly accepted the application of Toronto, which has since 1967 hosted one of the company's major laboratories. IBM attracted thousands of programmers to the city, and cumulative processes of new firm formation and organizational building helped create a major software cluster in central Canada. The early 1950s' move of William Shockley from Bell Labs in New Jersey to California and his 1955 founding of Shockley Semiconductors decided the location of the semiconductor industry and nurtured the rise of Silicon Valley; he won the Nobel Prize for physics in 1956.

Complex Dynamics and Innovation Systems

System dynamics has inspired theories about innovation systems without dominating them. Jay Forrester founded the discipline at MIT about 1957, and the last 50 years has seen its extensive application to demography, ecology, economics, geography, management, sociology, and other fields. System dynamics helps to reveal the properties of dynamic systems, studying the evolution of causal links, feedback mechanisms, flows, stocks, and temporal delays in complex systems, such as economic ones. Its micro-foundations are almost identical to those of evolutionary economics (Sterman, 2000). It assumes a population of bounded rational agents, who pursue different strategies and adapt their behaviour as other agents alter theirs. Co-adaptation makes predictions difficult and creates non-linear, out-of-equilibrium dynamics, positive feedback, and balancing loops. Thus, despite adaptive behaviour of agents, there are patterns in these interactions (Axelrod and Cohen, 2000). An example may help.

In the late 1970s and the early 1980s, some North American universities started conducting research in the new field of biotechnology, and a few academics launched spin-offs to commercialize the results of their research. At that time, venture capitalists showed little interest in the new science, but much more in information technologies. University administrators were not attentive either. However, the initial public offerings of some of the new dedicated biotechnology firms (DBF) attracted the attention of both venture capitalists and university technology managers. In the late 1980s and the 1990s, venture capital adapted to the new situation and created biotechnology portfolios. Universities also adapted and created or revamped their university–industry liaison offices. Because the DBFs emerged near these scientists' universities, clusters (regional innovation systems) appeared in biotechnology. The creation of portfolios of venture capital in biotechnology, and the interest of university technology managers, spurred other academics to start up biotechnology firms. The number of firms in regional innovation systems (RSIs) increased. This positive feedback loop began to balance itself (balancing loop) when venture capital for the field started to stabilize and diversified out of biotechnology, when new technologies (e.g., nanotechnology) attracted their attention, and when the growth of existing firms dried up the labour market. The stock-exchange crash in 2000–1 also helped balance the situation, and expansion slowed (Niosi, 2003, 2005). Figure 2.1 summarizes the model in the preliminary form of an influence diagram.

The process starts with university R&D in biotechnology, often a product of government programs. Academic research produces university patents, which in turn attracts venture capital. New DBFs emerge, which in turn increase R&D in the private sector; these enterprises obtain patents, encouraging creation of firms and expansion of university research. This positive feedback loop becomes a reinforcing mechanism that can last decades. It occurred in several agglomerations in North American biotechnology between 1980 and 2000. Yet several balancing loops reduced growth, including depletion of labour markets and the rise of venture capital, which attracted new technologies, such as nanotechnology.

National systems of innovation are equally amenable to modelling with system dynamics. The following case, similar to Canada, may illustrate its usefulness. A country may try to diversify out of its dwindling stock of natural resources into high-technology industries. To this end, it may invest some of its surpluses into creation of human capital for a few industries that it has targeted. It may direct another part of the surplus to attracting foreign competitors by subsidizing creation of new plants and R&D laboratories, as well as by nurturing domestic firms through special programs. The new companies may deplete the labour market and encourage the government to set up new programs relating to the new industries. New enterprises will spin off from the growing companies and will reinforce the sectoral system of innovation within national borders. Other foreign firms may join the growing regions within the national system. In time, balancing loops would arise: the labour market may shrink, other countries may copy successful strategies and attract domestic companies, and urban congestion may make regional or national systems less attractive. Figure 2.2 summarizes the argument.

Some government program (e.g., a set of policies for development of computers) creates human capital and attracts new firms from abroad, or new entrants in the industry, or diversification of existing firms in the new sector. Industrial growth follows, nurturing innovation and the rise

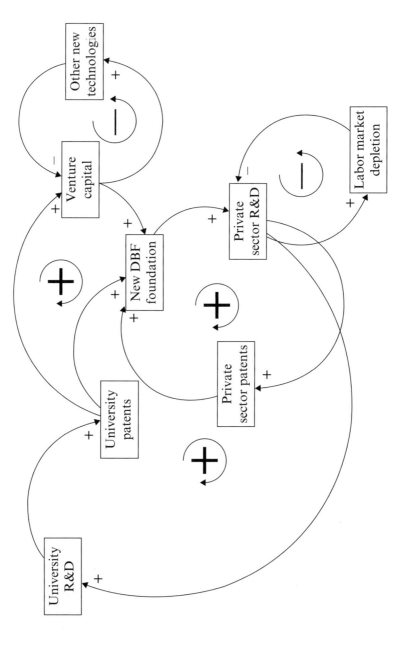

Figure 2.1 Dynamics of a biotechnology regional system of innovation

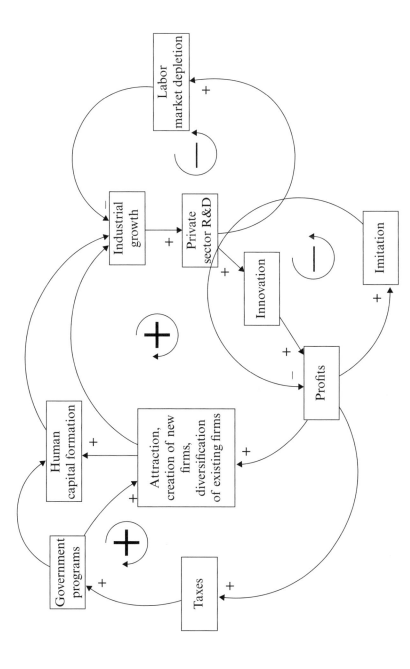

Figure 2.2   The dynamics of a national system of innovation

39

of industrial profits. This process attracts new firms, and some of them promote the formation of human capital, perhaps by subsidizing new graduate programs in information technology. Innovation brings profits, which government taxes. Government may pick another industry to diversify; new, advanced university programs may emerge; new firms enter the industry; and additional positive-feedback loops emerge. But balancing loops arise to slow the system's growth. The labour market is shrinking, and imitators (most often catching-up countries) copy the original innovators.

As these examples show, system dynamics can help to develop theory, as well as more precise description and exploration. System dynamics is a discipline that, through simulation, uses computer software to model the operation of complex systems and their processes. It does so by different methods (Davis et al., 2007). System dynamics is not the only simulation approach available; other methods include cellular automata, genetic algorithms, NK fitness landscapes, and stochastic processes.

Yet this book employs system dynamics, which I consider the most useful approach, for several reasons. First, it clarifies the underlying causal relationships between multiple variables. Innovation-system theories contain many variables. Second, it is particularly useful in dealing with time. Third, it is also very helpful when data are scarce, particularly because theories of innovation systems are simple and still need development. Fourth, it can summarize and simplify the main assumptions and hypothesis when they are purely verbal. Fifth, it can also help uncover data to clarify the relative weight of different variables, or the cost of different policies and programs, and the payoffs that one can expect from them or has already obtained. Finally, it permits exploration of new possibilities; for instance, its ability to explain the construction of different national, regional, or sectoral innovation systems over time may facilitate development of new development paths or borrowing from other experiences. Sterman (2000: 4) observes, 'The challenge facing us all is how to move from generalizations about accelerated learning and systems thinking, to tools and processes that help us understand complexity, design better operating policies, and guide change in systems.'

The issue of complexity and economics is now a major topic, but bibliographical bases unduly inflate the number of publications: the word 'complexity' may be much more fashionable than its analysis. Yet the subject appears in an increasing number of economics articles, papers, and books. The literature on innovation systems has also considered the subject. Noteworthy analysts include Janszen and Degenaars (1998), with their dynamic simulation model for Dutch biotechnology; Fischer (2001, 2002) and Lee and von Tunzelmann (2005), who use system dynamics for the integrated-circuit industry of Taiwan; and Frenken (2006a and 2006b) and Caminati (2006), who both employ NK models.

According to Brock and Colander (2000), the complexity approach possesses distinctive elements:

- Institutional design is its most central policy input.
- It is neutral about policy.
- The key initial step is determining the boundaries of the system the analyst wishes to study.
- It is much more inductive than deductive, because complex systems are not intuitive.
- The temporal dimension is central to the analysis.
- Policy recommendations are less certain.

And the approach differs radically from the traditional perspective, as Table 2.3 summarizes. Systems of innovation are complex adaptive systems and as such open, receiving matter, resources, and information from the rest of the economy. In other words, they are subsystems within the economy. A comparison with human biology is useful: it is possible to study the respiratory or the digestive system in partial isolation from the entire human organism, considering only its main links (entry of energy and release of entropy) with the rest of the body (see Beinhocker, 2006). Analysis of innovation systems can study the NSI's functioning without examining the entire economy; this is exactly what numerous publications have done for many countries (e.g., Nelson, 1993).

Also, the innovation system is in flux, and one can study its birth, growth, and eventual maturity. Neoclassical economics does not examine the creation of economic systems: it takes them as givens and often makes inferences about the economies of ancient civilizations using models it has built to analyse those of today. Economics thus simplifies the difficulty of its endeavour (Hodgson, 2001). We can study the building and eventual depletion of a pool of human capital, creation of public and private demand for it, promotion of innovation in public and private organizations, and outcomes of that innovation, as well as its links with the rest of the economy.

Complexity, as evolutionary economics, has its critics. The definition of complexity is not universal, and more than 45 versions were found (Horgan, 1995). The concept's use in disciplines as different as biology, chemistry, computer science, mathematics, and physics makes a universal definition highly unlikely. Yet, one definition for economics, which researchers at the Santa Fe Institute prepared, attracts general agreement,

Table 2.3   Complexity and evolutionary economics versus traditional economics

Issue	Complexity and evolutionary economics	Traditional economics
Micro-foundation	Bounded rational agents learn and adapt their behaviour; knowledge comes in different forms (e.g., tacit, codified) and is different from information	Perfect rational agents make no errors, do not learn, and have complete (or almost-complete) information
Dynamics	Open, non-linear systems usually out of equilibrium	Closed systems, static, linear systems in equilibrium
Links among agents	Many different types of links (technological, financial, personal, regulatory), including co-operative and competitive	Links among agents occur through market mechanisms
Relation between micro- and macro-economics	No division between micro- and macroeconomics; macro-patterns emerge from micro-level behaviour and links	Micro- and macroeconomics are different disciplines
Evolution	Evolutionary processes of variation, selection, and retention at many levels (technologies, firms, industries) provide novelty	No explicit mechanism for novelty
Theory development	Basically inductive: systems are discovered, as in natural science	Basically deductive
Policy	Specific to national, regional, and sectoral systems	One-fits-all policy prescriptions
Models	Complexity models, game theory, statistics, scientometrics	Calculus, algebra
Economic growth	Occurs through creation of new products, and sectors	Occurs through addition of capital and labour and increase of productivity
Technology	Studied as endogenous and key determinant of growth	Exogenous
Time	Time scales are key (i.e., for learning, institutional change)	Time is usually out of the models

Sources: Niosi, adapted and developed from Beinhocker (2006: 97).

and I employ it here because it suits the purposes of my research (see Chapter 1 above). In addition, this book is not dealing with general systems theory, or complexity in general, but only analyzing the economic system, or a subsystem within it.

Other criticisms have related more to its application to economics. Complexity deals with variation and uncertainty; thus policy recommendations deriving from complexity and evolution are less straightforward (but probably more accurate and useful) than those from neoclassical analysis. It is easy to theorize a world of homogeneous firms, homogeneously perfect rational consumers, a small set of well-known technological choices, and neutral governments, in a world of industries where returns do not increase with scale. It is much more difficult to deal with a range of national systems hosting varying sets of sectors, as happens in the real world, than to imagine a unique economic system in which one small set of solutions would apply to all nations. Again, the comparison with the human body is useful: for centuries the church taught that God had made humans in his own image. Then scientists started to analyze the human body and discovered that people looked pretty much like other mammals. In the last three decades, we have come to know that people differ genetically from each other, and the study of these differences may help to explain illness and evolution.

Conclusion: Innovation Systems and Economic Development

If technological and social innovation is the mother of riches, then countries possessing national and regional innovation systems in specific sectors will become wealthier, and those continuously harvesting the same resources will deplete them. Those that are unable to increase the variety of their industries will probably suffer from competition from new entrants. Richer countries and regions grow richer; poorer nations become poorer, as do poorer regions even within rich countries. This is the Matthew effect when we apply it to national or regional economies.

Economic development thus requires the introduction of variety into the economy. One can expect markets to provide variety by themselves. The history of the growth of national innovation systems (as well as regional and sectoral) shows that governments always give some guidance and direction. In their search for national defence, employment, or well-being for domestic populations, governments have by trial and error tinkered with the nurturing of different industries. Often they failed, and sometimes they succeeded. History is full of false starts: some 50 countries, including Argentina, Hungary, Indonesia, and Taiwan, tried to foster the development of aerospace industries, and they failed. Brazil succeeded.

Western Europe had a false co-operative start with Concorde, but its governments and industries learned, and they had a much better experience with Airbus. France tried to build large computers with the Plan Calcul and failed. Japan tried the Fifth Generation Computer with little success. Usually, countries copied the successful institutional and organizational innovations of their neighbours, showing that transmission of knowledge includes the explicit component of institutions, while the tacit elements move more easily through interactive learning and personal communication. Clusters of rich countries thus appear in geographical spots: North America, western Europe, South East Asia.

We can now study the process through which those national and regional systems of innovation emerge, develop, and intertwine with economic systems. We do not need to take them for granted or consider that they have always existed. In fact, they have emerged in the last 150 years in a handful of countries. They helped to make those societies rich, and their effectiveness and efficiency help us to understand why international gaps in wealth and productivity have increased and continue to do so.

In these innovation systems, agents (entrepreneurs as well as inventors and innovators and government officials) are far from possessing perfect information; they try and err, and sometimes they learn and correct their behaviour. Thus time is critical: learning takes time and resources; no innovation system emerges overnight either through market processes or through government incentives. National innovation systems are not in equilibrium: some are falling behind; a few are pulling ahead. Institutional and technical novelty in innovation systems occurs often. Also, the systems are open: they receive resources (people, funds, regulation) and information from the wider economic systems of which they form part. They receive in particular incentives from national and regional authorities, but not identical policy inducements; yet there are some similarities, the nature of which this book will try to discover. One of the main constants is that government intended these policy incentives at creating new sectors, to bolster defence, diversify the economy, or exploit opportunity.

Finally, these national systems are not all equal, yet groups of them do possess similarities. One can consider that Anglo-Saxon countries have many characteristics in common, and so do Japan and South Korea, or the Nordic countries, or Continental western European countries. In addition, there are similar dynamics in regional systems because of the industries they contain; regional systems of innovation in biotechnology are similar among them but differ noticeably from RSIs in information technology or in aerospace. Ideally, thus one should build a model for each country and each RSI within each national system. These models would be the product not of armchair speculation or theorizing, but of extensive empirical work, collecting data from countries and regions, like Darwin did during his voyage on the *Beagle*. The task is far from impossible, but this book will try only to show the way.

NOTE

1. They are [in size order] the United States, Japan, Germany, the United Kingdom, France, Italy, Canada, Russia, Sweden, Switzerland, Belgium, the Netherlands, Austria, Norway, Denmark, Finland, South Korea, Spain, Australia, Israel, Ireland, Iceland, Singapore, New Zealand, and Luxembourg. Mexico and Turkey, not advanced countries, also belong to the OECD.

3.   Industrial and technology policy

Policies to advance industry, innovation, and technology (which I group under the rubric 'industrial policy') constitute separate yet convergent domains. They are public tools that governments use to modify industrial structures, by either adding new sectors or renewing existing ones. Industrial policies have existed for several centuries, from Britain's prohibiting export of wool in the sixteenth century in order to provide cheap and abundant raw material to its nascent textile industry to the German and U.S. governments restructuring their domestic automobile industries through massive funding and partial nationalization in the twenty-first century.

Institutions to advance science, technology, and innovation (STI) are much more recent (I refer to them collectively as 'STI policy'). Their first elements appeared in the nineteenth century, with publicly funded university research in Germany and agricultural research laboratories in Germany, the United States, and Canada. Patent legislation is the precursor of today's STI policy. It overlaps both industrial and STI policies and has been in use in Britain and the United States since the late eighteenth century.

This chapter defines the policies, provides historical examples of their use, and links them with economic development and catching up.

3.1   DEFINING THE DOMAINS

Industrial policy is a set of government interventions that the wealthy nations have used during their industrial development (Lall, 2004; Reinert, 2007; Chang, 2003). Its main components include protective tariffs for infant industry, government procurement, direct subsidies for industrial investment, founding of public companies that government may later sell to the private sector, promotion of exports through preferential credit, industrial espionage, attraction of skilled personnel, protection or imitation of intellectual property, direct funding of existing firms to restructure them, and manipulation of exchange rates. Table 3.1 summarizes some industrial policies in developed countries.

Table 3.1   Industrial policies in early industrializing countries

Policy	Country	Period	Sources
Tariff and non-tariff protection	England	1721–1846	Nye, 1991; O'Rourke, 2000
	France	1892–1950	Nye, 1991; O'Rourke, 2000
	Germany	1879–	O'Rourke, 2000
	USA	1816–1945	O'Rourke, 2000
	Italy	1875–1950	O'Rourke, 2000
Skilled worker recruitment in foreign countries	England	17th Century	Basalla, 1988: 84–6
	France	18th Century	Harris, 1998
	Germany	19th Century	Landes, 1972: 140–2.
	Holland	19th Century	Landes, 1972: 148.
	Austria	19th Century	Landes, 1972: 148–50.
	Japan		
State companies	Italy	20th Century	Samuels, 1987; Holland, 1972
	Japan	19th, 20th Centuries	Samuels, 1987; Johnson, 1982
Public financing of industrial facilities	Japan	20th Century	Odagiri and Goto, 1996
	Italy	20th Century	Holland, 1972
	Germany	19th, 20th Centuries	
Public industrial missions to advanced countries	Japan	20th Century	Odagiri and Goto, 1996
	France	19th Century	Landes, 1972: 151
	Germany	19th Century	Landes, 1972: 151

Industrial policy can involve four general types of intervention – ownership, co-ordination, tariffs, and incentives. At one extreme, governments set up, own, and control enterprises. All wealthy countries use this method in energy, which they consider too vital economically and militarily to leave to the vagaries of the market. This is the case of state oil companies since the early twentieth century (BP in Britain, CFP in France, ENI in Italy), or later (JNOC in Japan, Petro-Canada, Statoil in Norway, and many others), electric-power generation and transmission utilities afterwards (ENDESA in Spain, ENEL in Italy, Hydro Ontario and Hydro Quebec in Canada, Norsk Hydro in co-ordination, Norway, the Tennessee Valley Authority in the United States, and others), and government holding companies for industrial firms (such as INI in Spain and IRI in Italy) (Holland, 1972; Samuels, 1987). In the 1930s and 1940s, government enterprise in production of energy was also very common in developing countries. But the formula involved risks of corruption, inertia, and favouritism. After the Second World War, government enterprises slowly faded away, and most enterprises went private.

A slightly less direct method of industrial policy was governmental co-ordination of industry. It was popular with authoritarian governments, such as those in Germany – Kartells from the late nineteenth century up to the Nazi regime – and in Japan – *zaibatsu* from the time of the Meiji restoration in 1868 up to American occupation beginning in 1945. But industrial co-operation was often difficult to obtain, and it derogated increasingly fashionable anti-trust laws. Industrial co-ordination gradually withered as a tool of industrial policy.

The third major tool of industrial policy was tariff protection. Governments employed it either to nurture domestically owned and controlled industry (as in Germany and the United States in the nineteenth and twentieth centuries) or to attract foreign firms (as in Canada's industrialization by invitation after 1867). Non-tariff barriers and manipulation of exchange rates sometimes complemented tariffs.

Fourth and finally, there were public incentives. They included tax, financial, and regulatory stimuli, as well as encouragements to attract skilled technicians. Such incentives usually did not discriminate against foreign enterprises or individuals. Skilled technicians would find employment in domestic firms or found new companies, as happened in nineteenth-century Continental Europe and North America. Some governments began to protect intellectual property in the late eighteenth century. Methods have included patent systems and later copyright, trademarks, and regulation of industrial design. Thus incentives progressively displaced the three other approaches to industrial policy during the twentieth century.

Industrial policy is distinct from, and older than, science, technology, and innovation policy (STI policy). The former is several centuries old; the latter took shape gradually in the late nineteenth century. Perhaps the first person to explain policy intervention in science, technology, and innovation was Vannevar Bush (1945), a scientist who worked for the U.S. government during the Second World War and wrote an influential report to the president, *Science: The Endless Frontier*. Bush argued that science was the engine of industrial and social progress. In the following decades, theoretical support emerged from the work of Arrow, Myrdal, and Solow. Solow (1956) proved that technology, not the incorporation of capital and labour, was the main cause of economic growth. Myrdal (1957) demonstrated that developing countries often stagnated because they suffered from inefficient institutions and vicious circles of low education, bad health, low productivity, and small revenues. Perhaps only government intervention could end these self-reinforcing loops. Arrow

(1962) showed that under pure market conditions externalities would limit companies' investment in STI. The R&D executants would recoup little of their investment because science, technology, and innovation consist mostly of knowledge that is easy to copy. Under conditions of externalities, the investors would then produce free, beneficial knowledge for both competitors (producer surplus) and consumers (consumer surplus). Yet these social benefits were substantial enough to justify government investment in in-house R&D in the firms.

The first institutions to enter this emerging area of policy were the government agricultural R&D laboratory and the research university. Germany set up the first agricultural labs about 1850, and Canada and the United States soon followed. Germany's federal agricultural research stations inspired the North American ones (Finlay, 1988). At the same time, botanical gardens appeared in several European countries to study the properties of plants as well as their eventual uses in industry. The U.S. Department of Agriculture has conducted research since 1862, even if the government set up the U.S. Agricultural Research Service only in 1953. In the twentieth century, full public agricultural laboratories emerged in western Europe, including INRA in France (in 1945).

Germany also established the first research universities (under the so-called Humboldt model) by 1850; the model emigrated to the United States and the United Kingdom as early as 1900, and other advanced nations soon did likewise. Germany and the United Kingdom created councils to fund scientific research in 1920; the same happened in the United States (the National Science Foundation, 1950) and Canada (1960).

Finally, national science and technology laboratories appeared in Britain in 1900 (the National Physical Laboratory), in the United States in 1901 (the National Bureau of Standards), and in Germany in 1910 (the Kaiser Wilhelm Institute, later the Max Planck). The Great War spurred government research, and new laboratories opened in Canada (the National Research Council, or NRC, 1916) and then in Italy (CNR, 1923), France (CNRS, 1938), and Spain (CSIC, 1939). The institution crossed the Atlantic to South America only in the 1950s (Table 3.2).

Yet most direct measures to stimulate industrial R&D appeared after 1945. They included tax credits for R&D, direct subsidies for R&D both in large and in small-and-medium-sized enterprises (SMEs), industrial research in government laboratories, specialized academic graduate programs, co-operative private-public research centres, government creation of non-profit research centres, public subsidies for employment of scientists and engineers in industry, and industry-related higher education programs (such as the many areas of engineering and more recently computer science and biotechnology).

*Table 3.2   The founding and diffusion of large-scale scientific and
industrial research*

National laboratories	Science funding agencies
1900: National Physics Laboratory (U.K.)	1920: Medical Research Council (U.K.)
1901: National Bureau of Standards (U.S.A.)	1920: NDW: 1st German research foundation
1910: Kaiser Wilhelm Institute (Germany)	1951: National Science Foundation (U.S.A.)
1916: National Research Council (U.S.A.)	1960: Medical Research Council
1916: National Research Council (Canada)	1965: Science Research Council (U.K.)
1923: CNR (Italy)	1970–75: NSERC and SSHRC (Canada)
1938: CNRS (France)	1988: Australian Research Council
1939: CSIC (Spain)	2006: European Research Council
1951: CONICET (Argentina)	
1951: CNPQ (Brazil)	

The international trend in industrial countries has been towards increasing development, refinement, and diversification of STI policies (Table 3.3). Through emulation, STI policies have crossed borders. On the basis of repeated evaluation, they have become more inclusive, efficient, and effective.

Also, STI policies receive much more respect from policy-makers and economists than does pure industrial policy. Yet they remain a specialized topic in economics and the policy science.

3.2   INDUSTRIAL POLICY: RATIONALE, HISTORY, AND TODAY

Rationale

Traditional theory admits government intervention to correct 'market failures.' The implicit assumption is that unfettered markets will produce economic development, despite a few deficiencies. But industrialization involves much more than simply correcting market failures. In fact, free markets have seldom created industry. The reasons are threefold.

First, industry requires the simultaneous development and further combination of temporary protection against more experienced competitors,

Table 3.3 STI policies in selected industrial countries

Policy	Country	Year started	Main characteristic
IP protection	Venice	1474	Protected for declared inventions 10 years
	England	1623	Protected projects of new inventions
	U.S.A.	1790	Protected declared inventions for 14 years
Scientific research funding	Germany	1920	Science Research Foundation
	U.K.	1920	Medical Research Council
	U.S.A.	1952	National Science Foundation
Tax credits for R&D	Japan	1967	20% of expenditures deductible
	Canada	1977	20% to 35% of expenditures deductible
	U.S.A.	1981	20% of expenditures deductible incremental
	France	1983	50% of incremental expenditures deductible
Direct subsidies for SME R&D	Canada (IRAP)	1962	Non-refundable grants for SME R&D projects
	U.S.A. (SBIR)	1982	Non-refundable grants for SME R&D projects
	Japan SBIR	1995	Non-refundable grants for SME R&D projects
Grants for private and public R&D	EU framework programs (1984–)	1998–2002	5th European Framework Research Programme (13.7 billion Euros)
		2002–6	6th European Framework Programme (17.5 billion Euros)
		2007–13	7th European Framework Programme (51 billion Euros)
Loans	South Korea (KDB)	1976	Loan program for technology development
	Canada (TPP)	1986	Conditional loan: repaid if project succeeds
Procurement	U.S.A. Germany	1940>	Defence-related procurement policies (Mowery, 1998)
		1970s>	Energy technology procurement (Klaasen et al., 2005)
Venture capital: tax measures	U.S.A. (SBIC)	1958	Private equity invested in SMEs supported by U.S. SBA
	U.S.A. (ERISA)	1978	Private pension funds admitted for VC Investment

Table 3.3   (continued)

Policy	Country	Year started	Main characteristic
	Canada (LSVCC)	1983	Private pension funds admitted for VC Investment
Government venture capital	Germany (WFG)	1975	Direct government funds invested in new firms
	Netherlands	1981	Government guarantees for private VC
	Israel (Yozma)	1993	Government supplies funds to privately managed VC
Thematic or vertical policies	U.K.–France	1962>	Concorde aircraft program
	Canada	1983	National Biotechnology Policy (Niosi and Bas, 2004)
	Germany	1995	BioRegio Contest (Dohse, 2000)

a specialized pool of human capital, risky financial investments, market knowledge and promotion, and above all, technology, some of it perhaps proprietary and difficult of access. Only governments can orchestrate the import, production, and co-ordination of so many different and costly inputs. Most often, governments in catching-up countries have to create a skilled labour market, a technology market, and a specialized venture capital market and also become the first market for new products through public procurement.

Second, development is a learning process. Backward countries aiming to industrialize would need to learn the new technologies, the organizational forms, the appropriate government and private sector routines, and the policies, as well as setting up other institutions. In the second half of the twentieth century, such countries would have had to foster the mastering of the appropriate process and product technologies by domestic private firms and orchestrate the policy incentives that new industry required, including protection of intellectual property, direct subsidies or tax credits for R&D, and so on. In addition, the new industrial firms would need to learn the appropriate organizational forms (i.e., the corporate organization) and the required routines, such as R&D management, quality control, concurrent engineering, management of supply chains, and 'benchmarking.'

Third, during the several decades it takes to absorb these physical and social technologies, local companies would be at a disadvantage vis-à-vis older rivals. Some kind of protection of infant industry, tariff or non-tariff, would thus be essential. All industrial nations, starting with England in the fifteenth century, implemented these policy instruments. Canada, France, Germany, Italy, Japan, Norway, Sweden, the United States, and today all industrializing countries (including China, South Korea, and Vietnam) have used different combinations of industrial policies (Amsden, 1989, 2001; Chang, 2003; Johnson, 1982; Kim, 1977b; Lall, 2004; Okimoto, 1989; Parayil, 2005; Reinert, 2007; Wade, 1990). In the aftermath of the Second World War, South East Asian countries applied non-tariff protection and undervalued currency to protect nascent enterprises.

In conventional economics, and in most OECD countries, industrial policy has become synonymous with 'picking winners,' corruption, and 'pork barrel.' Yet in the real world all governments in industrial countries continue their use in one form or another, ranging from direct subsidies to agriculture, through procurement contracts involving subsidies for military industry with substantial 'trickle down' effects into civilian industry (e.g., from aerospace since the 1930s to semiconductors, software, and other sectors after 1945) (Mowery and Rosenberg, 1989), to massive financial support to declining manufacturing sectors such as automobiles in 1979 (United States: Chrysler) and again in 2008–9 (France: Peugeot and Renault; Germany: Opel; and the United States: GM and Chrysler).

History

From the fifteenth century on, industrial policy began to emerge in European countries. It started in England, where Henry VII (reigned 1485–1509) subsidized shipbuilding and protected manufacture, prohibited export of raw materials (wool), and attracted artisans and industrialists, as did all governments there until well into the nineteenth century. Attraction of foreign human capital was a key industrial policy. Basalla (1988: 84–6) documents English industrial espionage of French and Italian silk technology through the attraction of silk weavers in the seventeenth century and the sending of British industrial spies to Italy. Britain forbade its possessions, from India to its North American colonies, to develop any type of manufacture that could compete with its own.

The government of France developed its internal market through controlling transportation ways and imposing tariffs, as well as promoting textile and glass industries under Colbert (minister of finance 1665–83), who also built a merchant shipping industry. Like England before, France sought inventors and industrialists from other countries (List, 1841). Also, in the eighteenth century it brought in British 'technological immigrants' in order to upgrade its metallurgical technologies (Harris, 1998). Yet France remained far less protectionist than Britain throughout the nineteenth century (Nye, 1991).

Economic historians find the United States the most protectionist among the new industrial countries of the nineteenth century (O'Rourke, 2000). As soon as they obtained independence, the Americans adopted strong protection to support domestic manufacturing. They reduced tariffs only after 1945 when Europe and Japan were recovering from war and did not threaten their industries.

In the meantime, the United States had in 1854 forced Japan to maintain an 'open door policy,' while its own protection was the highest in the industrializing world. Japan did not obtain tariff autonomy until 1911 (Johnson, 1982: 25). Because it could not use the most traditional tool of industrial policy, it built an active state, which applied other instruments and a more sophisticated industrial policy, which included sending trade missions and students abroad and building new industries under government control and ownership and later privatizing them. Among the many visits that Japanese officials and industrialists paid to more advanced countries, the Iwakura mission to Britain, Continental Europe, and the United States in 1871–3 has been well documented (Beasley, 1995).

Today

The economic and intellectual environment in which post-1945 potential candidates for catching up have sought to industrialize differs radically from the one under which Continental Europe and the United States caught up with Britain in the nineteenth century. First, both protectionism and industrial policy have become anathema for policy-makers. The economic profession has stipulated, referring to Ricardo's law of comparative advantage (1817) and the Heckscher-Ohlin-Samuelson model of international trade (1937), that countries should specialize in producing goods and services for which they had the best (static) factor endowment. Nations with abundant natural resources should produce agricultural products or minerals. Those with lots of capital would specialize in capital-intensive goods, and those with large labour forces, in labour-intensive goods. These theories suffered from fundamental economic changes after 1945, as well as from our new understanding of economic development.

Economists today generally agree that knowledge and technology, not capital, labour, and natural resources, are the most important factors of production and that science and technology are most often the result of government investments. Countries, whether their strength lies in capital, in labour, or in raw materials, should seriously consider developing knowledge and technology through the appropriate institutions (such as higher education, public laboratories, and STI policies). Their industrial and economic development will depend not so much on how much labour they possess as on workers' level and quality of education and not so much on the amount of capital it has but on how well it has invested that capital.

The actual or potential catchers up have applied different types of policies. Two models seem to dominate: the 'flying geese' model of South East Asia and the import-substitution model of Latin America.

Flying Geese

Japanese economist Akamatsu Kaname (1896–1974) first proposed the flying-geese model of South East Asian industrial development in the 1930s. After the Second World War first Japan and then South Korea, Singapore, and more recently China and Vietnam applied it.

The model has three complementary dimensions. It is, first, an intra-industry model of the dynamics of a successful industry in a catching-up country, as it evolves from importing products, through importing machinery, to locally manufacturing those products for the internal market, to exporting the final products, and finally to exporting its machinery. We should link it to the product-life-cycle (PLC) model; some authors consider the flying geese a predecessor of the PLC theory that Raymond Vernon proposed in 1966 (Cummings, 1984).

It is, second, a model of a catching-up country acquiring one industrial sector at a time and concentrating public resources on the industry it wishes to develop, as well as on the supporting institutions of higher education, government laboratories, and specialized public policies; once this industry is internationally competitive, the country turns to the next one. Japan has provided the model to the region, and South Korea, Singapore, and other countries have followed it. In historical order, textiles, metal products, automobiles, electronics, and biopharmaceuticals have been the priority of such countries as Japan and South Korea in the last 50 years. Anchordoguy (1989) offers a fascinating picture of how the Japanese government, through its Ministry of International Trade and Industry (MITI), created a domestic computer industry *de novo* by concentrating financial and institutional resources and planning on this sector during the 1960s and 1970s.

The third interpretation of the flying-geese model is a pattern of changing comparative advantage in South East Asia, where Japan is the leading goose, with South Korea, Singapore, China, Vietnam, and others following (Edgington & Hayter, 2000; Kasahara, 2004; Kumagai, 2008; Kwan, 2002; Ozawa, 2001 and 2002). Whatever the particular application, the model is far from being a particular case of import substitution. The model depicts governments as not simply setting up tariffs but as supporting each new sector with human capital, money, new institutions such as public

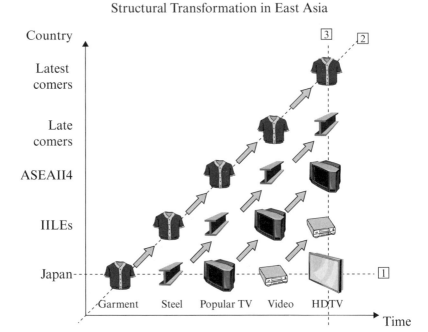

Structural Transformation in East Asia

Source: The Flying Geese Pattern of Development, Dr. Sabro Okita's Presentation (4th Pacific Economic Cooperation Council Conference, Seoul, 1985).

Figure 3.1   The flying-geese model

R&D laboratories and new STI policies, and other incentives. Their goal is to allow new entrants to move rapidly from imitation to innovation. Also, tariff and non-tariff protection has limits of time and scope. Figure 3.1 illustrates the argument.

Import Substitution

Industrialization by import substitution, or import-substitution industrialization (ISI), promotes industrialization in order to overcome the secular decline in the price of raw materials. As vocal promoter Argentinean economist Raul Prebisch observed: 'Formerly, before the great depression, development in the Latin American countries was stimulated from abroad by the constant increase of exports. There is no reason to suppose, at least at present, that this will again occur to the same extent, except under very exceptional circumstances. These countries no longer have an alternative between vigorous growth along these lines and internal expansion through industrialisation. Industrialisation has become the most important means of expansion' (Prebisch, 1950: 6).

The ISI model emerged in Latin America after an era when many countries there exported raw materials to Europe and to the United States. In the words of Hirschman (1968), such export-propelled growth lasted from the late nineteenth century until the Depression and ended about 1950. Yet 20 years later it became evident that inward industrialization was also running into problems. The reasons were many.

First, ISI encompassed across-the-board protection (Amsden, 2001), with no limits to time or scope. Governments protected industries for decades, even when they did not have the obligation to become internationally competitive. Such an approach did not create incentives for sheltered companies to upgrade their technology or to compete in foreign markets. Thus ISI promoted imitation, but not innovation with its associated increasing returns. Governments applied ISI policies some decades too late and omitted the essential STI institutions that South East Asian governments included in their flying-geese experiments. Finally, Latin American ISI merely replaced imports with local production and did not contemplate exports as a final goal of industrial policy. Conversely, South East Asian planners promoted industrialization for export in order to obtain foreign currency (Table 3.4).

The results of import substitution were predictable and similar throughout Latin America, but also in India, Turkey, and other developing countries: industry mushroomed but produced mature goods at high prices, was incapable of improving them, and found its manufactured exports marginal as a proportion of total exports: Latin America had continuously to rely on mineral and agricultural products to earn foreign currency. India and Turkey, which adopted this ISI model, were also exporting labour-intensive manufactured goods. Trade imbalances increased, and government deficits followed suit. For Latin America (but also for India, Turkey and other developing countries), the easy period of import substitution (textile, leather, furniture, basic metals, and petrochemicals) soon ended. The second stage ISI (machinery and equipment, electronics, pharmaceuticals, and fine chemicals) required inputs and institutions that governments had neglected: investments in STI and human capital. Also, internal markets could not support such sophisticated investments, either by local or by foreign companies. ISI policy was weak on exports to foreign markets. By the late 1970s, it became clear that the ISI experiment was running into an impasse. The rise in oil prices aggravated trade deficits. Higher interest rates made external debt unbearable for many countries in the region. Inflation increased. When governments reduced protectionist

Table 3.4   Comparing Asian flying-geese and Latin American ISI catching-up models

Policy	South East Asian flying geese	Latin American ISI
Identification of national priorities	Central government directed	No particular policy
Tariff protection	Limited in time and industry: one or two sectors at a time	No limits of time or industry
Technology import policy	Control over in-licensing	Technology transfer register
STI policies to stimulate learning and local BERD	Central government directed: e.g., tax credits and subsidies for R&D	No particular policy
Manpower policy: human-capital formation	Central government directed: upgrading of local education and extensive use of foreign higher-education institutions	No particular policy
Manpower policy: human-capital attraction	Central government directed: hiring of foreign experts	No particular policy
Financing	National development bank executing national priorities	National development bank with no priorities
Financing	Several strong sector programs linked to national priorities	Few sector programs not linked to priorities
Cluster and technopolis	Government directed through science and technology parks	No particular policy
Public procurement	Central government directed	No particular policy
Industrial structure	Preference for large national firms and/or multinationals	No particular policy
Foreign direct investment	Control over foreign direct investment	No policy or attraction of foreign direct investment
Export promotion	Tax deduction for exports	No particular policy
Export promotion	Currency manipulation (undervaluation)	No particular policy
Countries that adopted	China, Japan, Singapore, S. Korea	Argentina, Brazil, Mexico
Representative promoters	Kaname Akamatsu (Japan)	Raul Prebisch (Argentina)

tariffs in the 1970s and 1980s, some labour-intensive industries simply collapsed (Hirschman, 1968; Cardoso and Fishlow, 1992; Bruton, 1998).[1]

In the 1980s and 1990s, many Latin American countries turned to free trade. During the ISI period, foreign direct investment by multinational corporations (MNCs) had grown in such industries as automobiles, petrochemicals, and pharmaceuticals. Between 1980 and 2000, economic and industrial growth was at best erratic under free trade. MNCs increased their investment in such fields as food and beverages, and mining and energy, but also in privatized utilities: telecommunications, gas, and electricity services. The economic crisis of 2000–2 played havoc with free-trade experiments in the region. In the meantime, South East Asia was forging ahead through its carefully planned industrial policy, which included accumulation of learning and knowledge through various stages by addition of increasingly complex sectors and the accompanying institutions.

Another major difference between the flying-geese and the ISI models was that in South East Asia salaries started to rise soon after industrialization gained momentum (as did productivity, with learning in the lead). Conversely, in Latin America's ISI, governments sought to expand exports by devaluating currency or freezing wages. Amsden (1991: 284) sensibly maintains that a low-wage advantage of ISI countries could not offset a high-productivity advantage of flying geese. South East Asian nations achieved higher productivity by subsidizing R&D, investing in industry, controlling quality, and exporting goods from industrial firms in exchange for strong industrial commitment to absorb existing technologies and generate new ones. Amsden suggests that the flying-geese model is part of a more general pattern of 'industrializing by learning,' in contrast to a strategy in the 1990s that sought to nurture industrialization through free trade.

The flying-geese model gained the support of labour in a positive-sum game and reduced inequality. In contrast, the ISI model led to conflicts over distribution, which freer trade exacerbated in the late 1980s and the 1990s. As a result, South East Asia became more egalitarian and politically stable, while in Latin America income disparities increased and countries became less stable.

3.3 TECHNOLOGY POLICY

Technology policy is widespread in industrial and industrializing countries. Why does it exist? Equilibrium (neoclassical) and evolutionary approaches to economics have produced very different views of technology policy (Lipsey and Carlaw, 1998). In neoclassical economics there is one equilibrium position, all agents tend to maximize under perfect or quasi-perfect behavioural assumptions, and technology is observable only through its effects on productivity. In the evolutionary models, conversely, agents are bounded rational; therefore learning becomes central, and technological institutions are key. The main arguments of both currents are as follows.

Neoclassical

The central piece of the neoclassical argument in favour of technology policy is market failure: left to themselves, markets tend to produce reduced investment in science and technology. Market failure would result from five types of problem:

Externalities   Imperfect or unenforceable property rights would create productivity spillovers: firms investing in new technology would be unable to capture the full rents stemming from these investments. Consumers tend to benefit from lower prices (consumer surplus), and other enterprises (competitors) thrive from receiving free knowledge about this new technology (knowledge spillover) through several channels, including reverse engineering and the mobility of engineers and technicians between firms. Thus governments can legitimately subsidize the original innovators in order to compensate them for losses they incur on technology investments. Mansfield (1977) put the argument in another way: because of these spillovers, social returns from investments in science and technology are larger than private returns. It may thus be socially beneficial to subsidize private investment in science and technology.

- Risk and uncertainty may pervade research into new science and technology. Governments may justifiably support R&D on the frontiers of existing knowledge, particularly in science, where knowledge presents the characteristics of a public good and is difficult to protect.
- Strategic trade: In industries that experience economies of scale and first-mover advantages, such as aircraft, software, and pharmaceutical products, governments may subsidize new firms in order to ensure that the benefits accrue to the country (Krugman, 1983).
- Competition policy: Governments may subsidize new entrants in a given industry in order to increase competition.
- National missions, such as defense, health, environment, and communication, need public support to develop technologies in which private firms may curtail investment (Ergas, 1987). Governments intervene to increase production of these technologies and ensure that their supply corresponds to the public goal.

Several criticisms of this approach have surfaced. While most experts accept externalities, several have emphasized that governments may lack the knowledge to decide which technologies the market will adopt effectively or what the public or national need is. Externalities give rise to a policy failure, which may occur either because the government is subsidizing technologies that the market would have produced anyway or because the market does not adopt the new technologies. Also, a multi-country analysis shows that countries differ widely in their support for various industries. What is the optimal support for defense industries when the United States spends close to half of its public investment for technology in defense and Japan less than 2 per cent? The decision to subsidize one industry instead of another seems a matter more of governmental choice than of market failure.

Evolutionary Perspectives on Technology Policy

In the evolutionary approach, economic agents are bounded rational: their picture of the world is blurry, and they proceed mostly by trial and error, via search and later adjustments; therefore learning is a key component of human action and organizations. Also, pervasive path dependencies, dynamic increasing returns, and cumulative processes characterize markets (Arthur, 1994; David, 1994; Nelson and Winter, 1982). In such a context, narrow targeting of firms, industries, and technologies may produce government failure as well as government success. Conversely, horizontal, non-targeted policy may be beneficial. In evolutionary economics, the goals of such policy are four in number:

Creating variety and diversification
Economic variety and diversification may be beneficial for an economy. This was the stance in the 1950s of Latin America's structuralist school of development (Prebisch, 1950a and 1950b). Countries should produce high-value added goods and reduce the share of basic commodities in their exports in order to enter fast-growing markets. We can now understand why South East Asia did so well in contrast: high-growth, high-technology industries there succeeded dramatically, unlike the renewed emphasis on food, minerals, and other basic commodities in Latin America (Freeman, 1996).

Creating technological infrastructure
There are economies of scale in the collection and production of information. Governments may create public research centres, technological observatories, or other facilities to produce and disseminate knowledge

to small- and medium-sized enterprises that cannot sustain such activities as in-house R&D and monitoring of markets and technology (Tassey, 1991). This type of intervention has been frequent in agricultural R&D, as it has been clear since the nineteenth century that most farms lack resources to conduct research on plants, animal vaccines, and so on. Consequently, governments in most developed countries created agricultural research laboratories and disseminate both information and research results throughout the farms. Canada started agricultural R&D in public laboratories in 1868, and Argentina created the Instituto Nacional de Tecnología Agropecuaria (INTA) only in 1956.

Creating new routines in private and public institutions
Because of bounded rationality, firms do not invest in such a complex activity as R&D unless government promotes this routine. Learning here is the key issue. The idea is to build a community of users and producers of R&D, able to generate and adopt novelty. Such a policy may be necessary in developing countries, once the society has exhausted the learning opportunities that the opening of the economy has offered (Teubal, 1996, 1997).

Market failures
Evolutionary economics usually recognizes that market failure of the sort that I analyse above may arise. However, it does not accept either the maximizing behaviour of agents or the unique-equilibrium axioms of neoclassical theory.

Evolutionary economics also accepts that government or political failures occur. The emphasis on learning through government policy raises the possibility that public institutions may suffer from obstacles to learning. In other words, some public and private organizations may be reluctant to learn (Niosi, 2002). In market contexts, where most private firms operate, competition may take care of organizations that do not learn and that lag in competition. More awkward is the possibility that governments (which supposedly design, implement, evaluate, and adjust accordingly their policy incentives in science and technology) may be slow learners and become unable to measure the results of their intervention and incapable of modifying public inducements correspondingly. Evolutionary theories often assume that public institutions and private firms co-evolve and learn. Still, one should not take learning for granted: without appropriate dissemination of information, as well as incentives and contracts, public and private institutions do not learn. While the market teaches private firms, public-sector learning depends on adequate and independent periodic assessments. However, periodic policy evaluation may jeopardize the careers of bureaucrats, politicians, and managers, who may resent such evaluation and therefore not learn. Government's learning depends on some degree of competition among political actors, with the aim of modifying – and eventually even abolishing – policy instruments and technological infrastructure. Managers learn through incentives, plus real competition in the market.

Technology and institutions often co-evolve (Nelson, 1994a), as we can see in the development of STI policy after the Second World War. The rise of high-tech industries (electronics, aerospace, biopharmaceuticals, advanced materials, and nanotechnology) required new incentives and new governmental supports. Protection could not expand such sectors or attract foreign experts. Governments had to create this human capital, together with industrial demand for it. Substantial grants for academic research, direct subsidies for R&D, and government procurement and tax credits for innovative companies produced both the supply and the demand for cutting-edge skills.

Ergas (1987) classifies technology policy in two main types: 'mission-oriented' and 'diffusion-oriented'. In the first type, present in France, the United Kingdom, and the United States, governments subsidize production of technology in order to serve specific missions, such as defence and public health. U.S. military procurement and government-supported R&D took place through such programs as the Minuteman missile program and the Defense Advanced Research Program Agency (DARPA) (a response in 1958 to the launching of Sputnik). Also the Department of Defense's Very High Speed Integrated Circuits (VHSIC) program helped launch the American semi-conductor industry. Yet the strong role of U.S. government markets in semi-conductors probably discouraged their use in commercial markets, such as consumer electronics, in which Japan's Nippon conglomerates soon took the lead (Uenohara et al., 1984: 24–5). Similarly, in the 1960s and 1970s, DARPA helped fund development of ARPANET, precursor of the internet.

The second type of technology policy, diffusion-oriented, exists in Germany, Sweden, and Switzerland; governments intend intervention primarily to diffuse technology across the industrial structure. Ergas puts Japan in a separate class, in which government directs technology policy to both missions and diffusion.

Today we need to revise and add to Ergas's valuable and much-cited typology to accommodate the fast rise of South East Asia's newly indus- trialized economies. Countries catching up now implement technology policy to speed economic development. Ergas's Japanese 'outlier' case is becoming more frequent. Those governments that have taken Akamatsu,

Myrdal, and Solow seriously, including China, Singapore, and South Korea, are putting technology policy at the core of their long-term growth goals. This new third type of technology policy is one where the 'mission' of economic development includes both a major element of industrial mission and diffusion of new technology across the industrial structure.

But there is more to this than simply catching up. This 'economic development type' is now widespread also in OECD countries. Since the 1950s, the simultaneous revolution of advanced materials (now part of nanotechnologies), biotechnology, and information technologies is changing the industrial structure and renewing the basis of competition in North America and western Europe. Hundreds of thousands of new enterprises are exploiting new technology in semi-conductor design, editing and design of computer software, biotechnology, and advanced materials. These companies require more permanent government support, which now encompasses a panoply of measures, including financial and non-financial incentives (Table 3.5).

One of these measures is the fiscal credit for R&D. The U.S. government introduced tax credits in 1981, some years after other countries such as Canada, but before France (1983) and the United Kingdom (2000). In 1996, 12 OECD members provided such incentives; in 2008, 21 have adopted them. In many countries, tax credits represented the main public instrument for innovation. Also, U.S. states and Canadian provinces have instituted their own systems of tax credits. And a growing list of developing

Table 3.5   Measures to combat private under-investment in R&D

	Financial measures	Non-financial measures
Public provision of goods and services	Subsidizing exchange of R&D personnel between public and private sectors	Direct production of knowledge by public laboratories and universities
Modification of market incentives	Tax support for R&D Grants Soft loans Loan guarantees for R&D	Public procurement IP rights Competition policy for R&D projects
Support of the improvement of market mechanisms	Public venture capital	Creation or improvement of specialized financial-market mechanisms

Source: J. Guinet and H. Kamata (1996), 'Do tax incentives promote innovation?' in *OECD Observer*, 202, 22–5.

nations, including Argentina, Brazil, Chile, China, India, Mexico, Russia, Singapore, South Africa, and Taiwan, have implemented such policies to support innovation (Wajda, 2007). Yet tax credits penalize firms that have no tax liabilities. New technology companies usually have no profits to declare and so cannot take advantage of tax credits. Two types of policy incentives have resolved this problem: refundable tax credits for smaller firms (as in Canada and the Netherlands) and new programs of direct subsidies for SMEs, such as the Advanced Technology Program (1988) and the Small Business Innovation Research (SBIR) program (1992) in the United States.

R&D is not only about innovation (generating new products or processes) but also about learning existing technologies (Cohen and Levinthal, 1989). If catching up involves learning technological and related organizational novelties, developing countries would stress promotion of R&D, especially for business (BERD). Yet some such nations discovered only late the advantages of such programs, often a decade or two after their wealthier counterparts. Most LDCs, particularly in Africa and Latin America, have not discovered them yet. And, except for China and South Korea, most did not invest in or design the complementary incentives for innovation.

South Korea is one of the few developing countries that put technological learning at the forefront of its economic policy. In three decades, from the mid-1960s to the 1990s, it moved in a 'flying geese' pattern, moving from exporting textiles, toys, and other light manufactures in the 1960s, through steel, ships, and consumer electronics in the 1970s, to automobiles, computers, machinery, and semi-conductors, since the mid-1980s (Kim, 1997a). South Korea's government understood that a society catching up needed to import technology, diffuse it, and conduct indigenous R&D, both to assimilate it and to improve it as well as to produce new technology. For that purpose, it founded research institutes, which trained advanced researchers, many of whom moved to private R&D centres when these emerged later. Also, it created a ministry for science and technology as early as 1967; that department was in charge of preparing first the public R&D infrastructure and later the entry of the private sector into R&D. Over the decades, the government introduced many incentives. University R&D funds rose from U.S.$1.5 million in 1971 to $790 million in 1994, or 7.2 per cent of GERD, to $3.2 billion in 2005, or 9.9 per cent of GERD in purchasing parity power (PPP) (Kim, 1997b: 49; OECD, 2007c). Also, the government created numerous incentives for R&D, including tax credits, R&D loans, and preferential financing for industrial R&D (Kim, 1997b). Under so many stimuli, BERD expanded from U.S.$28.6 million in 1971 to $10.25 billion in 1994 to $24.6 billion in 2005. The number of corporate laboratories grew from one in 1970 to 2272 in 1995 to 12 104 in 2005 (Invest Korea, 2006). Similarly, the number of researchers in the private sector rose from 112 in 1965 to 2655 in 1975 to 137 700 in 2005.

South Korea had to build R&D capabilities from scratch. China had a more difficult task; it had to reorganize the R&D capabilities that it inherited from the Soviet-style regime, as well as building modern research organizations in the public and private sectors. In 1985, China started to dismantle its previous institutional systems, which had public research institutes separate from industry (Liu and White, 2001; Motohashi and Yun, 2007). The government privatized many public corporations, and new private firms appeared, both domestically and foreign-owned. From the late 1980s on, the government stimulated private and public companies to conduct R&D; also, it allowed universities and government laboratories to market their intellectual property or to conduct research for private firms. The Torch Program of the mid-1980s supported creation of incubators, as well as 53 academic science parks and over 40 000 spin-offs by 2005. In the 1990s, China revamped intellectual property by signing the Trade-related Aspects of Intellectual Property Rights (TRIPS) agreement. The Medium- to Long-Term Strategic Plan for the Development of Science and Technology (for 2006–20) has multiplied government investments (OECD, 2007c, 2008). By 2002, China had 600 foreign R&D laboratories. The ratio of R&D to GDP increased from 0.6 per cent in 1995 to 1.35 per cent in 2005. By 2006, China was the world's second-ranking country in GERD, ahead of Japan, and BERD represented two-thirds of total GERD (OECD, 2007c: 29). The new National Science Foundation (1986) and other agencies boosted academic R&D; by 2007, university research represented over 10 per cent of GERD; government research institutes spent the rest. In 2007, there were some 700 institutions of higher education, of growing but varied strength and visibility. The rise of scientific publications has been spectacular: by 2004, China was fifth in the world in numbers of scientific articles, after the United States, Japan, the United Kingdom, and Germany (Table 3.6). Despite so many achievements, however, there are several glaring weaknesses in the emerging national system of innovation, including the relatively strong need for venture capital (despite sizeable government investment), the scarcity of links between innovative organizations, and the uneven quality of academic teaching and research. Regional inequalities are also very extensive between the overdeveloped eastern coast and the hinterland.

The vast majority of developing countries are still unaware of the central importance of STI institutions. They leave higher education to itself, often under the guise of nurturing academic autonomy. Their STI

Table 3.6   Twenty countries with the largest number of scientific articles in the world, 2006

Country	2006
United States of America	283935
United Kingdom	74352
Germany	71174
Japan	71033
China	69423
France	50520
Canada	42841
Italy	39162
Spain	30338
Australia	26963
India	25610
South Korea	23200
Netherlands	23041
Russian Federation	20005
Brazil	16872
Switzerland	16781
Taiwan	16545
Sweden	16428
Turkey	13693
Poland	13002

Source: Thomson ISI.

policies are few in number and usually badly designed. For instance, Argentina, Brazil, and Mexico have implemented tax credits for R&D. But in both Argentina and Mexico, governments decide every year the size of these credits. In 2008, credits totalled U.S.$8 million in Argentina and $450 million in Mexico. Mexico abandoned tax credits in 2009. However, because law fixes these amounts, and demand far outstrips supply, civil servants decide which companies will receive credits. This system limits total national BERD and increases the potential for corruption. Brazil has several times modified the law of 1993. No evaluation was available as to its effects, but Brazilian BERD, at 0.4 per cent, is low as a proportion of GERD compared to almost all OECD countries.

Conclusion

Organizations, like the people who inhabit them, avoid risk and uncertainty and prefer easy tasks to complex ones. Industrial policy before 1939

Table 3.7 *Argentina, Brazil, Mexico, and South Korea, USPTO patents, 1981–2008*

Years	Brazil		Argentina		Mexico		South Korea	
	Requested	Granted	Requested	Granted	Requested	Granted	Requested	Granted
1983	57	19	35	21	73	34	78	26
1984	62	20	40	20	77	43	74	30
1985	78	30	39	11	81	35	129	41
1986	68	27	56	17	69	37	162	46
1987	62	34	42	18	70	54	235	84
1988	71	29	32	16	74	45	295	97
1989	111	36	32	20	77	41	607	159
1990	88	41	56	17	76	34	775	225
1991	124	62	59	16	106	42	1321	405
1992	112	40	59	20	105	45	1471	538
1993	105	57	56	24	82	50	1624	779
1994	156	60	75	32	105	52	1354	943
1995	115	63	65	31	99	45	1820	1161
1996	145	63	78	30	97	46	4248	1493
1997	134	62	77	35	110	45	1920	1891
1998	165	74	119	43	141	57	5452	3259
1999	186	91	96	44	147	76	5033	3562

Year								
2000	240	122	138	65	180	107	5882	3699
2001	247	127	146	58	220	95	6792	3783
2002	288	113	109	54	167	93	7757	3755
2003	333	150	123	68	213	93	9614	4198
2004	287	192	118	57	211	113	13388	4590
2005	340	93	92	37	217	88	16643	4811
2006	333	152	133	39	229	93	21963	5835
2007	385	112	166	52	216	89	23589	6882
2008	–	131	–	46	–	78	–	8410

Table 3.8   BERD and GERD, selected countries and blocs, 2006

Country	GERD (Million current U.S.$ PPP)	GERD as % of GDP	BERD (Million current U.S.$ PPP)	BERD as % of GDP
Developed countries				
U.S.A.	348 658	2.66	247 669	1.89
Japan	138 782	3.39	107 078	2.62
Germany	66 716	2.54	46 630	1.77
U.K.	35 590	1.78	21 943	1.10
France	41 508	2.1	26 186	1.32
Canada	23 306	1.94	12 755	1.06
Italy	19 384	1.14	9455	0.55
EU 27	244 655	1.77	154 376	1.12
South East Asia				
China	86 760	1.42	61 666	1.00
South Korea	35 890	3.22	27 725	2.49
Singapore	4780	2.31	3143	1.52
Latin America				
Argentina	2320	0.49	705	0.15
Brazil	17 950	1.00	7180	0.40
Mexico*	5919	0.46	2927	0.23

Note: * Figures for 2005.

Sources: OECD (2008), *Main science and technology indicators*, Paris, vol. 2. De Britto and de Mello (2006), 'Boosting innovation performance in Brazil', OECD Working Papers 532.

was about creating new sectors through the unsophisticated but effective tools of tariff and non-tariff protection, public financing of new industrial plants, imitation and attraction of artisans, industrialists, and inventors from more advanced nations, and founding of state companies. Such tools are still in use, as witness agricultural subsidies in industrial nations, as well as many policies (e.g., the still-active Buy American Act of 1933 or the recent intervention of the Canadian, French, German, and U.S. governments in their automobile industries), but they are receding in favour of subtler tools within science and technology policies.

Within organizations and academic, private, and public laboratories, R&D and innovation are among the most difficult tasks because they involve risk and uncertainty. Industrial learning – both organizational and technological and the breakdown of inertia – requires a major effort from governments. This endeavour can succeed if government places technology policy at the centre of its long-term plans of economic development. In this sense, the South Korean achievement is nothing less than remarkable, with over 12000 private firms active in R&D and its BERD now larger than that of France and the United Kingdom. China is now in third place in the world for its BERD (Table 3.8). Latin American countries – even the largest of them, Brazil, the 9th major world economy – are not in the same league.

Technology institutions are not simply about reducing market failures. They are at the same time about creating human capital (through the appropriate higher education and research institutions) and markets for it through promotion of business R&D and other best practices in industrial companies. Their goal is creating markets for innovative products and processes as well as the capacity to produce these goods and services. They aim at providing incentives for academic institutions to conduct advanced research and transfer the results to industry and society, including through incubation of new technology-based companies. Their objective is also about helping government laboratories move beyond agricultural and industrial extension into R&D and spinning off new firms. Finally, they also can affect the industrial structure by introducing new industrial sectors that are more intensive in research and development, technology, and innovation.

The two main approaches that developing countries have applied are the 'flying geese' model of South East Asia, which centred on learning and innovation, and the import-substitution model of Latin America. The relative fates of countries applying these two models are clear in Tables 3.6 and 3.7. In science, only Brazil approaches the rank of advanced countries; in technology, it lags far behind its South East Asian competitors.

NOTE

1. Katz (2000) argues that Argentina, Brazil, and Mexico increased productivity under ISI and augmented technological sophistication in several industries.

4. Building blocks of innovation

All systems are composed of elements and relationships between these elements. Innovation systems are made of economic agents (different types of organizations with their routines) and links between them.

This chapter looks at seven crucial building blocks of systems of innovation – human capital, academic institutions, government laboratories, horizontal policy, vertical policy, government investment, and absorptive capacity.

As I did above, I distinguish here four types of institutions: independent organizations, practices of organizations (e.g., R&D, production, and marketing routines), institutions that represent the environment of organizational routines and shape the relationships between organizations, such as laws, public policies, and regulations, and other institutions. The four-class typology presents an advantage, because public policies usually are independent variables that determine organizational routines. For instance, tax credits or direct subsidies for R&D may trigger new R&D or innovation or innovation practices in private firms. It is convenient to distinguish between these kinds of institutions when our goal is to understand the development of innovation systems.

The chapter also develops the concept of 'absorptive capacity of nations' – a notion that derives from Cohen and Levinthal (1990), Zahra and George (2002), and other scholars: institutions that support R&D increase a nation's capacity to use existing technical knowledge.

4.1 HUMAN CAPITAL

The relationship between human capital and economic development has generated an extensive and convincing literature. However, problems of definition and measurement have precluded precise estimation of the impact of human capital on economic development (Griliches, 1997; van Leeuwen, 2007). Three matters have proven particularly intractable: quality of education, workforce participation of people with higher education, and links between education and productivity.

The catching-up process has always happened at the same time as a rapid rise in education – particularly of the technical sort. Catching up is not the automatic and costless transfer of information from advanced to developing countries, but instead requires an understanding of the technologies that a society is to import, assimilate, and master, that in turn presupposes educated personnel.

In the nineteenth century, France and Germany created a whole set of technical institutes to train engineers, in order to catch up with Britain (Landes, 1972: 170). In the United States, catching-up industrialization after 1850 went hand in hand with foundation of dozens of institutions of higher education following the Morrill Act of 1862, which gave federal lands to states so they could create universities specializing in agriculture and mechanical arts (Nelson and Rosenberg, 1994). The U.S. university system, with its emphasis on education and scientific research, learned and adapted extensively from Germany. The coupling of basic and applied research with teaching accelerated transfer of technology from university to industry, as both academic researchers and graduates moved frontier knowledge from the former to the latter (Feller, 1999: 83).

In Japan, the College of Engineering (which started in 1873 and merged in 1886 with the University of Tokyo of 1877) and other post-secondary institutes, which followed the British and German model, accompanied rapid industrialization. The government emphasized technical education and collaboration with industry, rather than pure science and scientific publication (Odagiri, 1999; Mazzoleni, 2008). Also, it invited foreign scholars to teach during the two decades after the Meiji Restoration of 1868. Another novelty found echoes throughout South East Asia: strong incentives for local students to study abroad in order to nurture inward technology transfer.

All OECD members have created grant programs to lure students to higher education. A few others, such as Canada and the United States, have also set up large programs through which students receive interest-free loans while studying and pay them back when they complete their degrees and leave university or if they abandon their programs.

There has been extensive study in OECD countries of the impact of education on revenue and productivity. For instance, one study has found that, on average, each extra year of schooling over ten years raised output per capita by 6 per cent (Temple, 2001). Annual private rates of return for an extra year of education ranged between 5 and 15 per cent. Other benefits, even more difficult to estimate, included greater life expectancy, more social capital (trust), and better quality of life.

There were also wide differences in scientific and technical education between the rapidly catching-up nations in South East Asia and the 'falling-behind' countries of Latin America, which were 40 years ago way ahead of their Asian competitors (Amsden, 2001; Freeman, 1996). Asian university training was strongly emphasizing technical and scientific education, while Latin American universities were stronger in traditional careers such as law, medicine, and humanities. Enrolment in higher education in South East Asia soared, and thousands of students went abroad to study. As of 2004, India, China, South Korea, Taiwan, and Japan (in descending order) occupied five of the six top positions in number of foreign graduate students in the United States (NSF, 2006). In addition, between 1992 and 2003, more than 30 000 Chinese students obtained PhDs there, along with over 12 000 Indians, 11 500 Taiwanese, and 11 300 South Koreans. Most of those doctorates were in science and engineering. Fewer than 8400 Latin Americans earned PhDs in the United States during the same period.

Among developing countries, Arab nations display much lower rates of adult literacy than Latin America (64.1 per cent against 89.6 per cent) and education indexes (0.61 against 0.87) according to the United Nations (UN, 2006). Some Arab states, like most Latin American countries, do not lack natural resources (usually hydrocarbons), and their GDP per capita is not low. As in Latin America, these societies may face institutional barriers to education and formation of human capital.

In sum, a vast literature from economics and economic history shows that a rapid rise in education, particularly post-secondary technical and scientific education, accompanies catching up. This process is one of institutional and organizational build-up that includes creation and/or revamping of universities and technical institutes, hiring of foreign academics, and encouragement of local students to obtain postgraduate degrees abroad.

4.2   ACADEMIC INSTITUTIONS

We may start by distinguishing three types of universities: teaching (the Bologna type), teaching and research (the Humboldt type), and teaching, research, and industrial development (like MIT). The first model is the most ancient. It may be 1000 years old and emerged in the Middle Ages (Foray, 2003). The second began to appear in the mid-nineteenth century in Germany and produces human capital as well as new knowledge. The United States started setting up the third type of institution in the early twentieth century. It has strong ties to industry and produces useful knowledge with a commercial goal.

Development of human capital and human resources, essential for absorbing foreign technology or creating new technology, results from investments by individuals, firms, and governments. In less-advanced countries, individuals can barely invest in education, particularly after secondary school. Firms will not invest either, because of the 'free rider' problem: individuals can use the skills that firms pay to create to bargain higher salaries elsewhere, even abroad. Governments thus must invest in higher education and have done so in all countries catching up.

Industrializing countries tend to develop the Humboldt type of university, in which teaching and research coexist. Such organizations, both public and private, favour transfer of technology to industry through many channels, including hiring of trained researchers by industry, contractual research that industry pays for in universities, consultation of academic researchers by industry, and patenting and licensing by universities. Universities compete for top-level teachers and students, as well as for public and industrial research funds, and look abroad for teachers and researchers.

The United States has created hundreds of universities since passage of the Morrill Act in 1862. In 1930 it set up the National Institutes of Health, and in 1950 the National Science Foundation (NSF), both to support university research, as well as setting up other programs to support transfer of university research results to industry. Prominent legislation included the Bayh–Dole Act (1980), the Small Business Innovation Research Act (SBIR) in 1982, and the Small Business Technology Transfer Research Act (STTR) of 1992. Bayh–Dole transferred the intellectual property of academic research (and other public research laboratories) to the performing institutions inasmuch as public funds financed the research. SBIR helps small and medium-sized enterprises absorb new technology and provides up to $850 000 in early-stage R&D to small technology companies or to entrepreneurs who launch a firm. The STTR program provides up to a similar sum to small companies working in co-operation with academic researchers at universities, or with government researchers in public laboratories, to explore the commercial feasibility of new ideas emerging from these public institutions. Of the federal departments that allocate R&D funds to private firms, the most important is Defense, which runs both types of programs. All departments combined, SBIR constituted $1.14 billion in FY2007, and STTR $131 million.

In Canada, the federal government created the Medical Research Council (now Canadian Institutes for Health Research) in 1960 and the Natural Science and Engineering Research Council (NSERC) and the Social Sciences and Humanities Research Council (SSHRC) in the 1970s to support academic research and give incentives to universities to conduct advanced research. In 1997 it founded the Canada Foundation for Innovation (CFI) to fund research infrastructure. In 2000 it set up Genome Canada to support genomics research with a total fund of $700 million. By 2007 the combined annual budget of the five organizations was in excess of $2.5 billion. Since the 1970s provincial governments have supported university research. However, Canada has no equivalent to the Bayh–Dole Act, SBIR, or STTR, although there have been discussions about new mechanisms to support commercialization of academic research.

In Latin America and Continental Europe, most notably in Latin countries, the Bologna model is prevalent: research and teaching remain separate, with universities performing mostly teaching and a new type of institution launched in the 1920s and 1930s (of which France's Conseil National de la Recherche Scientifique, or CNRS, is the paradigm) doing only research. The French model has been dominant in Italy, Portugal, and Spain and all of Latin America since the 1950s. Such a system is less conducive to transfer of technology from university to industry, which occurs instead through the movement of graduates to the private sector.

During Japan's industrialization, universities were far less autonomous than those in western Europe or North America, and few imperial universities – most notably the University of Tokyo – boasted much of the nation's academic talent. Kyoto University started in 1897 and emphasized engineering. Tokyo, Kyoto, and five other imperial universities completed the elite system before the Second World War and still are among the country's top institutions of higher education. Since 1945 the government has created numerous funding agencies for university research under various ministries. By 2005 their annual budgets totalled over 467 billion yen (U.S.$4.1 billion), a small sum in relation to U.S. and western European budgets. Because the university system emphasized technical disciplines over pure science and humanities, Japan has many fewer Nobel prizes in science than comparable countries; 9 by 2007, against 240 from the United States, 81 from Germany, 80 from Britain, 31 from France, Canada and Italy 12 each.

Among developing countries, in South Korea enrolment in tertiary education increased from 38 400 students in 1953 to 1.15 million in 1994 and over 2 million in 2004, mostly in engineering programs (Kim, 1997a and 1997b: 63). In 2004, the rate of attendance in college and university (the percentage of students in the corresponding age cohort receiving post-secondary education) was over 60 per cent. By 2004, the country had 200 universities. Yet, like in Japan, a handful of universities did most of the advanced research, including Seoul and Pohang National Universities and KAIST (Korea Advanced Institute for Science and Technology). The Korean Science and Engineering Foundation (KOSEF, 1977) is the domestic equivalent of the U.S. National Science Foundation and the nation's only public funding agency for academic research. Overseas training in the United States was and remains very extensive, with over half of South Koreans graduating abroad going there, but with others studying in Japan, Britain, and Canada. As of 2007, South Korea had no Nobel Prize in science; like Japan, it has traded scientific excellence for economic growth.

Latin American universities reproduced the Latin European system. Each boasts several large national public universities and a few private ones. A CNRS type of research system developed in the 1950s and 1960s and takes research capability away from the universities. France founded the CNRS in 1938; Argentina's CONICET and Brazil's CNPq both emerged in 1951, Chile's CONICYT in 1967, and Mexico's CONACYT in 1972. These systems of higher education feature low funding for university research, low levels of university attendance, particularly in natural science and engineering, modest scientific excellence (four Nobel prizes in science for the region – three from Argentina and one from Mexico), fairly low publication rates, and little patenting. As for university attendance and fields of study, Table 4.1 and Figure 4.1 are eloquent: in Japan and South Korea, by 2002 over 10 per cent of 24 year olds had a university degree in natural science or engineering, against about 1 per cent in the three largest Latin American countries (Argentina, Brazil, and Mexico).

Also, Latin American universities produce few commercial results. In

Table 4.1   Field of first university degree and ratio to 24-year-old population, 2002 or most recent year

Country	Ratio of 1st university degree to 24-year-old population	Ratio of 1st university degree in natural science and engineering to 24-year-old population
Argentina	8.9	0.8
Brazil	14.9	0.9
Mexico	17.4	1.6
Germany	21.1	2.1
Italy	28.9	4.0
South Korea	31.7	13.5
Canada	36.7	4.4
Japan	36.8	11.6
U.S.A.	39.8	3.1
U.K.	45.8	4.8
France	48.7	6.7

Source: National Science Foundation, *Science and Engineering Indicators 2006*.

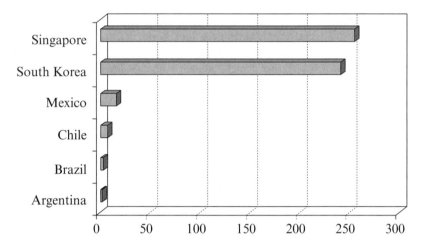

*Figure 4.1   U.S. patents granted to universities, selected countries,
1976–2007*

over 30 years, Argentina's have produced two U.S. patents, Brazil's two,
Chile's seven, and Mexico's 17. In the meantime, South Korea's received
242, and Singapore's 255. Singapore has only 4.5 million people and was
poorer than any of these Latin American countries 40 years ago. In 1962,
South Korea, with a population of 48 million today, was one of the poorer
nations in the world.

In publication, despite some improvements in Latin America, most
conspicuously in Brazil, proportionate figures are disturbing (Table 4.2
and Figure 4.2). Singapore (4.4 million inhabitants) publishes as much as
Argentina (40 million). With 49 million people, South Korea produces as
much as Argentina, Brazil, and Mexico, with 330 million.

The picture is even more dismal for patents. Between 1976 and 2007,
the United States Patent and Trademark Office granted Argentina's and
Brazil's universities two patents each, against 250 for South Korea's
and 255 for Singapore's (Table 4.3). CNRS-type institutions are equally
patent-poor in all leading Latin countries.

The comparison of expenditures on R&D in higher education in several
countries completes the picture (Table 4.4). In 2004, the most advanced
Latin American countries spent less than U.S.$20 per capita, against $75
in Singapore and between $100 and $233 in the G-7 countries.

In sum, rapidly growing South East Asian countries have imitated
Anglo-Saxon university systems but concentrated in applied science and
engineering and on developing human resources. Also, starting from low
levels in the 1960s, they have pursued human development and are now

Table 4.2   Science and engineering articles, selected countries, 2003

Country	S&E articles 2003	Articles per million population
U.K.	48 288	804
Canada	24 803	800
Singapore	3122	710
U.S.A.	211 233	704
Germany	44 305	547
France	31 917	523
Japan	60 067	481
Italy	24 696	426
South Korea	13 746	305
Chile	1500	100
Argentina	3096	81
Brazil	8684	51
Mexico	3747	37

Source: National Science Foundation, *Science and Engineering Indicators 2006.*

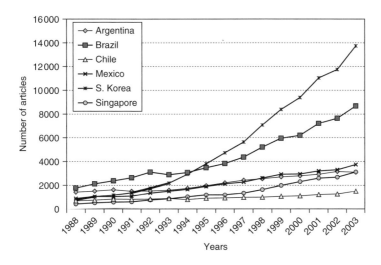

Source: NSF: *Science and Engineering Indicators.*

Figure 4.2   S&E articles, selected countries, 1988–2003

*Table 4.3   U.S. patents granted to universities of selected countries,
            1976–2007*

Country	Number of university patents	Number of patents of CNRS-type research institutes
Argentina	2	2
Brazil	2	3
Chile	7	0
Mexico	17	3
Spain	109	6
S. Korea	250	n.a.
Singapore	255	n.a.
France	278	249

Source: USPTO.

Table 4.4   Higher-education expenditures on R&D, 2004

Country	Higher education expenditures on R&D	Higher-education expenditures on R&D per million population (U.S.$ current PPP)
Argentina*	156	4
Mexico*	947	9
Chile*	203	14
Brazil*	2881	17
Singapore** (2005)	332	75
South Korea (2005)	3131	64
Italy	5880	101
Germany	9752	120
Japan	15847	123
France	7444	124
U.K.	7537	126
U.S.A.	42431	141
Canada	7231	233

Notes:
*   RiCYT: Expenditures on science and technology in higher education by performance
     sector.
**   *Statistics Singapore Newsletter* March 2007.

Source: OECD: *Main science and technology indicators*, 2006.

approaching the ranks of G-7 countries. In contrast, most developing countries, including those of Latin America, are experiencing 'low skills equilibrium' – self-reinforcing, vicious circles where state institutions invest little in human capital and new sectors do not develop and do not demand high skills (Bae and Rowley, 2004).

4.3   GOVERNMENT LABORATORIES

Economic development in catching-up Asian countries received reinforcement with creation of a large number of national laboratories. Yet the missions and structures of these facilities vary enormously from one country to another. The basic dichotomy is between extension laboratories, which provide such services as analysis of plants, soil, water quality, and waste in agriculture, as well as metrology, quality control, and standards in manufacturing, and R&D laboratories, which do science more than applied research. Crow and Bozeman (1998) provide a much more complex typology of U.S. government laboratories, which include 'public science' laboratories, such as the Fermi National Accelerator, the Lawrence Berkeley Laboratories, and many laboratories of the National Institutes of Health (NIH), which generate pure scientific knowledge. They also find 'public science and technology laboratories' producing both science and industrial knowledge and public technology laboratories creating only industrial technology, such as the Kentucky Center for Energy Research. Another valuable type is the hybrid science-and-technology laboratory, which produces articles and conferences, but also prototypes and internal reports and research for industry in specific projects; these organizations include the U.S. Geological Survey (USGS, under the Department of the Interior), which has existed since 1879, and the National Institute for Standards and Technology (NIST), 1901. The USGS studies earth and water in the United States and helps industry in use of mineral and water resources. The NIST produces infrastructure technology for industry (see Table 4.4). Even though mission laboratories have always formed the majority of public U.S. research organizations, the authors note an evolution towards increasing numbers of civil-technology industrial laboratories. Sematech, founded in 1987 to support research on semiconductors, is one of them; a non-profit R&D organization, it drifted to the private sector as public support gave way to industrial funding (Crow and Bozeman, 1998: 32).

In the United States, according to the NSF, the rationales for federal laboratories, besides pursuit of particular missions, were those of 'scale' – conducting R&D on magnitudes that exceed the capabilities or resources

Table 4.5 Representative U.S. government laboratories

Name	Year Founded	Web site	Size of S&E Staff, 2007	Mission	Responsible department	Budget, annual (most recent)
Agriculture	1862	www.ars.usda.gov	2100	Agricultural research	Agriculture	n.a.
U.S. Geological Survey	1879	www.usgs.gov	>10000	Earth sciences, mineral and water resources	DOI	$971 million
NIST	1901	www.nist.gov	2900	Infrastructure technology	DOC	$843 million
Naval Research Lab	1923	www.nrl.navy.ml	1500	Naval research	DOD	n.a.
NIH	1930	www.nih.gov	6000	Human health research	DOHHS	$2.8 billion
Lawrence Berkeley	1931	www.lbl.gov	3800	Energy, biology, nanoscience	DOE	$500 million
Los Alamos	1943	www.lanl.gov	9000	Nuclear, security	DOE	$2.2 billion
Oak Ridge National Lab	1943	www.ornl.gov	4200	Energy, life sciences, nanomaterials	DOE	$1.2 billion

Name	Year	Website	Employees	Research area	Agency	Budget
Argonne National Laboratory	1946	www.anl.gov	1000	Nuclear reactors	DOE	$475 million
Brookhaven National Lab	1947	www.bnl.gov	3200	Biology, chemistry, security	DOE	$445 million
Ames National Laboratory	1947	www.ameslab.gov		Energy, materials	DOE	$30 million
Princeton Plasma Physics Lab	1951	www.ppl.gov	400	Magnetic fusion	DOE	$83 million
Lawrence Livermore	1952	www.linl.gov	>8000	Nuclear weapons, bioscience, security	DOE	$1.6 billion/year
Goddard Space Flight Center	1959	www.gsfc.nasa.gov	12 500	Earth, solar, space science, satellites	NASA	$2 billion
Fermilab	1967	www.fnal.gov	2100	Physics, accelerator	DOE	$300 million

of private organizations – security, and knowledge management – basically long-term memory in specific sectors (NSF, 2006, vol. 1, pp. 4–22). In 2005, the government spent $25 billion in R&D in federal laboratories, more than half of it in facilities under the aegis of the Department of Defense. The next two largest spenders were Health and Energy. The government owns and runs some of these laboratories and owns others that industry or universities manage. The Stanford Linear Accelerator is a public laboratory of the Department of Health, but an academic organization operates it. In 2003, federal laboratories participated in 2936 cooperative R&D agreements with industry (NSF, vol. 1, pp. 4–6). They also received 1607 patents and 3656 licences from their inventions (ibid.).

In Canada, as in most countries, agricultural and geological research is historically the first area of public R&D. The Geological Survey of Canada (GSC) started in 1842 with a mission similar to the USGS's and is still one of Canada's largest public R&D laboratories. Public agricultural research started in 1868. Its rationale is and has always been what we call today 'correcting market failures': farms do not often conduct R&D, and the agro-food industry lacks size and capital to do so (Carew, 2001). The federal government has always paid for most agricultural R&D, even if its share has declined over time as university and provincial efforts have expanded. Ottawa has also long supported manufacturing research, mainly through the civil-industry research laboratories now under the aegis of the National Research Council (NRC), which it set up in 1916 and where it, to provide advice, created its first laboratories in the Department of Industry in the 1930s. The Second World War and the federal government's intention to diversify the economy fuelled development of public laboratories to undertake industrial research. The NRC had initially created mostly science laboratories, but after 1945 it launched a set of science and technology institutes, emphasizing support for industry. Today, NRC facilities employ some 4000 people across Canada and cover fields from aerospace and industrial machinery to biotechnology and nanotechnology. Federal departments ranging from Agriculture to Defence, Industry, and Natural Resources also support R&D, but their laboratories are smaller than their U.S. counterparts and focus less on national security.

South Korea's development of public research infrastructure started with industrialization in the 1960s. Up to that time, it had few capabilities in science and technology (Han, 1999; Kim, 1997a and 1997b). In 1959 it created a nuclear research institute (KAERI), and in 1966 twin organizations: KIST (Korea Institute for Science and Technology), as its central R&D laboratory, and KAIST (Korea Advanced Institute for Science and Technology), for advanced training (later 'South Korea's MIT'). It then established a series of more specialized research facilities (Table 4.6), most

Table 4.6   Selected South Korean government R&D laboratories

	Year Founded	Mission	Staff	U.S. Patents
KAERI	1959	Nuclear energy	ND	102
KIST	1966	Industrial R&D	654	7
KRIBB	1995	Biotechnology	293	45
ETRI	1976	ICT research	3000	0
SERI	1981	Engineering	NA	0
STEPI	1984	ST policy	54	0

Notes:
ETRI = Electronic and Telecommunications Research Institute.
KAERI = Korea Atomic Energy Research Institute.
KIST = Korea Institute for Science and Technology.
KRIBB = Korea Research Institute for Bioscience and Biotechnology.
SERI = Systems Engineering Research Institute.
STEPI = Science and Technology Policy Institute.

notably ETRI (1976) – 'South Korea's Bell Labs' – to support and co-
ordinate the embryonic electronics and telecommunications industry.

But the government was willing to give up even on very ambitious enterprises that were not so successful. It cancelled a nuclear reactor, a midsize
passenger aircraft, and a neutrino project. This approach suggests that
industrializing countries do not need to start with public science laboratories. Such a need will appear later, when the nation has almost caught up
and needs to open new research paths. One example in South Korea is the
Science and Technology Policy Institute – a small, highly skilled government think tank that provides the government with policy alternatives and
works to improve the national innovation system. Out of its 54 employees,
30 have PhDs.

In Taiwan, research institutes that the government supports play a dominant role in the national innovation system – most notably the Industrial
Technology Research Institute (ITRI), which it set up in 1973 to address
the technological needs of industry (Chu et al., 2006). It has become
a model of good governance and industrial incubation for developing
countries as well as an engine of industrial growth at home. It acquires,
develops, and transfers technology for the civilian sector. It has greatly
assisted rapid assimilation and catching up in the semi-conductor industry (Jan and Chen, 2006), and the country's two largest semi-conductor
foundries, which are among the world's top competitors – namely United
Microelectronics and Taiwan Semiconductor Manufacturing – are both
ITRI spin-offs. ITRI has also been instrumental in development of other
industries: automobiles, information technology, machine tools, and

optoelectronics. It also helps the chemical, pharmaceutical, and computer industries with dedicated laboratories. By mid-2009, ITRI had over 6000 employees, and more than 60 per cent of them had at least a master's degree. It has received more than 3300 U.S. patents since 1976 and has spun off an entire cluster of firms in the Hsinchu Science-Based Industrial Park (Hu et al., 2005).

4.4   HORIZONTAL POLICY

Building public organizations for science and technology represents a challenge for industrializing nations. Incorporating R&D in firms is a much more complex issue. For such purposes, governments need to induce private companies to change their behaviour and incorporate new R&D routines. These routines are prone to risk and uncertainty, demand long periods of investment before any return appears, and face strong competition from incumbents. In addition, firms must compete with the public sector (universities and public laboratories) for the best talent. All organizations by nature suffer from inertia, and private enterprises are reluctant to enter the R&D game because of all these factors.

In order to alter the structure of (at least some) companies, governments should avoid thinking of them as 'black boxes' and start monitoring their internal organization. Governments in all wealthy countries do this through statistical offices and other departments. We see above that in 2006 South Korea had more than 12000 industrial firms with internal R&D laboratories. Canada has a similar proportion, and close to 20000 companies each year request tax credits for R&D. (Some ask for the credits and outsource R&D to academic and government facilities.)

Another crucial point is that no single policy will overcome R&D inertia. What all industrial countries have implemented is a battery of complementary policies (Mohnen and Röller, 2005). A few examples can suffice for our purposes.

Almost all OECD countries apply tax credits for R&D, so a huge empirical literature examines their varying experiences. Tax credits have a major advantage: they do not favour any sector. If, unlike the situation in Argentina and Mexico, there is no maximum to their amount, they may attract both domestic and foreign firms. If governments design them well and build in larger incentives for SMEs, they will serve both large and smaller enterprises. However, tax credits do not serve to launch new firms or create new sectors. And they are usually not enough of an incentive to convince small companies to join the game of innovation.

In order to lure SMEs towards innovation, governments have created a panoply of programs, which include direct, non-reimbursable subsidies for R&D. Canada's Industrial Research Assistance Program (IRAP), the U.S. Small Business Innovation Research Program (SBIR), and the Japanese SBIR, which the American incentive inspired, are interesting cases.

With a view to incorporating skilled human capital in industrial firms, many countries provide grants to pay the salaries of young engineering or science graduates for a short period – perhaps six months.

Joint industry–university research centres with government funding often find homes on academic campuses. Such a trend often breeds close links between academic and industrial research, facilitates transfer of technology both ways, and familiarizes students with industrial R&D.

Governments invest in private-sector innovation, but how much should they invest? In most industrial nations, governments have for decades supported the largest share of private sector R&D. While aggregate data for OECD countries are available only for years since the 1980s (and reveal diminishing government support to BERD), historical analyses show strong support early in industrialization, as companies slowly adopt new routines (Kim, 1997a and 1997b; Teubal, 1996; Trajtenberg, 2001).

Because STI policy takes time to produce results (firms do not react instantaneously), policy-makers need to be patient and attentive to outcomes. In Canada since the 1970s the number of firms conducting R&D and building in-house labs has grown slowly towards the present level of more than 12 000 (Niosi, 2000a). Yet policy-makers need to pay attention to the double danger of corruption from public bureaucracies and moral hazard from private firms that may keep profits and transfer losses to government.

All wealthy countries and a few developing nations have tried to build a venture capital industry to support new technology firms (Dossani and Kenney, 2002), but there are few success stories. The United States possesses perhaps the only flourishing such sector and represents over half of the world's venture capital. Canada, Israel, and the United Kingdom have had some success in this area. For most of the world, such factors as macro-economic instability, lack of capital, absence of adequate financial institutions including stock markets, and lack of experience in such a risky type of management have been major obstacles in this field.

Horizontal policies such as those I mentioned before present advantages and disadvantages. On the positive side, they limit corruption and moral hazard. On the negative side, most countries that have to pick sectors and horizontal policies cannot help to choose sectors. The median country has a population of 4.5 million. If the United States developed with few sectoral policies, nations such as Finland and Singapore had to choose sectors in order to avoid dispersing scarce resources too broadly and thinly.

The historical record does not show a best practice of incorporating these complementary policies in a particular order, but several useful findings have emerged. First, policy stability counts. A study of 17 OECD members finds that direct government funding of BERD increased business expenditures on R&D and that tax incentives were particularly effective; as well, both direct funding and tax incentives increased BERD when they were stable over time (Guellec and Van Pottelsberghe, 2003). Similarly, Zhu et al. (2006) note that in China the stability of policies increased their effects. Once a government launches a STI policy it should evaluate, improve, and enhance it. In contrast, Chudnovsky et al. (2000) observe that the many changes in STI policy in Argentina harmed industrial R&D.

Second, it is difficult to start the institution-building sequence with vertical policies, because governments need to understand the industrial life cycle of the sectors they choose. It is not realistic to expect them at the start to know about complex industrial and product life cycles. Dozens of governments tried to nurture a domestic aircraft industry and failed, for picking sectors is not easy.[1] If STI policy must be stable, then vertical policy should arrive after years of designing and implementation of horizontal policies.

Third, vis-à-vis human capital it is important to balance supply and demand. Creation and development of higher education must accompany policies that stimulate the private sector to conduct R&D. Former communist countries in central and eastern Europe found themselves, after the fall of the Berlin Wall, with educated personnel for which the private sector had no demand because governments had not aimed adequate innovation policies at the private sector.

Fourth and finally, policy evaluation should play a key role. To judge whether private firms are responding to incentives, governments must create a statistical office (or revamp existing ones) to track businesses' expenditures on R&D, industrial use of different programs, and their effects on performance. They should invite independent third parties to assess companies' reports about the programs and the factors that eventually render them obsolescent. Policy evaluation has helped improve STI policies and institutions in all OECD nations (Capron and van Pottelsberghe, 1997; Jaffe, 2002; Georghiou, 1997; Kuhlmann, 1997; Papaconstantinou and Polt, 1997; Pianta and Sirilli, 1997).

4.5 VERTICAL POLICY

Once horizontal policies have levelled the technology field for all firms of all sectors, allowing unexpected innovators to pop up through market processes, and after the government has gained experience in the design, evaluation, and implementation of institutions for the entire economy, it may be able usefully to pick sectors. The case of Finland (see Chapter 5) is one where government successfully moved from static comparative advantages to dynamic ones by selecting information technology in the 1990s. Singapore chose electronics first and then biopharmaceuticals to nurture economic development. Israel was also successful in information technology because of government support (Trajtenberg, 2001). Canada picked aerospace, telecommunications, and nuclear energy after 1945 and then biotechnology, information technology, and new materials in the 1980s. In all these cases, small to medium-sized countries gained experience about STI institutions and then chose sectors and built appropriate organizations and programs.

Picking sectors is a complex process. A nation must gain critical mass in a few activities in order to compete on a global scale. All industrial activities present increasing managerial and technical complexity as they evolve. Even large countries cannot master all sectors and in fact generally tend towards national specialization. Governments must right from the start aim policies at only one or two sectors. The failure stories surrounding (for example) the aircraft industry illustrate the dangers of investing public funds in impossible bets. And developing countries have no monopoly on failures: many OECD governments retreated from sectors they had chosen after they lost large investments there.

4.6 GOVERNMENT INVESTMENT

National paths are so diverse that they discourage any attempt at valid comparisons. South East Asian countries began catching up with very modest public investments and increased them as soon as they gained experience and could see results. The fate of public investments also depends on the sectors that authorities have chosen. Catching up in traditional sectors (textiles, garments, furniture, leather products, plastic products, tools) requires less public investment. This is why South East Asian countries have set out there on their 'flying-geese' route.

Entry into high-tech industries (such as aerospace, information technologies, and biopharmaceuticals) is usually more costly: it demands more government investment in academic salaries, research funds for industry and higher education, and sophisticated government laboratories. Also, the proportion of tacit and institutional knowledge is much higher there, and this usually requires human capital. Again, governments in South East Asia have invested in education by sending people abroad to study (and striving to bring them back through repatriation or networking programs). Also, competition for high-level scholars and skilled professionals can be costly, as Singapore found vis-à-vis salaries in universities and public laboratories. Large countries such as China and India can count on thousands of expatriates with foreign degrees to build their high-quality pool of human capital; smaller nations such as Singapore have had to attract human capital so as to build critical masses quickly.

Countries that do not develop are those with abundant natural resources (mainly in Africa and Latin America), and those that are experiencing rapid development (especially in South East Asia), have few natural resources and have had to rely on science and technology to achieve affluence. The cost of STI institutions, including policies, is not a major issue for them.

A basic goal of developing countries should be to catch up with the OECD average of U.S.$700 in GERD per capita in 2006. (Mexico, a member of the OECD, spends $60 in R&D per capita and is representative of Latin America.) The Mexican effort represents 0.5 per cent of GDP against an average of 2.2 per cent in OECD countries. In the OECD, higher education consumes on average 17 per cent of that $700, or $117. (Mexico spends $16 per person on R&D in higher education.) To that end, the number of researchers should increase, along with – most important – the number of private-sector researchers, as well as BERD. For that purpose, governments should use public funds (or fiscal credits) to stimulate and expand industrial R&D. Such goals are not ambitious: the OECD includes both rapidly advancing countries but also laggards.

4.7   ABSORPTIVE CAPACITY

The absorptive capacity of firms depends in great measure on whether or not they possess an R&D organization (Cohen and Levinthal, 1989, 1990). Empirical studies of OECD nations have suggested that human capital and R&D activities over time influence productivity (Kneller and Stevens, 2006). Yet R&D requires organized activities in private and public firms, government laboratories, and research universities. Organizations ground R&D. It thus seems clear that the absorptive capacity of nations depends on the quantity and quality of their R&D organizations. Human capital is not enough, particularly if it lacks order. Such a hypothesis explains the apparent paradox of educated countries that have a high level of educational attainment (thus human capital) and a low to medium level of economic development – for example, Argentina, Chile, the Russian Federation, and Uruguay (UNESCO, 2005a). The institutional hypothesis explains why nations with a fairly large stock of human capital can also lag in terms of intellectual property (e.g., patents).

In order to increase productivity, developing countries should increase their stock of human capital and the number and quality of their R&D organizations, particularly those that use human capital to produce goods and services and increase national wealth. Therefore STI policy appears to belong at the top of the government agenda for economic development.

Conclusion

There is no universal path to successful technology policy and institution building. Societies catching up have often imitated wealthier ones and while importing foreign institutions have modified those they found useful. In the process they have often created new models, new combinations of policies and organizations, more suitable to their cultural history, mores, and resources.

Industrializing countries trying to build their systems of national innovation would do well to start with horizontal policies to construct a pool of human capital and the related demand policies that will ensure that private firms hire the human capital. Only then can they pick sectors and apply vertical industrial and technology policy after they have gained experience in designing, implementing, and evaluating institutions. Once they have put in place STI policies and institutions, they should assess, modify, and improve them, but only gradually, as policy stability is a gauge of success. Companies investing in R&D laboratories, whether domestic or foreign-controlled, will back away if government withdraws the incentives they had expected. Bringing them back will be an uphill battle.

Existing science and technology is a quasi-public good. It is available only to countries that have built the absorptive capacity to understand and use it. Their absorptive capacity depends on the size and quality of their stock of human capital and on the number and quality of their R&D organizations.

NOTE

1. See Amir (2007) for Indonesia, Chiang (1999) for Taiwan, Texier (2000) for South Korea, and Eriksson (1995) for a review of several Asian countries.

5. Building systems of innovation: three phases and three cases

While innovation systems include various combinations of institutions, organizations, and policies, their raw material is always human capital. There have been many attempts to measure and theorize about links between human capital and economic development. Nelson and Phelps (1966) suggest that countries with more human capital might more easily absorb technical knowledge from abroad. Romer (1990) argues that human capital is the key input to the research organizations that generate technical progress. In a sample of 98 countries between 1960 and 1985, Barro (1991) shows that economic growth correlated positively with initial human capital; also, nations with more human capital had lower fertility rates and greater investment in physical capital. Frantzen (2000) reveals how human capital increases productivity, while Benhabib and Siegel (1994, 2002) develop the Nelson–Phelps analysis and suggest that the spillovers of international knowledge that developing countries receive directly depend on education rates.

Yet divergences continue. In the Nelson–Phelps approach, education speeds diffusion of technology, while in the opposite approach, education is a factor of production (Krueger and Lindhal, 2001). As Benhabib and Siegel suggest, the policy implications of both perspectives differ markedly. If technology diffusion is not instantaneous and firms are heterogeneous, any catching-up policy must be patient and focus on the long term. If, in contrast, education is a factor of production and agents are rational, then companies will hire educated labour and increase productivity quickly. This is closer to Gary Becker's original concept of human capital. Catching up would thus be fairly rapid and straightforward. In this chapter, I argue that absorption, diffusion, and use of technology depend not only on the amount of human capital but also on its institutions. Also, I suggest that Say's law – that supply creates demand – is particularly misleading vis-à-vis the market for human capital. Government policy has to create both supply and demand.

This chapter looks at three phases in building systems of innovation: promoting human capital, choosing sectors, and launching virtuous circles. The rest of the chapter then examines three cases of nations that have caught up since the end of the Second World War: Canada, Singapore, and Finland.

5.1 PROMOTING HUMAN CAPITAL

If the economic history of the last two centuries can teach us anything, it is that markets do not produce human capital (or demand for it) by themselves. Governments have always subsidized its formation, because it is partly a public good: the persons who embody it and have invested in its accumulation cannot recuperate all the returns on the investment. Such an investment 'spills over' the economy in the form of faster adoption of new technologies, better management, and thus higher productivity, revenues, and so on.

Also, organizations tend to display a high level of inertia and stick to their routines, whether they are education systems, public laboratories, or private and public firms. All these types of organizations often reduce costs and complexity by sticking to low-value added activities, thus incorporating little human capital. On its own, the market usually produces a low-skill equilibrium economy.

5.2 CREATING HUMAN CAPITAL

Human capital consists of the skills and knowledge that the labour force embodies. These skills are the results of previous investments, most of which take place during schooling; this is why years of education usually serve as proxy for the level of human capital in a population. The adoption of modern technology requires a fairly high level of education. Functional literacy is not enough to use, let alone produce, new drugs, information and communication technology, numerically controlled machinery, or robots. The number of years of university education, or the percentage of the population with post-secondary degrees, is a good indicator for human capital.

Besides, R&D activities, whether they occur in government laboratories, private firms, or universities, require advanced, usually postgraduate, education. The costs [salaries] of highly skilled scientists and engineers make up half or more of the costs of conducting R&D (Hall, 2002). Catching up and economic development will seldom emerge from a population with simply functional literacy or even some level of post-secondary education. For firms to conduct R&D they must hire personnel with some training in R&D – usually the function of research universities.

In the absence of government incentives and funding, traditional universities will conduct teaching but little research and technology transfer. Teaching is less complex and costly than conducting research and publication, patenting and licensing research results. Prussia set up research universities in the early nineteenth century, and this organizational innovation diffused slowly across industrial nations. Before 1939, for instance, U.S. governments scantily financed research in higher education, and only a handful of institutions could qualify as research universities (Atkinson and Blanpied, 2008). The Second World War showed the many advantages that the country was obtaining from these new facilities, and the government created the National Science Foundation in 1950 to support them. U.S. graduate studies expanded rapidly thereafter.

In most developing countries, universities teach undergraduates and grant first degrees. Yet research is normally the purview of more senior studies, which require permanent provision of government funds, expensive libraries, and professors with advanced degrees. Traditional universities will thus produce graduates with only basic academic skills. The Bologna model does not demand or produce highly skilled personnel. Yet people with college and undergraduate degrees will produce fewer positive externalities than those with higher degrees. Also, higher-education R&D is a major factor determining the intensity of business R&D, as Martin Falk (2004) discovers in a study of 17 OECD countries for the period 1970–2002.

In developing countries today, as was the case in North America and western Europe before the Second World War, most government laboratories are agricultural extension units (Alic, 2008). They usually teach good practices (agricultural and sometimes industrial) to local firms; conduct basic tests, such as analyzing soil, diagnosing cattle, and certifying products; and offer courses to upgrade human resources in firms. Few of them, however, perform much advanced R&D. As in the case of universities, breakthrough research requires much more money and personnel than they tend to possess. Extension units, like traditional universities, do not demand highly educated human capital either.

Innovation surveys (European Commission, 1992, 1996, 2001) define innovative firms as those that introduce new products or processes ('new' meaning new to the firm, the industry, the country, or the world) during a reference period. In this 'soft' sense, buying a computer to process a firm's financial information is thus an innovation. However, in a more restrictive meaning, innovative firms are those that create (not simply adopt) new materials, products, or processes or introduce better materials, products, or processes to the market. Traditional firms innovate in the first, more general and softer sense. Superior enterprises innovate in the restrictive sense, usually through R&D. They may conduct such activities in house ('intramural' R&D) or under contract, in a university or public laboratory or in another company. They do so because new or better products, processes, or materials can confer a temporary monopoly, and the large profits they earn can fund capital investment, R&D projects, or hiring of more skilled personnel. Companies with in-house R&D capabilities usually employ highly skilled people. Studies show that R&D-active businesses are on average more profitable, grow faster, require more human capital (Baldwin et al., 1994; Del Monte and Papagni, 2003), and tend to export more products than inactive companies. The demand for personnel is much less where governments do not directly fund private R&D or give tax incentives to business R&D.

5.3   STIMULATING BUSINESS R&D

Thus the market for human capital is a construction of public policy. Without incentives, no country will supply or demand highly skilled workers. Any wealthy nation with a mature base of human capital shows the efforts of government, against the inertia of the economic system, to create both supply and demand for personnel.

Tax credits for R&D, as well as tax deductions and allowances, are the most universal incentive to innovate in OECD countries. In 2007, some 20 OECD members used such a stimulus to increase R&D. Also, a few non-OECD nations, including Argentina, Brazil, China, India, Mexico, and South Africa, have recently implemented such policies. As an incentive for business R&D, tax credits have several advantages: they are non-discriminatory, easy to implement and evaluate, and less prone to corrupt practices.

Yet governments vary in their use of tax allowances and credits (Tables 5.1, 5.2 and 5.3).

These tables show that Canada relies more on tax credits, while the United States is more likely to disburse direct subsidies for R&D. Australia, France, and the United States are 'medium promoters' of such indirect support for business R&D, while Argentina, Japan, and Mexico are 'small' ones.

Direct subsidies for business R&D have a few advantages: they may more easily target specific industries, technologies, regions, or sizes of firms. They are easier to monitor than tax credits and allowances. However, they can also serve as political favours, and only constant review, evaluation, and public access to such information may keep such

Table 5.1 Direct versus indirect financing of business R&D, selected countries, 1995, U.S.$ millions (PPP)

Country (year)	Cost to government of tax credits (1)	Direct government funding of business R&D (2)	Industry R&D expenditures (3)	$(4) = \dfrac{(1)*100}{(3)}$	$\dfrac{(2)*100}{(3)}$	(4)+(5)
Australia (1997)	138	84	3233	4.3	2.6	6.9
Canada (1995)	685	441	5143	**13.3**	8.6	21.9
France (1997)	376	1778	14159	2.7	2.7	5.4
Japan (1997)	202	828	65173	0.3	1.3	1.6
Netherlands (1997)	207	210	3269	6.3	6.4	12.7
U.S.A. (1999)	2393	23595	152617	1.6	**15.4**	17.0

Source: OECD: *Science, technology and industry outlook 2002*, 115.

Table 5.2   Gross expenditure on R&D by main sector, 2005

Country	Percentage of GERD performed by sector			
	Industry	Higher education	Government and PRO	Non-profit
	As % of GERD	As % of GERD	As % of GERD	% of GERD
Canada	53.9	36.4	9.2	0.4
Singapore	66.0	10.0	24.0	ND
Finland	70.8	19.0	9.6	0.6
OECD average	68.0	17.6	11.8	2.6

Sources: OECD *Main science and technology indicators* 2007; ASTAR, *Results of the national survey on R&D 2005*, Singapore, 2006.

Table 5.3   Revenue losses from tax credits for R&D, 2005

Country	Year launched	Characteristics	Revenue losses from tax credits, U.S.$ million (PPP), 2005	Number of companies claiming credit (Year)
Argentina	1997	Small promoter	8	ND
Australia	1985	'Medium promoter'	356	ND
Canada	1977	'Leading promoter'	2290	19 700 (2004/5)
France	1983	'Medium promoter'	1010	ND
Ireland	1997	Small promoter	65	ND
Japan	1967	'Small promoter'	3	ND
Mexico	1977	Medium promoter	450	ND
U.K.	2000	Medium promoter	937	5500 (2003–4)
U.S.A.	1981	'Medium promoter'	5110	10 388 (2001)

Note: The qualification 'small' or 'medium promoter' between brackets refers to Warda (1999); otherwise it is the author's qualification.

Sources: OECD, *STI Outlook 2007*; Warda (1999); United Kingdom, House of Commons (2005).

a system honest. Finland and the United States are among the most conspicuous users of direct R&D subsidies.

Reimbursable loans for R&D, repayable to governments if projects succeed, usually support private firms undertaking large research projects, such as aerospace R&D. Europe's EADS uses them for Airbus R&D in

Table 5.4   Building supply and demand for human capital

Building the supply of human capital	Building the demand for human capital
Grant loan systems for students	Tax allowance and credits for R&D for private firms
Research grants and fellowships	R&D subsidies for private SMEs
Immigration of skilled labour	R&D loans for private firms
Import of foreign teachers	Subsidies aimed at the attraction of foreign R&D laboratories
Incentives to create graduate university programs	Intellectual property laws (patent, copyright, industrial design, trademarks)
Tax exemptions to foreign researchers	Tax deductions for venture capital
Academic research funding councils	Public venture capital
Accelerated immigration for foreign university students	Public R&D laboratories

Belgium, Britain, France, Germany, and Spain, among other countries. Canada also supports its aerospace research through this policy tool. Belgium supports R&D by SMEs via refundable loans covering up to 40 per cent of project costs. Finland uses such loans to cover capital and industrial costs of R&D projects.

Table 5.4 shows some of the main levers that governments in advanced countries use to create a human capital base.

5.4   CHOOSING SECTORS

While the first step in implementing science, technology and innovation (STI) policy and building institutions is massive investment in post-secondary education and general incentives for firms to hire college and university graduates in business and government, generating a national system of innovation (NSI) requires other measures. Most, if not all NSI, consists of a small set of sector systems. In addition, nations tend to specialize technologically over time (Archibugi and Pianta, 1992). Only such populous countries as the United States and China can spread their support over many industries. Most governments must choose their areas of specialization if they want to be competitive in at least a few industries.

Specialization is often the result of decisions by governments to support specific sectors. In the 1990s in Finland, public R&D and government support for private R&D laid the foundations for the spectacular growth of the communications equipment industry, which expanded innovative output and energized the economy while increasing per capita revenue towards the top levels of western Europe (Walwyn, 2007). Singapore chose electronics first and then biopharmaceuticals.

Larger countries have also supported rising industries, often several of them. Kim (1997b) has thoroughly analyzed South Korea's choices. As that country began to industrialize, the government enacted the Automotive Industry Promotion Law of 1962 and later added incentive policies and market protection. Similarly, the Electronic Industry Promotion Act of 1969 and other related policies launched South Korea as a major manufacturer of both consumer and industrial electronics. The government targeted aircraft in the mid-1970s and started assembling U.S.-built helicopter subsystems to gain production technology, then moved to assemble military aircraft in the 1980s. However, even South Korea does not always choose wisely: in 1987 it implemented an ambitious Aircraft Industry Development Promotion Law to produce commercial aircraft. However, 20 years later it had produced only a small number of military turboprops, which the country's military purchased. As Texier (2000: 158) concludes, 'Developing an aircraft, even a simpler model, proved far more difficult than anybody . . . would have ever thought.'

Picking industries is much harder than giving horizontal support to creation of human capital, providing tax relief to generate demand for human capital in R&D, or even granting subsidies or loans for R&D and technical advances in smaller firms. There are at least six reasons for this difficulty.

First, when governments support innovation in all industries, through horizontal policies such as tax allowances and credits, they leave no particular sector behind. But domestic opposition may emerge when they target one or a few industries and hence postpone the demands of others. Besides, some sectors will probably bear the costs of the support that goes to any particular industry.

Second, programs targeting specific industries require mobilization of many types of institutions and organizations. Universities will need to develop science or engineering programs in particular disciplines to provide specialized personnel in, for example, aerospace or electronics engineering. Government laboratories will need to enlarge or devote part of their resources to the new priority – for instance, build wind tunnels for aircraft or laboratories to design semi-conductors. Government will have to disburse fresh (and often substantial) funds for such complementary activities. According to Texier (2000), lack of public resources doomed the South Korean aircraft program.

Third, horizontal programs will probably not stir up trade disputes with other countries. All governments in industrial countries invest in higher education or R&D tax credits. In contrast, several types of domestic market protection, direct R&D subsidies, and export promotion to develop a specific sector will almost certainly fire up opposition from foreign producers. The aircraft industry experiences chronic American–European disputes about direct R&D subsidies to Boeing and Airbus and Brazilian–Canadian controversy about R&D and export subsidies to Embraer and Bombardier Aerospace (Goldstein and McGuire, 2004; Pavcnik, 2002).

Fourth, horizontal policies do not help specific companies. But governments may appear to be 'picking winners' when they support a new sector where one or a few companies dominate the domestic industry. Any support to wireless communication equipment in Finland may seem to be support for Nokia. Any plan for the aircraft industry in Brazil will undoubtedly look like public support for Embraer. Both domestic and international opposition, from other companies, foreign governments, and/or international agencies, will probably emerge.

Fifth, horizontal policies bet public funds on many companies, and nobody would expect success from all firms obtaining tax credits for R&D or all SMEs receiving small subsidies for innovation. These programs are 'statistically' effective, or they are not. Specialists evaluate them, and a handful of policy-makers pay attention; the general public seldom even knows they exist. But when major bets concentrate on one or a few companies, products, or industries, their fate is evident and a matter of public debate. The French TGV trains and the European Airbus both emerged through public support. But these success stories do not offset the ultimate and well-known failures of the French Plan Calcul (Jéquier, 1974), the Minitel (Moulaison, 2004), and the Anglo–French Concorde aircraft (Feldman, 1985), which attracted much public debate and criticism.

Finally, such vertical strategies are most often sets of policies rather than single ones. Tax credits for R&D are fairly simple. But launching a set of laws and regulations to nurture a particular industry requires detailed knowledge of the industry cycle, its technological trajectories and routines for appropriation, national competence in the sector, and international competition; as well as constant evaluation of the sector's capabilities and their progress. In the absence of such specialized knowledge, gaps and bottlenecks may appear in personnel, intellectual property may leak out, and/or the industry may miss technological paths. The history of industrial catching up abounds with stories of abandoned aircraft industries (Amir, 2007), semi-conductor plants that did not produce a wafer (Rasiah et al., 2008), and steel plants that shut down soon after they opened.

The case of Taiwan illustrates the right order of policy development. According to Saxenian: 'Most political leaders in Taiwan in the 1960s and 1970s . . . developed programs and institutions to develop Taiwan technological capabilities. They focused initially on improving the skill base and technical infrastructure. These policymakers began making substantial investments in technical education and in upgrading the capabilities of public research institutions' (Saxenian, 2004: 195).

The selection of the semi-conductor industry took place in the mid-1970s, through creation of the Industrial Technology Research Institute (ITRI, 1973) and the Electronics Research and Service Organization (ERSO, 1974), Taiwan's two model public-research organizations. ITRI and ERSO spun off some of the country's fastest-growing information technology firms, including United Microelectronics Corp. (UMC, 1980, from ITRI) and Winbond Electronics Corp. (1987, from ERSO). Grants, loans, and subsidies joined the series of incentives whereby policy-makers stimulated growth of the industry. In the early 1980s, the government sought to create a venture-capital industry, by promoting local capital and inviting overseas venture capital to locate in the island. Also, such a policy system served both local and foreign information technology firms. Semi-conductors became a cornerstone of Taiwan and allowed it to diversify into production of computers, numerically controlled machines, and telecommunications equipment. In 2006, Taiwan's exports were worth U.S.$244 billion, of which 28 per cent (or $63 billion) consisted of electronic products. Exporters of electronic goods enjoyed higher productivity, grew faster, paid higher wages, and conducted more R&D than traditional labour-intensive low-tech firms, thus accelerating the virtuous circle of growth in the island (Liu et al., 1999).

5.5   LAUNCHING VIRTUOUS CIRCLES

The building of an NSI often starts with implementation of general policies such as increasing tertiary education and horizontal policies to stimulate absorption of such personnel in companies and public organizations, particularly for R&D and other innovative activities. But the building of actual innovation systems is much more complex. In the meantime, Figure 5.1 shows the positive feedback effects of such initial incentives.

Tax credits for R&D are the natural starting point in building an NSI. They allow the most dynamic firms to increase their technological capabilities without government's having to consider industry, region, or size of firm. Numerous studies conclude that tax credits increase R&D in the private sector (Hall, 1992; Hall and Van Reenen, 2000; Bloom et al., 2002). Yet some scholars observe that companies take several years to adjust because of learning costs of R&D and other adjustment costs.

However effective, the virtuous circle that fiscal measures launch may

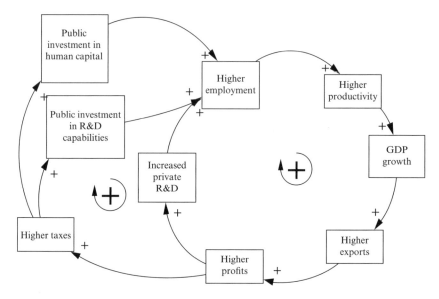

Figure 5.1   Starting the virtuous circle of growth

soon impede growth. Tax credits for R&D will go probably to a small group of enterprises, usually large and medium-size ones. Firms that are smaller or have no net revenue will tend not to use them. Several developing countries, including Argentina and Mexico, have implemented such credits, but with a fixed total sum that they divide among larger corporations and a few SMEs. Large firms that were already conducting R&D used public funds instead of their own, and national R&D did not increase. Even in most OECD countries, where there are no upper limits on credits, amounts that firms request, and the number that do so, increase only slowly. Most medium-size and large firms use that incentive, and smaller ones do not.

Governments employ other mechanisms to expand the pool of innovative firms. Direct subsidies for R&D in smaller firms are more effective. However, governments may face too many demands from many companies in different industries. Public funds may not engender critical masses of expertise in relevant sectors.

International venture capital to support smaller firms goes to developing countries only if new companies there have patents and enough highly skilled personnel. Few developing countries, apart from China and India, seem to understand the value of such signals.

Also, whether governments use tax credits or horizontal subsidies for SMEs, firms tend to direct R&D towards projects and products that promise the highest private returns, which may conflict with the state's goals. If the government wants to limit the effects of some tropical illness, increase local production of foodstuffs, or enter a new industry, it needs to invest in such efforts. Subsidies or loans to smaller (and larger) firms may be the way to induce them to participate in the public mission.

Three Cases of Catching Up

Since the Second World War, a handful of countries have joined the developed world. This convergence club includes several nations in Europe (Finland, Ireland, and Norway) and several in South East Asia (Singapore, South Korea, and Taiwan) that were not rich 40 years ago. Among these newcomers, a few deserve attention. The cases of Japan and South Korea have been the object of many studies; I thus prefer to concentrate on Canada, Finland, and Singapore, because of several characteristics. First, Finland and Singapore are small countries, as are the vast majority of developing nations. Canada has a large endowment of natural resources but a small population, like most African and Latin American countries. The rapid catching up of China, and the wakening of India, are fascinating, but these are the only two nations with more than one billion people. The median size of developing countries is about 4 million people, like Finland, Ireland, and Singapore. Second, these countries entered the industrial world after 1945. They are catching up in high-tech industries. Most new poor nations will not develop quickly by fostering traditional industries such as textiles, garments, and furniture. Rapid economic growth will require new industries in the early phases of industry cycles, when newcomers can still find promising niches. Third, any catching up will take place in an environment of free trade. Japan and South Korea are interesting cases in economic history, but their strong protectionist policies are a phenomenon of the nineteenth and twentieth centuries. The countries of this chapter (Canada, Finland, and Singapore) have managed to grow and enter new industries under free trade. As such, they can provide models for future catchers up. In 2008, by gross domestic product (GDP) per capita at 2008 exchange rates, Finland was 11th, Canada was 18th, and Singapore 22nd, according to the IMF. In purchasing parity power (PPP) Singapore was 4th, Canada 13th, and Finland 20th. Table 5.5 compares the three countries with several others on some key dimensions.

5.6   CANADA: INCHING TOWARDS THE TOP

In the period since the Second World War, Canada has joined the club of developed countries, as it organized a fairly efficient and effective NSI

Table 5.5   Some key indicators of the three countries in this chapter vis-à-vis other nations

	Canada	Singapore	Finland	Ireland	China	Brazil	India
Population million (2007)[1]	33	4.5	5.2	4	1322	190	1130
GERD/GDP[2] (2004)	1.99%	2.25%	3.51%	1.20%	1.23%	0.9%	0.7%
R&D by U.S. multinationals, U.S.$ million (2004)[3]	2702	711	106	876	622	340	163
S&E articles (2005)[4]	25836	3609	4811	2120	41596	9899	14608
S&E articles per million population	783	802	925	530	31	52	13
Exports of high-tech products, U.S.$ current, million (2005)[5]	28172	124490	15067	49847	440104	5797	5442
U.S. patents granted (2005)[6]	3177	377	751	156	565	98	384
U.S. patents granted per million population (2005)	96	84	144	39	0.4	0.5	0.3
Per-capita GDP, U.S.$ (PPP) (2007)[7]	38200	48900	35500	45600	5300	9700	2700

Notes:
[1]   Source: *CIA Factbook.*
[2]   Source: OECD (2007c, 2008).
[3]   Source: NSF (2008).
[4]   Source: NSF (2008).
[5]   Source: NSF (2008).
[6]   Source: USPTO.
[7]   Source: *CIA Factbook.*

(Niosi, 2000a and 2005). One of the world's largest countries (about 10 million square km), and with a sparse population, it added numerous sophisticated organizations and policies for STI to its large stock of natural resources.

Creating a Human Capital Base and Demand for Skilled Personnel

Today, Canada boasts one of the highest education levels in the world. In 2003, some 44 per cent of its population had completed a tertiary degree (UNESCO, 2005a). This is the result of two parallel trends: on the supply side, massive investments in the education of its native population and selective immigration of skilled labour; on the demand side, numerous policies to create a market for such human capital.

Such a large labour force emerged in the last 50 years. University education has become a major factor in Canada since 1945 (Figure 5.2). Policies to increase the supply of human capital originated in the 1920s and 1930s, when governments put in place the first systems of loans and grants for students. However, post-secondary enrolment grew slowly up to the 1950s, then rapidly between 1951 and 1975 (a six-fold increase);

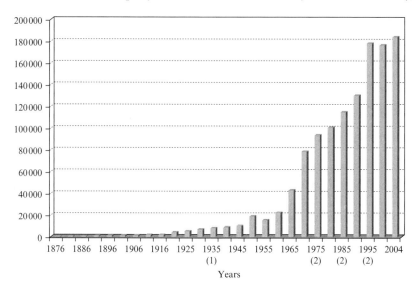

Note: Main university degrees; short programs not included.

Source: Statistics Canada.

Figure 5.2 University degrees awarded, 1876–2004 (selected years)

college (non-university) enrolment increased by eight times during the same period. Participation rates in tertiary education of people aged 18 to 24 rose from 6 per cent to 20 per cent and exceed 40 per cent today.

Thus the figures show a noticeable lag between the first policies and the results. Several reasons explain this lag. First, the institutions themselves adapted rather late – the majority of the country's 200 community and technical colleges emerged after the mid-1960s, and new universities and postgraduate degrees in the late 1960s and the 1970s. Second, this expansion followed creation of federal incentives for academic research. The Medical Research Council (MRC), the Natural Science and Engineering Research Council (NSERC), and the Social Sciences and Humanities Research Council (SSHRC) offered substantial funds to universities creating graduate programs. Between 1965 and 1980, the number of university graduates rose from about 20 000 per year to over 100 000; by 2006, it was close to 200 000.

Third, another landmark in the supply of human capital was creation of the federal Department of Manpower in 1965, amalgamating the Department of Labour and the Immigration Service. In 1967, the country established a point system that gave age and education priority for immigration applicants; the country would educate people at home and import many with high levels of skill. Despite changes in immigration laws, particularly in 1976, the link remained between immigration, education (human capital), and labour requirements. From the 1980s on, immigration has been adding over 45 000 skilled workers to the labour force every year.

Fourth, because of many government policies to stimulate business R&D, demand for educated labour increased in parallel fashion.

Creating R&D Activities

Demand for human capital soared through implementation of a long series of incentives. Creating inducements for companies to conduct R&D was crucial. The first tax relief for industrial R&D occurred in 1942. The number of active companies remained at about 300 for decades. After passage of a new law in 1977, the number rose slowly, as Figure 5.3 shows. By the late 1980s several provinces had their own schemes, and by 1999 the eight largest offered tax credits. When they use federal and provincial credits, companies may deduct up to 50 per cent of their R&D expenditures from their taxes. In sum, Canada has among the earliest, more user-friendly and most generous tax incentives in the world (Warda, 1999).

In Canada, as in any other industrial nation, tax credits for R&D attracted mostly large and medium-size firms: these have more resources to invest in R&D and more net profits, and so tax credits can be quite

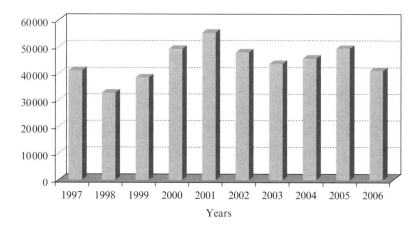

Note: Over 15 years old and planning to work.

Source: Citizenship and Immigration Canada.

Figure 5.3   Skilled immigrants to Canada in managerial, professional or technical occupations (1997–2006)

appealing to them. Other incentives were necessary for SMEs. In 1962, the Industrial Research Assistance Program (IRAP) created an expert group of technical advisers and a fund to nurture R&D and related activities in firms with fewer than 500 employees. Also, after the mid-1970s, the federal and provincial governments stimulated emergence of a venture-capital industry, which led to thousands of technology and R&D-intensive new firms. BERD soared.

Detailed analysis of the Canadian case shows that both the number of companies and industrial R&D expenditures react to public policy incentives, but in modest ways and slowly. Major lags suggest that firms have their own routines; initially, they either ignore incentives or experience uncertainty. Companies must learn the new routine of hiring highly skilled scientists and engineers to design new products or processes or to improve existing ones. Also, smaller firms usually conduct R&D in a more opportunistic way: since the early 1990s, among R&D-active firms, some 1700 (mostly large and medium-size) companies conduct R&D every year, and almost 30000 do so on a temporary basis (Schellings and Gault, 2006). The annual average fluctuates between 18000 and 20000 enterprises. Also, in the period 1997–99, according to the 1999 Survey of Innovation, some 35 per cent of manufacturers used tax credits (Czarnitzki et al., 2004). Companies that accepted both tax credits and direct subsidies for R&D were more

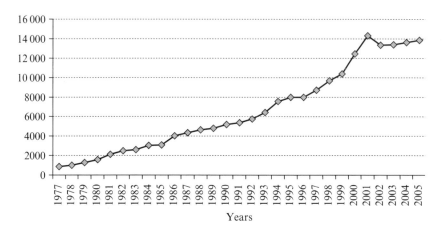

Source: Statistics Canada.

Figure 5.4   Canada BERD (1977–2005) C$M current

innovative, more often introduced world-first product innovations, and were more successful in commercializing their innovations (Bérubé and Mohnen, 2007), suggesting that these measures complement each other.

The large number of foreign companies that conduct R&D in the country shows that Canada's inducements for R&D have been extremely successful. Canada has always been open to foreign direct investment and has attracted hundreds of large R&D laboratories of major multinational corporations in high-tech industries, including aerospace, computer software, and pharmaceuticals.

Governments grant financial incentives to firms to conduct R&D either in house or under contract, because such activity produces the same kind of positive spillovers that human capital creates. New knowledge spills over to consumers and to other producers, increasing the general well being, not simply the profits of the original innovator. Similarly, governments finance new universities and advanced programs to create such human capital. Dozens of Canadian universities either emerged from scratch or evolved from colleges in the 1950s, 1960s, and 1970s, following the arrival of 'baby boomers' at university and the demand that the new incentives engendered. Also, the gains from higher education increased substantially, and the differences in salaries and employability between college and university graduates and high-school graduates also rose. The demand for higher education increased. Graduate programs proliferated when public figures showed that both incomes and chances of finding a job rose with each degree and after creation of the three granting councils. Yet the policy incentives for higher education did not immediately transform institutions: almost 50 years after creation of the first granting council, nearly half of universities still offer no postgraduate studies.

However, the planning capacity of the federal government in STI fluctuates regularly with the political party in power. For most of the twentieth century, the Liberal Party was in power, and it tended to reinforce STI organizations and policies. The shorter Conservative mandates[1] saw stagnation or even partial dismantling of the institutions. The party's economic and social base now lies in conservative Alberta, which is rich with hydrocarbons and strongly opposes federal planning and a developmental federal state. Living in a country with vast natural resources, Canada's policy-makers tend to believe in Ricardian static comparative advantages, instead of in dynamic ones, which emerge through creation and assimilation of knowledge and investment in human capital.

Revamping the Intellectual Property Legislation

Canada had created its own patenting system in 1869, right after Confederation. In 1923, it harmonized its patent legislation with that of other industrial countries and introduced a compulsory licence system for patented food and medicines. This approach provided for granting of licences to Canadian firms of patented products; in 1925, the country joined the Paris Convention Treaty. A further modification to compulsory licencing in 1969 allowed licences to import patented medicines. This change reduced the price of drugs and helped to create a competitive generic pharmaceutical industry. In the meantime, Canada sought to create a biopharmaceutical industry and, for that purpose, amended the patent act twice. In 1987, it increased the duration of patents from 17 to 20 years while creating a Patented Medicines Price Review Board to monitor the price of drugs. In 1993, a second amendment, under a Conservative government, abolished compulsory licencing. As a consequence, pharmaceutical R&D blossomed, but the price of drugs remained low in comparison with other industrial countries, while biotechnology thrived (Canadian Biotechnology Advisory Committee, 2001).

Conclusion on Canada's NSI

Canada developed an NSI over five decades, between 1945 and 1995. By the mid-1990s, the system had established most of its present-day organizations (research universities, government laboratories, and close to 20 000 companies each year conducting R&D). Most of its policy incentives were in place for decades and had undergone evaluation, modification, and

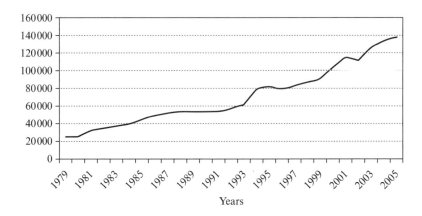

Source: Statistics Canada.

Figure 5.5   Industrial R&D personnel, Canada (1979–2005)

revamping as necessary. Human capital was among the finest in the world, and some studies started to show that in some fields the supply of university students and graduates exceeded demand. Besides, despite a large academic output, including in scientific disciplines, few companies become large. Many small and medium-size enterprises disappear, they remain small, or their foreign counterparts absorb them. The issues of growth factors of new science-based firms and commercialization of technology now appear high in the public policy agenda.

5.7   SINGAPORE: FORGING AHEAD

Singapore shows a different path to development. The city-state (4.6 million people and some 310 square miles) has been an independent nation only since 1965. It has no natural resources, and at independence its densely settled population had low levels of education, and so the government chose to develop technology. The island is close to China and Japan, and most of its people are bilingual (with Chinese and English predominant, but Tamil and Malay also official languages). In just 40 years, Singapore has become one of the world's richest countries.

Revamping and Inventing Institutions

The most important agency planning development has been the Economic Development Board (EDB), which the state set up in 1961. In 1967, the government created the Science Council, and in 1968, the Institute for Standards and Industrial Research (SISIR), the main government laboratory. In 1968, it also founded the Development Bank of Singapore to finance industrialization (Parayil, 2005) and the Ministry of Science and Technology, which it split in 1981 between the Ministry of Education and the new Ministry of Trade and Industry. In 1982, the Science Council took over from EDB the R&D Assistance Scheme and the Science Park, which opened in the late 1980s. In 1991, Trade and Industry took over the EDB and launched the National Science and Technology Board (NSTB). NSTB's first task was to formulate a National Technology Plan, which was to increase the ratio of GERD to GDP to 2 per cent and employ 40 researchers per 10 000 inhabitants by 1995 (Low, 1998). The plan's other objectives included increasing the private sector's contribution to more than 50 per cent of GERD and to urge more companies to conduct R&D. The plan also dealt with development of skilled personnel, public research laboratories, and policy incentives for the private sector.

The first plan invested S$2 billion in science and technology projects, and the second (1996–2000) raised the public investment to S$4 billion. The plan for 2001–5 had a budget of S$7 billion, and in the meantime the NSTB became the Agency for Science, Technology and Research (A*STAR), promoting projects to increase the understanding and absorption of science and technology and to attract and nurture a pool of talented people from abroad. Today A*STAR leads development of research and innovation in Singapore.

Building Human Capital

On the basis of such scanty comparative advantages, the government of Singapore chose to develop human capital through a rigorous and demanding education system and to create demand for such labour through foreign direct investment. Post-secondary enrolment increased rapidly (Figure 5.6), particularly in universities and polytechnics. In 2005, polytechnic alumni represented half of all post-secondary graduates in the country. And that year, Singapore added over 33 000 people with degrees to its workforce.

Education for women has expanded by leaps and bounds. In 1977, there were three male students doing post-secondary studies for each woman doing so; by 2006, they were 120 males for 100 females (see Table 5.7).

The country continuously revised and upgraded its policies on human capital as it attained new milestones and to keep them in line with its policies re industrial and technology development. By 2004–5, in international tests, Singapore was first in science and mathematics in the world, and its

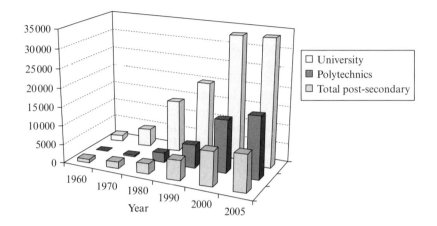

Source: Singapore (2007).

Figure 5.6   Singapore, post-secondary graduates, 1960–2005

Table 5.6   Tertiary education of population, ages 25–34 (%), selected countries, 1994 and 2004

Country	1994	2004
Canada	37.8	53.3
Finland	34.1	38.1
Ireland	24.4	40.4
Singapore*	12.1	35.3
USA	32.0	39.0
OECD average	22.2	31.0

Note: * For Singapore, reference years are census data for 1990 and 2000; figures for Singapore include both polytechnic and university graduates (Hong Kong University of Science and Technology, 2002).

Source: NSF (2008).

labour force had the highest productivity. Such results were the outcome of a national strategy and the highest per-capita expenditure on education in Asia (Osman-Gani, 2004). The country used a tripartite approach to human development, involving several government departments, employers, and trade unions (ibid.). The government established a \$5-billion Lifelong Learning Fund to upgrade workers' capabilities continually and established auxiliary funds to improve the skills of low-income workers.

Singapore has also attracted researchers and teachers from developed

Table 5.7   Singapore tertiary-education enrolment by gender, selected years, 1977–2006 (University and polytechnic only)

Year	Males	Females	Sex ratio*
1977	13 520	5890	299
1987	27 540	15 980	172
1997	53 190	41 050	130
2007	71 148	59 437	120

Note: * Males per hundred females.

Source: Singapore Department of Statistics, *Social progress of Singapore women*, 1998, Singapore: Occasional Paper.

countries to complement local capabilities. The new biotechnology cluster has close to 2000 foreign scientists working in collaboration with local ones. Such an approach allows faster absorption of cutting-edge science and technology from all over the world.

Singapore has put more emphasis than other South East Asian countries on non-university tertiary technical education (Lall, 2000: 43). Its polytechnics are high-level institutions, whose graduates are in strong demand by industry.

Creating Demand for Human Capital

Singapore's authorities decided to industrialize the country in order to diversify it and produce exports, and the process occurred in several stages, like in the flying geese model. From its origins as a British colony and commercial entrepôt, Singapore experienced a short first stage of labour-intensive economic development, mostly through textiles and clothing import-substitution. By the end of the 1960s, the government decided to create an Economic Development Board and embarked on high-tech industrialization by invitation, becoming one of the world's most successful magnets for foreign capital. This time, electronics (machinery, computer hardware and software, and consumer electronics) led the country's move away from low-skill, labour-intensive industry towards highly skilled industries. The explosion in higher education thus went hand in hand with insatiable demand for skilled labour. The state promoted petroleum refining, which became another success story, and shipbuilding followed. By fostering education and demand in tandem, the country expanded its GDP at a cumulative rate of 8.7 per cent per year 1960–70, 9.4 per cent 1970–80, 7.5 per cent 1980–90, and 8.4 per cent 1990–2000 (Goh, 2005).

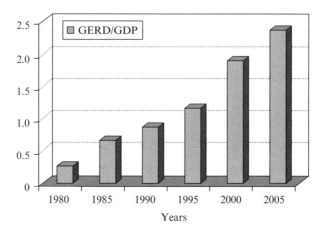

Source: Singapore (2007).

Figure 5.7   Singapore, GERD as % of GDP, 1980–2005

Gross expenditure on R&D (GERD) increased from 0.25 per cent of GDP in 1980, to 0.86 per cent in 1990, to 1.89 per cent in 2000, and rose again to 2.36 per cent in 2005 (Figure 5.7). By 2005, business expenditure on R&D (BERD) represented over 66 per cent of total GERD. These figures compare favourably with those of the European Union, Canada, and the United States. In 2005, the OECD countries spent 2.25 per cent of GDP in R&D; in the European Union, the figure was 1.74 per cent (OECD, 2007c). Also, in 2005 BERD in the OECD area was 68 per cent (ibid.). Numbers of research scientists and engineers grew accordingly (Figure 5.8).

In addition, many multinational corporations located R&D on the island, and in 2005 American multinationals spent more on R&D in Singapore than in China. Singapore's record in innovation is remarkable: with 4.5 million inhabitants, it has almost as many patents as India (1.1 billion people) and four times more than Brazil (190 million).

The island targeted its R&D efforts towards high-tech sectors that promised fast growth. By 2005, in terms of value, it exported more than twice as much high-tech production as Brazil, India (both members of the BRIC club), Canada, and Italy (members of the G-7).

By 2000, Singapore's government had launched its Biomedical Sciences Initiative to create a biomedical and biotechnology cluster and invested heavily in developing academic programs, attracting top-rank academic researchers, and creating six government research laboratories and a specialized science park (Parayil, 2005). It is working to become Asia's

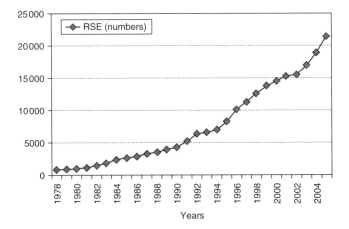

Figure 5.8   Singapore total research scientists and engineers (RSE, numbers), 1978–2005

centre of innovation in human health and to develop all the value chain, from basic research to drug manufacturing. For that purpose, it implemented tax holidays for multinational pharmaceutical corporations that set up R&D or production in the country. In October 2003, it opened the first phase of its Biopolis science park, close to the National University of Singapore, and it completed the second phase in October 2006. The park houses seven research institutes, legal and patent services, global multinationals, and emerging start-ups. By the end of 2007, prominent tenants included GlaxoSmithKline (GSK) from Britain, Novartis from Switzerland, and Takeda from Japan (JTC, 2007). At the end of 2007, the facility's buildings boasted 2 million square feet of space; the total cost was U.S.$392 million.

With such an active developmental state, Singapore had per-capita revenue in 2007 of close to $50 000 in PPP terms, placing it ahead of most developed countries.

Conclusion re Singapore

In just 40 years, Singapore has moved from the lowest to the highest ranks in the industrial world. Its achievement was the result of appropriate institution building, vast government investment in research and development training, and attraction of foreign direct investment in chosen industries. Despite rising wages and shortages of space and labour, the island has moved towards the leading edge of advanced technologies. Yet, unlike other East Asian 'tigers,' it has not grown its own technology-based multinational corporations. Its technical capabilities are embedded in both foreign multinationals and small and medium-size domestic firms.

5.8   FINLAND: FORGING AHEAD

Finland is another country that has since 1945 developed industry and built an NSI. Since the early 1980s it has changed from a low-innovative country to one of the most innovative in the world (Boschma and Sotarauta, 2007; Schienstock, 2007).

A Short, Agitated Economic History

Finland became independent from the Soviet Union in 1917, and for the next five decades its relationships with its giant neighbour shaped its political and economic life: Since the 1920s, Finland exported most of its small output of industrial products to the Soviet Union. In the late 1950s, Finland was an agrarian society, where half of the people lived in the countryside. Its industrial development up to the early 1990s depended on foreign debt, Soviet markets, and government spending. In 1991, after a badly designed financial deregulation, a severe recession reduced GDP by 14 per cent; unemployment reached 20 per cent in 1993 (Honkapohja and Koskela, 1999). Economic recovery took place while unemployment was still very high. By the early 1990s, Finland had started its transformation from dependence on natural resources and manufacture of light goods to innovation and high technology and from trade dependence on Russia to international competitor. Finland joined the European Union in 1995 and adopted the Euro in January 1999. By 2006, it was the most competitive country in the world.

Investing in Human Capital

Before and immediately after the Second World War, the average level of education of the Finnish population was low. Even in 1971, the country was near the bottom of the OECD distribution in terms of workers' average amount of education: 8.7 years. Only Belgium, Greece, Ireland, Italy, Portugal, and Spain ranked lower in western Europe. By 1998, the average adult Finn had 11.2 years of schooling, and the nation had surpassed France in human capital.

Yet problems persisted. In 2005, the Ministry of Education reported that only half of university students graduated in seven years or less, and one-quarter never graduated (Finland Ministry of Education, 2005, p. 89).

Also, investment in education per student was below the OECD average. Yet the education system was among the best in the world.

Finland has two types of post-secondary institutions: some 20 universities (focusing on science and research) and 32 polytechnics (more practical, with little or no research). Universities belong to the state and spend some 19 per cent of Finnish GERD in R&D. In 2003, the universities invested some 976 million Euros in basic and applied research. Universities charge no tuition fees, because the government wants to increase attendance and attract foreign students. The internationalization of universities has an economic as well as a cultural goal: the population is stagnating, and the country needs qualified immigrants. Yet by 1999 only 2.2 per cent of university students were not Finnish by origin (Dobson and Hölttä, 2001). Finland is less attractive than Canada to both foreign students and skilled immigrants.

The government set up the polytechnics in the mid-1990s to spur the tertiary-level professions. It found inspiration in German Fachhochschulen, British polytechnics, and similar institutions elsewhere (Lampinen, 2001; Kohtamäki and Lyytinen, 2004).

Out of Recession Into Innovation

During and after the 1991–3 recession, the government slashed public expenditures but increased funding for research and innovation (Boschma and Sotarauta, 2007). From just under 1 per cent in 1981, GERD grew to 3.5 per cent in 2007 (Table 5.9). That year, Finland was second only to Sweden in the OECD in the ratio of GERD to GDP. Also, its BERD counts: GDP ratio was extremely high, as government stimulated industrial research and development. Ireland, Canada, and Finland (in descending order) lead the world in the percentage of BERD that goes to high tech (OECD, 2006b: 32), and Finland is top in the number of business researchers per thousand employees in industry (ibid., p. 34). By the end of the decade, Finland plans to invest 4 per cent of GDP per year in R&D. Also, the *National Plan for Science, Technology and Innovation 2007–2011* proposes to expand and improve education, increase public investment in R&D, and develop links between economic agents in various spheres of activity. Like Canada and Singapore, Finland has invested massively in education during the last two decades.

Figures in Table 5.9 show that, in the midst of the 1991–93 recession, Finland continued to increase its investment in R&D. It also boosted expenditures in higher education, with an emphasis on science and engineering.

Unlike Canada and Singapore, Finland relies very little on foreign direct investment, or high-skilled labour, and students imported from abroad. Also, foreign affiliates conduct little BERD and generate fewer

Table 5.8   Public expenditure on education as % of GDP, selected countries, 1991 and 2002–5

Country	1991	2002–5 Average
Canada	6.5	5.2
Ireland	5.0	4.8
Singapore	3.1	3.7
Finland	6.5	6.5
United States	5.1	5.9
Argentina	3.3	3,8
Philippines	3.0	2.7
Morocco	5.0	6.7

Source: United Nations Development Program: Human Development Reports, 2007/8, www.hdrstats.undp.org/countries/data_sheets/cty_ds_IRL.html

than 10 per cent of the country's filings at the European Patent Office. In fact, one domestic firm, Nokia, represents one-third of Finnish GERD. In this sense, Finland represents an extreme opposite case to the other small industrial nations, where foreign affiliates conduct a large share of R&D and much national R&D takes place abroad.

New and Improved Institutions

In 1987, Finland created the Science and Technology Promotion Fund (STPF) within the Ministry of Education, under the prime minister as chair, with a mandate to follow and address science, technology, innovation, and education.

Also, it gave the universities a mission – namely, technology transfer to the private sector. Beginning in January 2007, university researchers must disclose all the inventions they make, and universities have the first right to intellectual property when public monies fund the research. Finland regulates academic research much like the U.S. Bayh–Dole Act does American research.

However, Finland (together with other OECD members Iceland, New Zealand, Sweden, and Switzerland) lacks tax incentives for business R&D and supports industrial R&D with direct grants. There may be a relationship between the country's use of direct grants for R&D and the small amount of R&D that foreign affiliates conduct.

Tekes (1983) is the main agency for funding innovative R&D projects in firms, universities, and government research laboratories. It covers a wide spectrum of technology, from traditional areas such as food, pulp

Table 5.9   Finland, GERD as % of GDP, selected years, 1981–2007

Year	GERD as % of GDP	BERD as % of GDP	Total researchers (FTE)	GERD: compound annual growth rate	Total researchers per 1,000 total employment
1981	1.20%				
1987	1.75%	1.03%	10 593		4.1
1988	1.80%	1.08%		7.8	
1989	1.83%	1.13%		7.4	
1990	1.91%	1.20%		4.2	
1991	2.04%	1.18%	14 030	ND	5.5
1992	2.18%	1.24%		1.4	
1993	2.21%	1.29%	15 229	0.4	6.1
1994	2.34%	1.45%		10.4	
1995	2.35%	1.49%	16 863	5.6	8.2
1996	2.59%	1.72%		14.3	
1997	2.71%	1.79%	21 149	13.5	12.3
1998	2.88%	1.94%	30 431	11.0	13.9
1999	3.23%	2.20%	32 676		14.5
2000	3.40%	2.41%	34 847		15.1
2001	3.42%	2.43%	36 889		15.8
2002	3.36%	2.34%	38 632		16.4
2003	3.43%	2.42%	41 724		17.7
2004	3.45%	2.42%	41 004		17.3
2005	3.48%	2.47%	39 582		16.5
2006	3.45%	2.46%	40 411		16.6
2007	3.43%	2.45%			

Note: FTE: Full Time Equivalent

and paper, and wood technologies to biotechnology and nanotechnology. Tekes pays half of project costs, and the host institution the rest. According to Tekes, every year companies participate in some 2700 projects, and universities in some 1100. A typical project lasts five years. Funding may consist of low-interest loans or grants. Foreign enterprises operating in Finland are fundable, as are international partners not based in the country. In 2003, Tekes's budget was 386 million Euros.

Sitra (1967) is an innovation fund. An independent foundation, it operates under the aegis of Parliament. It has four main areas: health, energy, food and nutrition, and the mechanical industry; it has recently added programs vis-à-vis China and India. By 2007, it had a capital endowment

Organization				Task
Parliament				
Government				General policy
Ministry of economy	**Ministry of Technology and Innovation**	**Science and Technology Policy Council**		STI policy
Academy of Finland	Tekes Centres	Sitra	Foundation of Inventions	STI policy formulation, implementation, funding
Public Universities Research institutes Centres of excellence		**Private** Enterprises Research laboratories		R&D performing
Semi-private Finnvera Sitra/VC Industrial investment/VC		**Private** Venture capital Banks		Business funding

Source: Kotilainen (2005).

Figure 5.9   Finland's national system of innovation

of 821 million Euros and employed 100 people. In 2003, its investment in R&D was 32 million Euros.

Figure 5.9 presents the links between and the responsibilities of the main actors in Finland's NSI. The general strategy of science, technology, and innovation policy come from Parliament and the government. The STPF develops the more precise regulations and puts those policies in operation. Tekes and Sitra are the main funding agencies, and firms, universities, and public laboratories conduct complementary research. Private institutions such as venture-capital firms and banks also help fund firms' R&D.

Finland has developed a strong venture-capital industry. In the 1980s and early 1990s, the state provided the capital, but the private sector replaced the public funds as main provider during the 1990s, and emerging high-tech firms receive support jointly from the state and private-sector venture capital. In 2003, private venture capitalists invested 294 million Euros in high-tech companies, and business 'angels' another 387 million Euros.

Conclusion on Finland

During its short history as an independent nation, Finland has transformed its economy from exploitation of natural resources up to 1939, through investment in light industries up to the 1960s, to investment in human capital from the 1960s to the 1980s, and most recently to technological innovation since about 1990 (Rouvinen, 2006). In the last two decades, Finland has developed a highly efficient NSI, relying on direct public funding of company and university research, rapid development of domestic human capital, and strong business participation in R&D and innovation. While tax credits on R&D tend to take more time to modify the behaviour of firms and to benefit medium-size to large corporations, direct funding reaches all sizes of firms and creates incentives that stimulate private-sector R&D faster and more adequately. However, Finland is a small, ethnically homogeneous country with little corruption and 'transparent' institutions. Its system of face-to-face negotiations between firms and the state for R&D subsidies is not easy to transplant elsewhere.

As with other catching-up countries that have developed an NSI, Finland still has problems. The one that appears most clear is its dependence on one firm, Nokia. Nokia represents 33 per cent of Finland's GERD (close to 60 per cent of its BERD), 31 per cent of the total capitalization of Helsinki's stock exchange, and 20 per cent of Finnish exports (Rouvinen, 2006). In the same vein, Finland has specialized its technology and industry more than any other country in the world, as telecommunication equipment dwarfs all other sectors. Internationalization brings it little foreign talent, foreign companies' R&D, or foreign direct investment in manufacturing or services (Schienstock, 2007).

Conclusion

The three countries represent different post-1945 ways of catching up. All can serve as examples to developing countries, as they caught up under free trade and so differ from the nineteenth-century protectionism of Continental Europe and the United States and the more recent cases of Japan and South Korea. They also had to cope with the emergence of high-tech industries and to develop not on the basis of such traditional sectors as textiles, garments, and steel and its products, but in aerospace, biopharmaceuticals, information technology, and other advanced industries. In high-tech activities, the quality of institutions, organizations, and policies matters, because these activities are skill-intensive and require public and private investments in R&D and innovation, massive inward knowledge, and technology transfer.

However, all of them promoted growth through the incorporation of new, advanced technology sectors, in a manner that reminds of both the flying geese experience of South East Asia, and theories of growth via the incorporation of new sectors, as argued by Prebisch in the 1950s and Pyka and Saviotti more recently.

These successful countries increased and tried to balance the supply and demand of human capital, as well as its quality. Yet two distinct models appear. The Canadian we may call 'human capital supply and R&D incentives.' The national and provincial governments invested more in education, fine-tuned immigration laws to attract foreign direct investment and skilled labour, and revamped R&D incentives to attract the innovative activities of multinational companies. By 1945, Canada had already had a century of experience of foreign direct investment, and many policy-makers saw that its value depended on the quality of the labour force and other resources and incentives. According to John Dunning (1998), location-specific advantages help explain where multinationals locate their activities. The Canadian path may be working also in Australia and could prove useful to many Latin American countries, which have substantial natural resources and average education attainment. Canada's early version of what we would call STI policy aimed to increase the supply of human capital (with grants since the First World War and grant-loans since 1934) and foster R&D activities in firms (R&D tax deductions since 1942).

Singapore's dynamics differed notably: it started by 'job creation and witnessed deferred human capital formation.' The government attracted foreign direct investment to create jobs (at the beginning, any jobs) to reduce unemployment and gain foreign currency through exports, and it succeeded, using local competitive advantages, including geographical location and labour cost. Decades later, it discovered that it could attract higher-value-added activities from the same multinationals, including R&D and innovation, if it upgraded its human capital. Much later, it figured out that it could nurture domestic high-tech companies using the same incentives in education, science, technology, and innovation. Such innovative domestic enterprises may help the country reduce the risk of massive investment outflows and a resulting decline in high-tech exports.

Finland moved from natural resources to light industry and from this to education and human capital and thence to fast adoption of policy incentives and related organizations to expand business R&D. It is similar to Canada in some respects (abundant natural resources and a large neighbouring market) but has to rely on its own people without immigration, and local industrial investment.

Canada's specialization in several high-tech sectors was the result of government policy. Singapore's government chose electronic products and then pharmaceuticals and biotechnology. Conversely, telecommunications equipment in Finland grew out of the strategy of a company that knew how to take advantage of domestic capabilities in the sector. Today, the Finnish government makes efforts to reduce specialization and invests in quite a few sectors as it seeks to diminish dependence on one company.

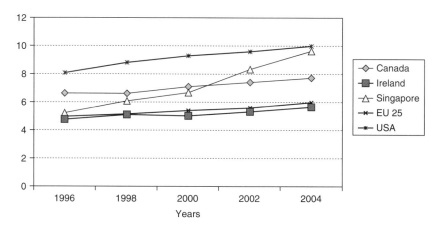

Figure 5.10   Researchers per 1000 employment, 1996–2004, selected countries

Among the three countries that I compare in this chapter, Singapore stands as the strongest in its efforts to incorporate human capital in industry (Figure 5.10). In per-capita terms it is the only one that has truly caught up with the United States. European Union countries, as well as Canada and Finland, seem to fall behind on this particular dimension.

The literature on NSI has insisted on path dependence and the inertia of institutions and organizations. Yet in these cases we find a process of 'path creation' that has been well documented. Such an endeavour involves the launching of one or a few new dynamic industries. Yet, as the case of Canada shows, there are limits to the 'science and technology push' approach to creating an NSI. Again, as Lall (2000) emphasizes, there is no single optimal path to technological development. The appropriate path depends on the original endowments of natural resources, capital, and skilled labour and the abilities of policy-makers. However, all these countries had to invest in creating or upgrading their human-capital base, inventing new institutions, attracting foreign technology and knowledge, and implementing incentives for foreign and local companies to conduct R&D. These nations have not closed their doors to foreign direct investment but on the contrary have attracted it and tried to learn better management practices from leading international firms.

NOTE

1. In the post-war period, Conservative governments ruled Canada between 1957 and 1963, 1979–80, 1994–83, and since 2006.

6.   Developing countries: four cases

More than 50 years ago, the Swedish economist Gunnar Myrdal (1957) enunciated his famous theory of underdevelopment, which he based on the vicious circle – cumulative causation among a series of factors that reinforced each other through feedback loops, such as low employability, low revenues, low education levels, low productivity, and bad health. With low incomes people cannot buy good health services or good education. Low education determines low productivity, which in turn explains low revenues and low employability. Bad health undermines productivity.

Myrdal sought to integrate political, social, and cultural factors in his analysis of the poverty trap. Thus he mentioned that rapid demographic growth in a society would hinder economic development. Advocating a restriction in the fertility rates of developing countries, he foresaw the spectacular economic growth of China under the policy of one child per family and the catastrophic situation of most Muslim countries with very high fertility rates. Myrdal also emphasized that governments should challenge traditional institutions that tend to perpetuate social and economic inequalities and also block growth; these include the caste system in India and religions that promote uncontrolled population growth. Also, he argued that markets by themselves would not eliminate obstacles to development: governments must plan new industries and remove rigidities, while opening new possibilities for private enterprises. Again, he anticipated the post-1945 planning activities of the governments of China, Japan, South Korea, and Taiwan that underlie the 'Asian miracle' (Deyo, 1987; Amsden, 1989; Okimoto, 1989; Wade, 1990; Johnson, 1982; Kim, 1997b; Kim and Nelson, 2000; Chang and Shih, 2004; Motohashi and Yun, 2007). But most often, Myrdal argued, in developing countries the state is a weak system, with an inefficient and sometimes corrupt public administration (Myrdal, 1957, chap. 7).

Myrdal's theory of underdevelopment is probably one of the first and most useful applications of the idea of reinforcing feedback loops, which is central to systems theory and complexity in economics and other social sciences. A majority of developing countries find themselves in such a low-revenue equilibrium, where a set of mutually reinforcing variables, to which one can add corruption, creates chronic poverty. Corruption redirects public funds away from social goods (such as education, institution building, and health services) and thus deprives developing countries of the mechanisms through which they could escape poverty. All these variables thus strongly correlate: low education, bad health, intense religiosity (and/or class or caste distinctions), high levels of unemployment, and pervasive corruption.

The same vicious circle exists in societies at various levels of development. For many decades, if not centuries, it kept such European countries as Ireland, Portugal, and Spain in poverty, where large families and low education and employability reinforced themselves. When a country seeks to diversify its economy, educate its population for future challenges, and slowly abandon more traditional sectors, it needs government initiative to break from the vicious circle.

In choosing the nations to illustrate the process of falling behind, I considered several. I thought of Spain, Mexico, and Morocco. Spain suffers from competition from developing countries because it has specialized in traditional manufactures, such as textiles, leather products, and garments, as well as construction and tourism. It has an inefficient public sector and is slowly but consistently moving towards the lower ranks of developed nations. Morocco was another candidate, as one of the largest countries in Africa, culturally and geographically close to western Europe. Ex-communist countries, such as Ukraine, have problems of their own, and their patterns do not correspond to the typical developing nation.

Mexico, despite entry into the club of rich North American and OECD countries (after the NAFTA agreement) seems unable to imitate the institutions of its wealthier neighbours, as Greece, Portugal, and Spain have done in Europe. I finally decided to analyze Argentina, Egypt, Mexico, and the Philippines. I wanted to illustrate similar mechanisms in various continents and under different cultures, endowments, and markets. Argentina was familiar to me; it also has a medium to high level of human capital and a large resource base. For several decades, between 1900 and 1940, it was one of the richest nations in the world. Mexico has the 12th-largest economy in the world and possesses oil. It also participates in one of the richest markets, NAFTA. Yet it faces daunting challenges. Egypt and the Philippines at some time held promise of development and had several advantages of size and links to Western institutions, science, and technology. These three countries – Mexico, Egypt, and the Philippines – rank respectively 66th, 111th, and 117th in the world in per-capita GDP at the exchange rates of 2007 and 48th, 111th, and 106th by GDP per capita at purchasing parity power (Table 6.1).

All four countries present deficiencies in human capital but are not in the bottom of the distribution, and they suffer from high levels of corruption. Argentina and Mexico have a low to medium level of human development (Tables 6.2 and 6.3), and Egypt and the Philippines are in the medium level.

Table 6.1 A choice of countries

Country	Population, million (2007)	Per-capita GDP, U.S.$ (2007)		Life expectancy at birth (2007)	Corruption index	Continent	Religion (majority)
		PPP	Official rate				
Algeria	33	8100	3815	73.52	3.0	Africa	Muslim
Argentina	**40**	**13000**	**6125**	**76.32**	**2.9**	**South America**	**Catholic**
Brazil	190	9700	6678	72.24	3.5	South America	Catholic
Chile	16	14400	10063	76.96	7.0	South America	Catholic
Egypt	**80**	**5400**	**1600**	**71.57**	**2.9**	**Africa**	**Muslim**
Indonesia	235	3400	1745	70.16	2.3	Asia	Muslim
Iran	65	12300	4276	70.56	2.5	Asia	Muslim
Lebanon	4	10400	6315	73.15	3.0	Asia	Catholic/ Muslim
Mexico	**109**	**12500**	**8128**	**75.63**	**3.5**	**North America**	**Catholic**
Morocco	34	3800	2147	71.22	3.5	Africa	Muslim
Nigeria	135	2200	939	47.44	2.2	Africa	Muslim
Philippines	**91**	**3300**	**1582**	**70.51**	**2.5**	**Asia**	**Catholic**
Tunisia	10	7500	3454	75.34	4.2	Africa	Muslim
Turkey	71	9400	6788	72.88	4.1	Asia/Europe	Muslim
Uruguay	3.5	10700	6000	75.93	6.7	South America	Catholic
Median	40	10700	6000	70	3.3		

Sources: CIA Factbook; Transparency International.

Table 6.2   Key indicators of countries in this chapter, 2008

Country	Population, Million (2007)*	Population Density* (per sq. km and rank) (2007)	Per-capita GDP, U.S. $*		Per-capita GDP (PPP), rank*	Human capital index**	Corruption index and rank (2007)***	Human Development Index and Rank (2007)****
			At PPP	Official Exchange rate				
Argentina	40	14 (206)	13 000	6125	48	69.27	2.9 (105)	0.869 (38)
Egypt	80	74 (127)	5400	1600	111	69.98	2.9 (105)	0.708 (112)
Mexico	110	55 (149)	12 500	8054	64	68.64	3.5 (72)	0.829 (52)
Philippines	91	277 (45)	3300	1582	116	63.85	2.5 (131)	0.771 (90)

Sources:
 * CIA Factbook.
 ** Altinok and Murseli (2007). This human capital index is based on several international tests on science, mathematics. and reading.
 *** Transparency International. www.transparency.org/policy_research/surveys_indices/cpi
 **** UN Development Reports. The index is a composite measure of life expectancy, human capital, and standard of living. In the UN report the index is 'a composite of the adult literacy rate and the combined primary, secondary and tertiary ratio, with two thirds of the weight given to the adult literacy rate and one third to gross enrolment ratio' (UN, 2004).

Table 6.3   Education expectancy, countries in this chapter and OECD mean, 2002–3

Country	Year	All levels of education		Upper secondary education	Tertiary education
		Male	Female	Male + Female	Male + Female
Argentina	2002	16.9	18.4	2.4	3.5
Egypt	2002/3	10.8	10.4	2.2	1.5
Mexico	2003	13.0	13.4	1.5	1.1
Philippines	2002/3	11.5	12.3	0.6	1.4
OECD mean	2003	16.9	17.6	0.2	2.8

Source: UNESCO: *Education Trends in Perspective*, 2005, Table 1.4, p. 175.

Such a choice of nations emphasizes the fact that human capital and human development may be present but may not be enough. As I argue throughout this book, institutions are just as important.

The mechanisms of poverty are several; some are common to many countries, while others are distinctive. In this section, we look at education, public morality, and health care.

6.1   EDUCATION

The strong and positive link between education and economic growth is clear. The poorer countries have neglected the education of their people. Their human capital index shows them below the richer nations in both literacy and enrolment in tertiary education.[1] But the simple count of the number of years of education is not a very good indicator of human capital. Several other factors are crucial, including quality of education. The institutions providing education may not necessarily impart similar training. Also, each year of supplementary education may not yield similar returns in terms of economic performance. In other words, there may be decreasing returns to education (Wössmann, 2002).

Besides, it is not enough to have educated citizens; it is also important to provide them with jobs that employ their skills. That requires several conditions. Adequate mobility (geographical as well as occupational) of skilled personnel is important; this is one of the goals of the European Union as the Lisbon Council of 2006 stated. But the European Union also found that countries varied in their use of personnel. Some, it observed, have a good endowment of human capital and harness it well (Ederer, 2006). In its estimation, the Nordic countries have the highest endowment of human capital and the best use.[2] Italy, Portugal, and Spain, are close to the bottom on both counts. Ederer (2006: 8) suggests: 'The most likely outlook for countries at the bottom of the Human Capital Index is long term economic stagnation.'

Effective employment of personnel depends on policies that encourage their use – especially science, technology and innovation (STI) policies for the business sector. Latin American and other developing countries share with Latin Europe their difficulty in using human resources.

6.2   PUBLIC MORALITY

'Corruption is an act in which the power of public office is used for personal gain in a manner that contravenes the rules of the game' (Jain, 2001, as cited by Aidt, 2003). Three conditions are necessary for corruption to exist and persist: discretionary power of the public official, economic rents to extract or create, and weak institutions that are unable to prevent such practices. Corruption reduces growth through several mechanisms:

- Waste of labour on unproductive activities (Mauro, 2004)
- Loss of tax revenue (Mauro, 1997)
- Selection of 'white elephant projects' where levies can be easier to collect (Mauro, 1997)
- Less government money reaches education or public works (Mauro, 2004)
- Corruption affects income distribution in an inverted, U-shaped way (Li et al., 2000)
- Political instability – endemic in Africa and parts of Latin America – as groups compete to capture corruption rents (Mo, 2001), reduces private investment and formation of human capital
- Inflation of costs of public works to include the bribes (Braun and Di Tella, 2004)

Corruption seems endemic in many developing countries, as we can see in the *Corruption Index* that Transparency International publishes every year, and in some regions within industrial nations, such as Italy (Del Monte and Papagni, 2003).

Also, corruption is difficult to eradicate because in most cases each citizen experiences a small loss, while the corrupt bureaucrat enjoys huge gains. No citizen is usually able to confront a corrupt public administration. Hence 'bad equilibrium situations' of extensive corruption and slow economic growth persist. In contrast, economic growth improves the quality of institutions, decreases the chances of corruption because people (including bureaucrats) have better education, and the public service receives better pay (Chong and Calderón, 2000). Corruption reduces the funds available for education and feeds on low education: it is easier to cheat a population with low education than one with higher levels of human capital. Thus corruption, poverty, and low education all reinforce each other mutually.

As to the causes of corruption, besides low education, authors have mentioned

- Low public sector quality, in terms of contract enforcement, potential nationalization, infrastructure quality, and bureaucratic delays (Chong and Calderón, 2000)
- The variability of macro-economic inflation increases monitoring costs and hence corruption (Braun and Di Tella, 2004)
- Low salaries in the public sector (Mauro, 1997) – some types of government policies may lead to corruption, including subsidies, trade restrictions and quotas, and multiple exchange rates (Mauro, 1997)
- Distribution of natural resources to politicians and their friends (Mauro, 1997)
- High turnover among public servants, especially in Africa and Latin America. Each new minister changes hundreds (if not thousands) of civil servants, who know that they have little time to collect bribes.

6.3   HEALTH CARE

Health has a strong and positive impact on economic growth, as Nobel Prize winner Robert W. Fogel has shown convincingly (Fogel, 1990; 1999). Ever since, experts have considered health a major determinant of economic growth. According to Bloom and Canning (2000), this impact occurs through four channels:

Productivity: Healthier people are more productive because they are more robust, physically and mentally. Also they miss fewer working days.
Education: Healthier people tend to invest more in education because they expect more returns on their investment over longer periods.
Investment in physical capital: A healthier population means more thrifty people and attracts more foreign direct investment.
Demographic dividend: Healthier populations mean that fertility declines and income per capita increases.

Using life expectancy as an indicator, we find that health clearly affects economic growth. Also, health and economic growth reinforce each other in a 'virtuous' circle of positive feedbacks. Mothers with fewer children can work and increase household income. Richer people have more resources to devote to health and education. Bloom et al. (2002) calculate that each year of additional life expectancy increases GDP by 4 per cent. In a more theoretical way, they argue that human capital is the product not only of education but also of good health.

Using other indicators of health, namely the probability of survival by age and gender groups, yields a similar result. In a study of 18 Latin American countries, Mayer (2001) notes the significant effects of better health on economic growth. He infers that such results occur through higher productivity, more and better education, greater female participation in the labour force, a lower burden of disease, and other channels. According to him, such effects – like those of education – on growth are long term and considerable.

Figure 6.1 summarizes the hypothesized causal loops between these variables.

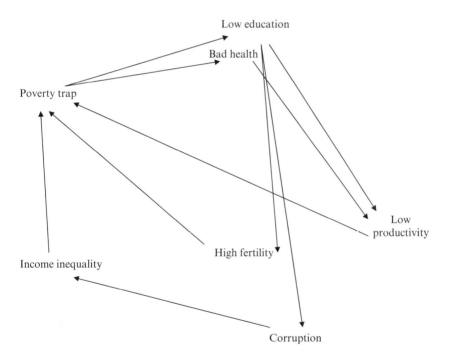

Figure 6.1   The poverty trap

I chose the particular countries for this chapter – Argentina, Egypt, Mexico, and the Philippines – because they all have large populations, high life expectancies – all being above the world average of 65 years – a great deal of corruption (all of them under the corruption median of the world), and fairly low incomes (two of them have a GDP per capita below the world median).

6.4   ARGENTINA

Experts have sometimes compared Argentina for the period 1860–1940 with Australia and Canada (Platt and Di Tella, 1985). The three nations enjoy huge territories and extraordinary natural resources, and in all three Europeans displaced aboriginal inhabitants. The three countries were wealthy and by the Second World War were among the world's ten richest. In the first half of the 20th century, they exported mostly natural resources (Argentina, the agricultural produce of its fertile pampas, including wheat and meat, to Europe; Australia, its wool, meat, and wheat; and Canada, its pulp and paper as well as minerals, to the United States). But there the similarities end.

The differences are much more important, in terms of the theoretical discussion above. First, Australia and Canada received mostly Britons who brought higher human capital than the Spaniards and Italians who chose Argentina. In Australia and Canada, settlers imported and adopted very early some kind of democracy and British institutions (and Canada also U.S. ones such as the organization of government).[3] More important, they also brought institutions of higher education and public research. If Canada created the National Research Council (NRC) in 1916, only months after the United States founded its own, and Australia established the Council for Scientific and Industrial Research (CSIR) in 1926, Argentina founded its Instituto nacional de tecnología industrial (INTI) only in 1956. Canada created its first agricultural research stations in 1868, and the Australian Department of Agriculture started using experimental farms and research centres soon after 1900; Argentina established its Instituto nacional de tecnología agropecuaria (INTA) only decades later, in 1956.

Second, Australia and Canada took advantage of preferential trade terms with Britain, as well as spillovers from British foreign direct investment. British corporations helped set up many industries in both countries, such as aerospace sectors. Canada benefited too from the proximity of the United States. Large American enterprises searched for minerals in Canada and during the twentieth century launched its copper, lead, nickel, and oil industries. Other American companies invested in Canada and created the automobile industry, but also aluminum, food, steel, telecommunications-equipment, and other sectors, transferring with them knowledge and technology. Argentina was far from the United States, the new centre of science and technology, and both its culture and its geography isolated it.

Third, and crucial, Canada borrowed extensively from U.S. institutions during the twentieth century, and Australia from Britain models. Both British dominions adopted public academic and science policies from the two most advanced countries on earth. Australian and Canadian universities adopted the U.S. model very early, with three cycles of study, open recruitment from around the world, and international research and publication. Argentina kept the old southern European, Bologna model, which emphasized undergraduate teaching and little research. Up to the 1950s, Italy had only three Nobel prizes in science (Guglielmo Marconi (physics, 1909), Enrico Fermi (physics, 1938), and Camillo Golgi (medicine, 1906), but Marconi had an Irish mother and set up his transmitting station in Newfoundland, and Fermi worked substantially in the United States) and Spain had only one (Ramon y Cajal in medicine, in 1906). By 1950, the United Kingdom had 30 Nobel prizes in science, and the United States 28; in the meantime, scientific and technical leadership of the world had passed from Britain to the United States. Spain and Italy were far from the scientific frontier.

Fourth, Argentina's mother countries, Italy and Spain, had little to teach it by way of public policy except military coups and dictatorship (notably those of Primo de Rivera and Franco in Spain and Mussolini in Italy), even if some of these governments favoured industrial development. Argentinian corruption seems to outperform some of the most fraudulent political practices in its mother countries. And it is textbook corruption, featuring big (unnecessary) projects and privatization. The TGV railway (costing U.S.$4 billion), which Argentina announced in 2006, is a classic big project, in a country where 30 per cent of people live in poverty.

Economic Development in the Twentieth Century

The economic development of Argentina is not easily understandable by traditional neoclassical theories. By the early twentieth century, the country was one of the richest in the world. By the end of the Second World War its per-capita GDP was still 90 per cent of the average for the G-7 plus Australia and New Zealand (Chudnovsky and Lopez, 2007). In 1930, its illiteracy rate was 12 per cent – high by the standards of the times. The country attracted both foreign direct investment and European immigrants, and it seemed both wealthy and industrializing (Clark, 1940). Yet after 1945, it dropped fairly quickly from 6th in GDP per capita at PPP (in Colin Clark's estimations for 1925–34) to 66th today. What explains such a dizzying collapse?

Political instability, institutional fragility, economic volatility, and social unrest are among the most important factors (Chudnovsky and Lopez, 2007).

- Political instability is most evident. 'In the 38 years between 1962 and 2000, Argentina had 18 presidents . . . and 37 ministers of the economy' (ibid.: 24). During the crisis of December 2001–January 2002 there were five presidents! Such a chaotic environment is not conducive to business investment and economic calculation.
- Institutional fragility is also overwhelming. Not only elected (or self-appointed) political leaders have short-term horizons. Unlike all other industrial countries, Argentina has no professional bureaucracy: each new minister appoints his or her own political clients to the civil service; under such conditions, public policy is improvisational, it frequently changes direction, and there is no learning in the government sector.
- Economic volatility is manifest in the high levels of inflation. In the last 50 years Argentina has had one of the highest inflation rates in the world: the consumer price index (CPI) rose by an average of 10.6 per cent per year 1940–49, 30.3 per cent 1950–59, 23.3 per cent 1960–69, 132.9 per cent 1970–79, and 750.4 per cent 1980–89. Volatility also affected economic policy. In the 1930s Argentina started import-substitution industrialization (ISI) to compensate for the decline of agricultural exports; from 1945 to 1955 ISI was the official policy of the Peron government, but after 1976 successive military governments slowly dismantled it. In 1989, the elected Peronist government of President Carlos Menem entirely abandoned it in favour of an open economy with lower public expenditures, fixed the peso at parity with the dollar, deregulated the economy, and liberalized foreign trade and investment. Inflation declined from 4923 per cent in 1989 to 0 in 1996, and unemployment soared from 7.6 per cent in 1989 to 19.7 per cent in 2002. The manufacturing sector slashed jobs to compete with cheaper and/or high-quality imports.
- Social unrest followed in the 1990s. Argentina had always had substantial income inequality: this increased after 1945. By the end of 2002, half of the country's population was living in poverty; in 2006, the official estimate was 31.4 per cent. Argentina is ranked 69th in the world in per-capita income, between Bhutan and Ghana (just ahead of it) and Brazil and Paraguay (just behind it).

Between 1930 and 1975, ISI protected industry, both domestic and foreign-controlled. Domestic firms had little access to frontier technology and few policy incentives to search for and adopt it. Foreign enterprises operated with obsolete technology, even if they were technologically ahead of local companies. Above all, local and foreign firms conducted little R&D or innovation. Public policy did not favour or reward novelty. The Convertibility Plan of the 1990s did not change technological activity, but competition destroyed many of the technical laggards in traditional industries. As a result, overall productivity increased, but employment dwindled.

Also, during the last two decades, foreign demand for agricultural products increased, and exports soared. Agriculture represents only 10 per cent of GDP, but meat, soya, and other food products constitute over 45 per cent of exports. After the crisis of 2001–2, during which GDP fell by almost 11 per cent, the economy began to grow again, and GDP increased annually by 7–8 per cent between 2002 and 2007. Manufacturing also expanded, reaching 23 per cent of GDP in 2005. Yet policies and organizations for STI did not receive adequate support.

Supporting Institutions And Organizations

In its almost two centuries as an independent nation, Argentina has been unable to build a national system of innovation (NSI); the (too) numerous governments were constantly revising, redesigning, and intervening in the institutions and organizations of the embryonic NSI. Three main periods of institution building – 1918, the 1950s, and the 1990s – deserve mention.

The so-called university reform movement came into being in 1918. In 1912, the federal government had extended universal voting rights to all men over 18 years old. The Mexican Revolution of 1910, world war in Europe, and the Russian Revolution in 1917 agitated the 15 000 university students of Argentina. They went on strike to request the autonomy of higher education from the central government, student participation in administration, extension of the university system, and adjudication of teaching positions by the public instead of nomination by government officials. They also insisted on free tertiary education, a 'routine' that still exists in all the national universities. The movement extended itself to other Latin American countries and shaped the structure of higher education in the region (Walter, 1969).

The second period was the 1950s. At this time, import substitution was the rule. Industry required technical support and skilled labour. The government created two national universities – most notably the National

---

BOX 6.1   MAIN STI INSTITUTIONS OF
           ARGENTINA, 1994

	SECYT	CONICET Institute for Continental Ices Other institutes
	Department of Environment	National Institute for Hydrology National parks
	Department of Agriculture	INTA INIDEP
President's Office	Department of Industry	INTI National Institute for Viniculture National Institute of Earthquake Prevention
	Department of Defense	DGFM, CITEFA National Institute for the Antarctic Other institutes
	Department of Health	National Institute for Microbiology National Institute for Epidemiology Other institutes
	Department of Education CONEA CNAE	National universities Private universities

Source: Bisang (1995).

Technological University, which is now one of the country's largest with 70 000 students – but also the national institutes of agricultural research (INTA, 1956) and industrial research (INTI, 1957), as well as the National Commission for Atomic Energy (CONEA), to design a nuclear reactor. In 1958, to boost academic research, it launched the National Council for Research in Science and Technology (CONICET), which it modeled on

Table 6.4   Argentina, main science and technology indicators, selected years, 1990–2005

	1990	1995	2000	2005
GDP, US $ billion	141	258	284	183
GDP, US $ (PPP)	240	361	445	554
GERD, US $ billion	n.d.	1.08	1.24	0.84
GERD/GDP	n.d.	0.42%	0.44%	0.46%
Science and engineering (S&E) publications	1627	1969	2792	2890
S&E articles per million inhabitants	51	58	78	76
U.S. patents granted (first inventor)	17	31	54	24
U.S. biotechnology patents	1		3	n.a.
Total researchers (FTE) (1)	n.a.	n.a.	21 602	24 680
Total researchers (FTE) per million EAP	n.a.	n.a.	1490	1592
Government researchers (FTE) as % of (1)	n.a.	n.a.	36.1%	41.7%
Business-sector researchers (FTE) as % of (1)	n.a.	n.a.	12.2%	11.8%
University researchers (FTE) as % of (1)	n.a.	n.a.	50.0%	44.6%

Sources: RICyT, *Indicadores de ciencia y tecnología, (2008)*; NSF, *Science and engineering indicators*, 2006, 2008.

the French CNRS; its cadre of researchers has grown to 3500, making it the country's largest research organization. By 1994, the Argentinian NSI appeared as Box 6.1 shows it.

In the 1990s, the government introduced a series of programs and policies to stimulate university research, private-sector R&D, and innovation. It created an interdepartmental co-ordinating committee for science and technology, a plan for science and technology, and a Secretariat for Science and Technology (SECyT). It also launched several funds to promote university research and private sector R&D; two of them, FONTAR and FONCyT, spent some U.S.$190 million between 1993 and 2001, and then their joint budget moved up close to $80–90 million per year (Table 6.4).

Table 6.4 shows that Argentinians have not grown richer in the last 20 years. Their GERD has not expanded either as a percentage of GDP. Scientific publications have increased in number, probably because of the incentives that the government introduced in the 1990s (Tables 6.5 and 6.6).

Table 6.5 Science and engineering articles in all fields, selected countries, 1995–2005

Country	1995	1996	1997	1998	1999	2000	2001	2002	2003	2004	2005	Average annual change			Arts per million population
												1995–2000	2000–2005	1995–2005	2005
Argentina	1967	2287	2451	2551	2636	2846	2931	3178	1919	2982	3058	7.7	1.4	4.5	76
Egypt	1388	1292	1266	1275	1293	1433	1463	1564	1717	1661	1658	0.6	3.8	1.8	21
Mexico	1937	2124	2302	2659	2884	2971	3203	3320	3659	3870	3902	8.9	5.6	7.3	35
Philippines	145	153	170	171	176	185	141	182	184	163	178	5	-0.7	2.1	2
Canada	23740	23842	22781	22201	22125	22701	21945	22342	23552	24230	25836	-0.9	2.6	0.8	807
Finland	4077	4330	4452	4513	4719	4844	4930	4904	4898	5018	4811	3.5	-0.1	1.7	1069
Ireland	1218	1254	1331	1520	1459	1581	1588	1629	1681	1935	2120	5.4	6	5.7	530
Singapore	1141	1141	1339	1584	1897	2361	2434	2632	2939	3384	3609	15.6	8.9	12.2	902

Source: National Science Foundation: *Science and Engineering Indicators 2008*.

Table 6.6   *US patents granted, 1997–2007, selected countries*

Country	1997	1998	1999	2000	2001	2002	2003	2004	2005	2006	2007	Change % in period 1997–2007	Patents per million pop. 2005
Argentina	38	46	46	63	58	58	70	50	29	47	53	39%	1.3
Egypt	1	1	3	8	6	5	6	4	7	4	12	1200%	0.1
Mexico	57	77	94	100	87	105	93	102	98	88	88	54%	0.8
Philippines	21	19	21	12	15	19	25	21	18	35	21	0%	0.2
Canada	2817	3537	3678	3925	4063	3857	3894	3781	3177	4094	3970	41%	120
Finland	468	629	695	649	769	856	944	954	751	1005	943	101%	181
Ireland	76	78	100	137	164	142	182	197	169	198	161	112%	39
Singapore	100	136	152	242	304	421	460	485	377	469	451	351%	98

Source: USPTO, Patent counts by country/state and year, all patents, all types, Washington, DC, 2008.

Patent statistics show Argentina low in the production of novelty; its scientific publications are more numerous than those of most developing countries, but far fewer than those of nations that have 'caught up' in the last decades (Table 6.6).

Besides, the number of patents fell between 1995 and 2005, a highly unusual pattern. Ireland and Singapore, each with slightly over 4 million people, generate far more patents than Argentina (40 million inhabitants) or Brazil (180 million). In every country, public sector R&D produces far fewer patents than business R&D (Falk, 2007). And in Latin America, particularly in Argentina, private sector R&D is rare because of the bad design, insufficient funding, and scarcity of public incentives.

One local observer (Carullo, 1999) summarizes the problems in the following way:

- Insufficient investment, with reduced participation of the private sector and the provinces;
- Absence of priorities;
- Lack of co-ordination among science and technology organizations;
- Strong fluctuations in budgets;
- Large imbalances among areas of knowledge;
- Lack of mechanisms to evaluate quality;
- Significant deficiencies in management;
- Technology institutes that centre on routine services;
- Absence of private-sector R&D efforts;
- Lack of incentives to increase SMEs' technical capabilities;
- Lack of links between technological and scientific institutions and large firms.

The Education System

At one time, Argentina was the most educated country in Latin America, even if it was lagging behind industrial nations. Today, it sits at about the OECD average in number of years of schooling, but other Latin American states are catching up with it: their education is probably also superior if one judges by expenditures as a percentage of GDP (see Table 6.7).

The volatility that affects the economy also affects education. Government expenditures on education, for instance, were 2.67 per cent of GDP in 1980, 1.12 per cent in 1990, and 4.7 per cent in 2000, according to the UN database. Chile's comparable figures moved from 4.63 per cent of GDP to 4 per cent in 1990 and to 7.5 per cent in 2003. In 2003, the adult illiteracy rate was 2.2 per cent in Uruguay, 2.9 per cent in Argentina, and

Table 6.7   Expenditure on educational institutions as % of GDP, countries in this chapter and OECD average, 2002–3

Country	Year	Primary, secondary, and postsecondary, non-tertiary education			Tertiary education			All levels of education		
		Public	Private	Total	Public	Private	Total	Public	Private	Total
Argentina	2002	2.9	0.4	3.3	0.7	0.4	1.1	3.9	0.8	4.7
Egypt	2002/3	–	–	n.d.	–	–	n.d.	–	–	n.d.
Mexico	2002	3.5	0.7	4.1	1.0	0.4	1.4	5.1	1.1	6.3
Philippines	2002/3	2.6	–	–	0.4	–	–	3.1	2.0	5.2
OECD average	2002	3.6	0.3	3.8	1.1	0.3	1.4	5.1	0.7	5.8

Note: n.d.: No data available.

Source: UNESCO: *Education Trends in Perspective*, 2005, Table 2.2, p. 191.

3.6 per cent in Chile, but much higher in Mexico (8 per cent) and Brazil (11.9 per cent). Comparative surveys by the International Association for the Evaluation of Educational Achievement (IAEEA) show Argentinian students performing at the average level in Latin America and far below the standards of wealthy countries (or Russia).

More than 90 per cent of Argentina's 1.1 million higher education students attend the nation's 38 public universities; the rest attend 49 private institutions. The University of Buenos Aires boasts over 300000 students, Cordoba 110000, and La Plata and Rosario 75000 each. The university system produced in 2005 some 76 articles in science and engineering per million inhabitants, which compares well with Egypt and the Philippines, but lags far behind Canada, Finland, and Singapore.

Only about a quarter of university students complete their degrees. Some 300000 students enter each year, but half of them leave during the first year. In 2004, only 1.1 million, or some 3.4 per cent of, Argentineans had a university degree – approximately the same number as the totally illiterate. Canada had a similar number of people starting university, but 80–90 per cent of them graduate; three-quarters of students there receive grants or loans from government. Also, in 2002 about 75000 Argentinians earned university degrees, but close to 15000 had studied accountancy, administration, or economics, about 10000 were lawyers, 5400 physicians, and 4300 architects, and only 3500 were engineers and another 3500 computer scientists. Thus only 9 per cent of graduates were in technical disciplines, and 4 per cent in science – low proportions for a country that aspires to catch up or even keep up with its Asian competitors.

Public Research Organizations

Argentina has few public research organizations (PROs) in its embryonic NSI, and they appeared fairly late. Some of them deserve mention.

The government set up the Instituto Nacional de Tecnología Agropecuaria (INTA) in 1956 to counter three decades of stagnation in agricultural production. It started out autarkic, with funds coming from a tax of 1.5 per cent on agricultural exports. Its budget evolved slowly downwards, from U.S.$250 million in 1980 to virtually 0 in 1988, but it averaged $150 million per year in the 1990s. Its mandate includes research, extension, and promotion of rural economic development, through creation of local stations throughout Argentina with different types of production. Government representatives and agricultural producers administer it jointly. INTA has a major research center close to Buenos Aires and some 40 experimental stations and extension centers across the country. By

2006, it had almost 5800 employees, 3600 of them permanent, in research (2396), extension (577), and support. Its budget for 2006 was U.S.$136 million. During its half-century history, INTA has developed hundreds of cultivars and some machinery and equipment, as well as vaccines and other novelties. Since 1995, it has requested 20 patents, and by early 2008 it had received four and was waiting for 16.

The Instituto Nacional de Tecnología Industrial (INTI) started out in 1957. In 2008, it had 29 research centers in many industries, including chemicals, leather products, wood and furniture, plastics, construction, rubber, electronics, energy, textiles, and milk products. Besides it had six extension units in different areas of the country. In all, INTI had 1900 employees, 1200 of them permanent. Since 1995, it has requested nine patents, and by May 2008 it had four patents and five pending.

Other institutes make a smaller contribution to economic development, such as the Atomic Energy Commission (CONEA), another large government research organization and one that has received public support for over 50 years (Adler, 1987). Nuclear energy is now high among public priorities, but Argentina does not seem able to take advantage of the new demand for technologies different from oil and gas. The country is unable to build nuclear reactors by itself, or to face the impending national energy shortage.

Policies re R&D

Argentina has been as slow and patchy in implementing public policies to induce business R&D as it has in creating public research organizations. Besides, the list of abandoned policies and technology projects is staggering.

Argentina's military institute for aeronautics produced its first aircraft in the 1920s, the Avro 504 'Gosport,' under British licence. In the late 1940s, the government's military plant designed and built a military jet, the Pulqui. In the late 1950s, the government abandoned the program that could have spun off an aerospace industry but had established some windows in the aircraft industry, out of which emerged two other military jets, the Pucará and the Pampa. The Cordoba plant also manufactured other trainer aircraft. Finally, in the late 1990s, the Peronist government sold its military aircraft plant (Fábrica Militar de Aviones) to Lockheed Martin, and aircraft production stopped entirely. In December 2008, another Peronist government renationalized the facility, which produced aircraft in small batches – none of them a commercial success – principally for the armed forces. In the meantime, Brazil switched from military to civilian aircraft and nurtured Embraer, which competes with Canada's

Bombardier for third place in the world as a maker of commercial aircraft.

In the late 1950s and early 1960s, Argentina produced an experimental computer, and in the late 1960s FATE (a tire manufacturer), with the help of INTI and the National University of Buenos Aires, decided to diversify into computer manufacturing. FATE manufactured both calculators and microcomputers and designed a larger computer, similar to the IBM 360. The prototype was working by 1975; yet the project ended after the military coup of March 1976 (Adler, 1987). Meanwhile Japan implemented policies to nurture a competitive domestic computer industry (Anchordoguy, 1989).

In the early 1950s, Edgar Kaiser wanted to produce cars and chose Argentina for that purpose. The firm created a subsidiary there in which it had minority control, and several Argentinians had some two-thirds of the shares. The company produced its first jeep in 1956 and several models of cars, jeeps, and small trucks. Up until 1960, Industrias Kaiser Argentina (IKA) was the largest car producer in the country. It remained large until its sale to Renault in 1966–67 (MacDonald, 1988). In the meantime, South Korea, starting from a much more difficult economic and technological background, began to nurture a car industry and created three producers (Kim, 1997b). Today, Argentina has a trade deficit in cars, while both Brazil and South Korea, under very different trajectories, have a large trade surplus in their competitive auto industries.

By the early 1960s, Argentina had advanced quite far in molecular biology, under the leadership of Dr Cesar Milstein. In 1963, Milstein moved to Cambridge, England, where he won the Nobel Prize for his discovery of monoclonal antibodies. Several of his best researchers followed him. While Singapore strives to attract high-level scientists and engineers in this particular set of technologies, Argentina makes an effort to export them.

In sum, technological laissez-faire complemented Argentina's late and incomplete organization for STI. The continuous battle for political power between political and military factions did not help it to maintain any direction in academic or industrial policy. Besides, industrial development policy was incomplete, because it did not include the key technological dimension. At no time did the government establish or upgrade laboratories to nurture local technological capabilities in specific industries. Technology policies for the private sector were (and still are) almost non-existent: while most industrial countries implemented tax allowances and credits for R&D between the 1940s and the 1980s, as well as subsidies to stimulate innovation in firms, Argentina launched them only in the late 1990s, but with very small maxima of a few million dollars per year for the total program.

6.5   EGYPT

Egypt is the second most populous country in Africa and the most populous in the Middle East. Through its tumultuous modern era, Egypt has experienced French rule (1798–1801), Ottoman government (1801–1915), a British regime (1882–1952), the republic (1953 to the present), the Anglo–French–Israeli invasion of 1956, and Soviet and later American influence since 1945.

Historically and up to today, Egyptian economic and social life has revolved around the Nile River, where close to 99 per cent of the population lives. Since the founding of the republic, Egypt has known intense government intervention in the economy under President Nasser and increasing liberalization under presidents Sadat and Mubarak. Yet the economy is still dependent on a few sectors, such as agriculture, hydrocarbons, and manufacturing, as well as tourism. Consequently, productivity, GDP per capita, and the standard of living are low by world standards.

Economic Development in the Twentieth Century

The Egyptian economy has historically depended on agriculture. The country has exploited oil since 1886, but only in 1976 did it achieve an oil trade surplus. In the 1970s and 1980s major discoveries of gas occurred, and mining of coal began (in the 1990s). In the last 20 years, oil, gas, and their products have become the major source of export earnings. However, reserves are not very sizeable in comparison with the Arab emirates or Saudi Arabia. Tourism accounts for 20 per cent of foreign-currency revenues.

Since the opening of the economy in 1974, Egypt has attracted foreign direct investment (FDI), particularly in oil and gas, but little R&D from foreign multinationals (NSF, 2008). The obstacles to FDI include economic uncertainty resulting from financial crises; incomplete, incoherent, or overlapping legislation; unstable exchange rates; a shortage of highly skilled professionals in many fields; and other problems. Besides, as Sadik and Bobol (2001) emphasize, FDI spurs growth more clearly in the presence of domestic human capital and if local businesses can absorb some of the knowledge and the technology that foreign firms bring with them. Unfortunately, local firms conduct little R&D and can collect few knowledge spillovers from foreign enterprises. Since 2005, however, FDI has been expanding rapidly, particularly in hydrocarbons. It represented less than 1 per cent of GDP up to 2004, but then jumped to 4.4 per cent in 2005, 5.7 per cent in 2006, and 8.5 per cent in 2007. By 2006, FDI represented over half of gross fixed capital formation in the country (UNCTAD, 2007).

Egypt R&D

The Egyptian R&D system and its institutions are weak. The *UN Human Development Report 2005* put Egypt as spending 0.2 per cent of GDP on R&D. The government spends most of it (86 per cent), while the foreign sector spent 10.6 per cent and the private sector the remaining 3.7 per cent. Several authors have concluded that the situation is not unique to Egypt; by the mid-1990s, the Arab world, with 20 countries and 310 million inhabitants, contributed 0.55 per cent to the world's science literature, in comparison with 0.89 per cent for tiny Israel alone (Anwar and Abu Bakar, 1997). By 2005, the share of Israel had not changed, while that of the Arab countries was 0.69 per cent (NSF, 2008). Egypt, with close to 23 per cent of the Arab world's population, represented 33 per cent of its science and engineering articles.

Despite its relatively good score in publications, Egypt's private sector R&D was dismal. Its exports in high technology were negligible: in 2005, they represented U.S.$122 million on total exports of U.S.$25 billion. In the period 1987–2007 Egyptian inventors received 92 patents from the U.S. Patent and Trademark Office, but just 19 of them belonged to Egyptian assignees. In the same period, Israelis had obtained 15 868 U.S. patents.

Yet some institutional building took place in Egypt. In 1963, the government created its first Ministry of Scientific Research (MSR), and in 1971, the Technology and Scientific Research Academy. The MSR oversees 13 research institutes (see Table 6.8 below).

Universities

Previous to creation of the republic, education in Egypt was not a priority. In 1947, 77 per cent of the population was illiterate, and there were only 15 000 university students in the country (Cook, 1999). The republic granted universal access to higher education, but quality did not follow quantity. University is free, but the university system is comparatively poor. The Nasser government guaranteed a job in the public sector to all graduates, thus inflating the civil service – a measure that effectively ended in 1986. But the system neglected science and engineering, and many graduates cannot find work.

In 1908, the government set up a national university; it merged that with a public one in 1925 and renamed it Fouad University in 1940 after the king. In 1953, the institution became Cairo University – today the largest national university. At the founding of the republic, Egypt had four universities. Seven state universities emerged under Sadat in the 1970s. In

Table 6.8   Some of Egypt's major research institutions

Ministry	Government laboratory
Agriculture	Agricultural Research Centre (early 20th century)
Agriculture	Agricultural Genetic Engineering Research Institute (1990)
Electricity	Atomic Energy Authority (1958)
Health	Central Public Health Laboratory
Housing, Utilities and Urban Development	Housing and Building National Research Centre
Planning	Cairo Demographic Centre (1963)
Scientific Research	National Research Centre (1956)
Scientific Research	National Standardization and Calibration Institute (1963)
Scientific Research	National Research Institute for Astronomy and Geophysics (1980/1905)
Scientific Research	Central Metallurgical R&D Institute
Scientific Research	Research Institute for Ophthalmology
Scientific Research	Electronics Research Institute
Scientific Research	Theodor Bilharz Research Institute
Scientific Research	National Authority for Remote Sensing and Space Sciences
Scientific Research	Egyptian Petroleum Research Institute (1974)
Scientific Research	National Institute for Oceanography and Fisheries Sciences
Water Resources and Irrigation	National Water Research Centre (1975)
	Desert Research Centre (1939)

1992, the state permitted private universities in addition to the American University in Cairo (AUC). By 1999–2000, some 1.5 million students were attending the 12 state universities and their eight branches. The nine private universities had 6000 students, and the AUC, 4000. Graduation rates are low; in 1998–99, the system produced about 140 000 graduates. Two observers summarized the problems of higher education:

- Egypt spends less on education than most Arab countries ($1191 per university student per year against ten times that amount in some oil-rich Arab countries, such as Bahrain, Kuwait, and Saudi Arabia).
- The pressure of numbers remains relentless, as more youngsters intend to pursue higher education.
- The ratio of professors to students is high (37:1) and continues to grow.

- Research spending is very low, and researchers in Egypt are among the worst paid in the Arab world.
- Oil-rich Arab countries have attracted some of the best talents from Egyptian universities.
- There is no system to monitor academic research and teaching.

The writers conclude that Egyptian higher education needs more money, better research facilities, and better teaching and research capacities (Belal and Springel, 2006). As in Argentina, so in Egypt low salaries push professors to consult, teach private courses, sell books and course notes to students, and reduce research. Richards (1992) concludes that government needs to increase employment for graduates in the private sector. I return to this issue below.

Government Laboratories

Some public research exists in Egypt: the 100-year-old Agricultural Research Centre (ARC) set up an Agricultural Engineering Research Institute (AGERI) in 1990. Agriculture represents 20 per cent of GDP and exports and employs 34 per cent of the labour force. With some 2500 PhD researchers, ARC is the nation's oldest and one of its largest research bodies, with 16 research institutes, six central laboratories, and 46 experimental stations. AGERI is the only Egyptian public laboratory that has received U.S. patents.

The National Research Centre is the largest such organization in Egypt, with over 60 per cent of all the research personnel in the Ministry of Science and Technology; it consists of 13 divisions, 106 departments, and about 4300 researchers. Between the 1960s and the 1980s it spun off six divisions as separate, autonomous units: the Central Metallurgical Research Institute, the Electronics Research Institute, the National Institute for Standards, the Petroleum Research Institute, the Ophthalmology Research Institute, and the Theodor Bilharz Institute.[4] The National Research Centre is one of the main sources of Egypt's foreign publications.

The Egyptian Atomic Energy Authority (EAEA) is 50 years old and undertakes applied nuclear research in four centers. It employs more than 1400 scientists, 2300 technical staffers, and 1300 administrative personnel.

The Central Public Health Laboratory in Cairo investigates diseases and food safety. It receives over 300 000 food samples for analysis every year.

Finally, several science and technology parks have emerged since 2000. The Mubarak City for Scientific Research and Technology Applications

(MUCSAT, 1993) is in Alexandria. *Science* heralded it as a move 'to create a homegrown biotechnology industry from scratch. Egypt must reverse a decades-long scientific exodus caused by hardships such as salaries of only about $200 a month, aging equipment, and red tape that can delay orders for months' (Frank, 2001). The first stage opened in 2000 with four centers: the Advanced Technologies and New Materials Research Institute, the Genetic Engineering and Biotechnology Research Institute, the Informatics Research Institute, and the Technology Capabilities Research Centre.

The Smart Villages Company (2001) fosters creation of technology parks. Smart Village Cairo already boasts more than 100 companies and 12000 professionals. Other such facilities on the planning board include one in Sinai (Sinai Technology Valley).

Foreign laboratories complement local ones. The Swiss-based multinational SGS, which specializes in inspection, certification, and testing, has operated in Egypt since 1965, with a series of laboratories aiming at basic manufacturing industries and/or to support tourism. SGS now has 250 employees at six laboratories and several offices in Egypt, including two food laboratories and one textile-testing facility in Cairo and laboratories for agriculture, for minerals, and for petroleum and petrochemicals in Alexandria. Besides, it helps the Egyptian Organization for Standardization and Quality to upgrade its laboratories and train personnel.

Since 1946, the U.S. Naval Medical Research Unit Number 3 (NAMRU-3) has been active in Cairo and has been investigating human health in collaboration with domestic and international agencies. Its mission is to study, prevent, and control epidemic and endemic diseases in subtropical areas where navy personnel work and live (Pellerin, 2007).

Innovation Policies

The private sector is so little active in science, technology, and innovation (STI) because of the total absence of policy incentives. That inactivity in turn explains the difficulty university graduates have in joining the business economy, the low prestige of scientific and technical careers, and the very few links between the large state universities and industry. The lack of policy incentives is as in Argentina, in Egypt the weakest link in the STI system.

However, as in Argentina, the government in Egypt has been waking up. In 2007, in response to public criticism and low productivity, it set up a higher Council for Science and Technology and a Science and Technology Fund. The Ministry of Science and Technology administers the Council, and the Fund, the Egyptian National Research Funding Agency, which it modeled on the U.S. National Science Foundation. Egypt has declared the years 2007–16 the Egyptian decade for science and technology and plans to increase funding for science and technology, expand GERD to 1 per cent of GDP (Koenig, 2007), stimulate international co-operation, and upgrade science and mathematics curricula. Similarly, in November 2006 African science ministers meeting in the Egyptian capital proposed in their Cairo Declaration to increase the continent's GERD to 1 per cent of GDP by 2010 and launch a biotechnology strategy.

Conclusion on Egypt

In sum, Egypt has built some of the STI organizations that Argentina has not established, but they have insufficient personnel and inadequate funding. Government spends little on R&D – about U.S.$100 million for 2006–7. The remaining R&D funds are university expenditures and the result of foreign R&D collaborations. Reaching the Cairo Declaration goals – $1.27 billion – would multiply national GERD in just three years. While MUCSAT, the National Funding Agency, and technology parks could absorb some of this money, such an increase appears as an unattainable goal for the national organizations.

6.6   MEXICO

Mexico has implemented more public policies to nurture innovation, higher education, and R&D than most developing countries. In addition, it and its education system were for almost a century open to professionals and academics from many countries, notably from Franco's Spain and Latin America. Yet, despite its openness and efforts, as well as some evident results, the Mexican NSI is still embryonic and requires urgent revamping.

Economic Development in the Twentieth Century

The republic of Mexico declared independence from Spain in 1810, lost one-third of its territory in the war with the United States 1846–48, and passed through several dictatorships, French occupation (1850–68), the Revolution of 1910, and finally a new constitution in 1917. It experienced a long period of economic growth between 1940 and 1980 and political peace under the rule of the Institutional Revolutionary Party from 1929 on. Growth occurred mostly through exploitation of mineral resources and manufacturing under tariff protection and after 1945 through import substitution. In the 1970s, oil became the main export product, and it remains so today. Mexico joined the General Agreement on Trade and Tariffs (GATT) in 1985 and is a member of the World Trade Organization. In 1994, its entry into the North American Free Trade Agreement (NAFTA) with Canada and the United States further redirected its trade towards its North American partners. Mexico's economy is the twelfth largest in the world, and, like Argentina, it is a middle-income country.

However, its economic challenges are daunting. First, the main source of foreign currency – and of 40 per cent of government revenues – is oil, which is beginning to run out, with 10 years of proven reserves remaining (Gil Valdivia and Chacon Domínguez, 2008). Second, the rise of South East Asia threatens its consumer manufacturing in terms of both exports and the domestic market. Third, Mexico does not create enough jobs for its rising population, which is still migrating to the United States in massive numbers. However, expatriates send back remittances that earn the country more foreign currency than anything but oil. Fourth, between 2000 and 2007, Mexico's GDP grew each year (between 3 per cent and 4.8 per cent at constant prices), but not enough to reduce substantially either poverty or vast social and economic inequality. Fifth, despite high expenditures in education, Mexico still lags behind the OECD and several Latin American countries in education expectancy (Tables 6.3 and 6.7). Finally, corruption remains a problem, even if it is not as acute as in the other three countries in this chapter.

The National System of Innovation

In the last quarter-century, Mexico has caught up with the main Latin American countries (Argentina and Brazil) in many areas of science, technology, and innovation (STI), as well as in GDP per capita. Scientific publication has more than doubled (Table 6.5), and patents in the United States increased by over 50 per cent in the last ten years (Table 6.6). After the mid-1990s Mexico implemented several laws to promote STI. The most recent was the Law of Science and Technology (2002), to reinforce elements of the national system of science and technology and improve their co-ordination. The Parliament voted new budgets, and improvements followed in several areas. By 2007, federal expenditure in science and technology reached 0.5 per cent of GDP, or U.S.$3.5 billion at official exchange rates.

However, this is a 'small miracle' in comparison with several South East Asian nations. Tiny Singapore, with 4.5 million people, publishes almost as many scientific and engineering articles as Mexico with 110 million and receives five times more patents in the United States. Singapore has 30 times more patents in real numbers and 100 times more patents per person.

Universities

As in Argentina, in Mexico most of the national and state universities, which number about 100, are public and almost free. The National Autonomous University of Mexico (UNAM) towers over the system. UNAM has more than one-tenth of all the country's university students and produces almost one-third of all of its international scientific information publications. It has 5400 full-time professors, 20000 part-timers, and 2550 researchers who belong to the National System of Researchers (NSR). It hosts 158000 undergraduates, over 20000 postgraduates, and 110000 students studying for certificates. The Instituto Tecnológico de Monterrey (ITESM) has 33 campuses across the country. By 2007, it had 92000 students, including 55000 undergraduates and 12000 postgraduates. It also boasts 2800 full-time and 6000 part-time faculty members. Despite its name, it is multidisciplinary but publishes little. The Universidad Autónoma Metropolitana (UAM, 1974) is another large public institution in Mexico City with over 45000 students and some 5000 professors, including 547 NSR members (on average 2000–4). UAM produced 7 per cent of all international scientific information articles from Mexico between 1990 and 2004 (Mexico, Foro consultivo científico y tecnológico, 2006a: 26).

The government created the NSR in December 1983 to fund and assess researchers' work and reward the most productive. The number of members is flexible. The NSR organizes periodical peer reviews of all researchers (in academe and government laboratories) and announces new members, who receive a bonus that may equal half of their pay. The NSR had unforeseen effects: it tended to reduce attention to and efforts in teaching, administration, technology transfer, and other activities in favour of publication. The system (like its counterparts in the United States and Canada) favours focus on short-term projects and brief articles. And, after 25 years, it did not transform Mexico's position in world science (Mexico, Foro consultivo científico y tecnológico, 2006b: 26–27) (Tables 6.9 and 6.10).

In 1984, the NSR had 1400 researchers in all disciplines; in 1992, it had 6600, and in 2005, over 12000. By 2006, natural sciences and mathematics occupied 51 per cent of researchers, the social sciences 27 per cent, engineering 12 per cent, and medicine and health sciences

Table 6.9 *Mexico: Main science and engineering indicators, selected years, 1990–2005*

	1990	1995	2000	2005
Population	81	91	97	104
GDP, US $, billion	262.7	286.7	581.4	767.5
GDP, US $ (PPP)	517.4	626.2	886.4	1114.4
GERD, US $, billion	n.d.	0.861	2.03	3.84
GERD*100/GDP	n.d.	0.30%	0.35%	0.50%
Science and engineering (S&E) publications	1038	1901	2950	3902
S&E articles per million inhabitants	12.8	20.9	30.4	37.5
U.S. patents granted (first inventor)	32	40	76	95
U.S. biotechnology patents	4	5	7	n.d.
Total researchers (FTE) (1)	n.d.	33 297	40 545	83 683
Total researchers (FTE) per thousand EAP	n.d.	0.54	0.55	1.03
Government researchers (FTE) as % of (1)	n.d.	31.0%	32.1%	15.0%
Business-sector researchers (FTE) as % of (1)	n.d.	10.3%	19.7%	45.3%
University researchers (FTE) as % of (1)	n.d.	57.8%	47.6%	38.0%
Non-profit organizations (FTE) as % of (1)	n.d.	0.9%	0.6%	1.7%

Notes: FTE: Full-time equivalent
EAP: Employed

Sources: OECD, main science and technology indicators, various issues; Science and Engineering Indicators, various years.

10 per cent (Mexico, Foro consultivo científico y tecnológico, 2006a). However, the soaring numbers did not allow Mexico to catch up with wealthy countries. Besides, few young recruits were entering the system, and the average age of researchers was rising fast (ibid: 17–20). And evaluation considers only domestic publications, thus downplaying publishing abroad (Mexico, Foro consultivo científico y tecnológico, 2006b, p. 27).

The Mexican university system hosts 2.5 million students. More than 60 per cent of them obtain their first degree in the social sciences and humanities, and about half take their graduate degree in the same areas. Natural sciences and engineering represent about 35 per cent of first degrees and 50 per cent of graduate degrees (ibid.: 35). Unlike in the United States and Canada, no major incentive channels students towards engineering and computer, health, or natural sciences.

By 2005, just 7.9 per cent of Mexican adults had a tertiary degree, against 25 per cent on average in OECD countries. Only 27 per cent of these Mexicans graduate in science and engineering. The private sector employs few scientists and engineers; Mexico is thus in a low-skill labour trap, where weak demand matches weak supply of human capital.

Government Laboratories

Public research institutions in Mexico fall into two categories: The National Council for Scientific and Technical Research (CONACYT) and sector centers that government departments operate (Mexico, Foro consultivo científico y tecnológico, 2006a, p. 25).

CONACYT runs 27 institutes:

- Ten centers in the natural and exact sciences, in such areas as computer sciences, ecology, electronics, material sciences, mathematics, molecular biology, optics, and physics;
- Nine centers in technological development and services, such as agro-food, chemicals and plastics, machinery, mechanical industries, metals, and the shoe and leather industry;
- Eight centers in the social sciences and humanities, in such disciplines as anthropology, economics, education, geography, history, and public administration.

These three subsystems employ in all some 4000 researchers and 2200 administrative personnel. The natural science group has almost half of the research personnel, technology 28 per cent of them, and the social sciences 23 per cent.

The sectoral centers have links to government departments in relation to specific industries, such as agriculture, energy, environment, and industry. Their common mission is generation and diffusion of knowledge in specific industries in Mexico. Among them some deserve special mention:

- The Mexican Petroleum Institute (IMP) is one of the largest. Operating since 1965, it had in 2006 some 738 researchers (of whom 205 were members of the NRS). IMP has developed many technologies and is one of the largest Mexican patent holders in both the United States and Mexico.

- The Institute for Electric Research (IIE) has functioned since 1975; it employed in 2007 517 researchers in such areas as alternative energies, controls, and electrical and mechanical systems.
- The National Institute for Nuclear Research (ININ), in operation since 1956, develops applications of nuclear technology in energy, material sciences, and medicine. It has close connections to the Department of Energy.

In the Department of Agriculture one finds the National Institute of Forest, Agriculture and Cattle Research (INFAP), operating since 1985 and including eight research centers and 38 experimental stations. It employs about 1000 researchers and has produced some valuable technologies in Mexican crops. Two other research centers deserve mention: the National Institute for Public Health (INSP) and the Mexican Water Technology Institute (IMTA).

The Mexican Foro consultivo (2006) calculates that all these research centers and a few others employed some 800 of the NSR's 12000 elite researchers. Their publication record was good, but they had received few patents, particularly international patents. Besides, universities seemed more attractive for researchers. Among the 12 organizations that gathered 50 per cent of NSR members, ten were universities, including UNAM and UAM, and only two were government research centers.

In comparison with its North American partners, Mexico had few research centers employing too few researchers. Canada had about 160 public research organizations (110 federal and 50 provincial) employing close to 10000 person-years in R&D. Also, some of these laboratories were active in frontier research areas such as biotechnology, nanotechnology, robotics, and telecommunications and in transferring results to the private sector. In the United States, the 800 or so federal research laboratories (NSF, 2008) have more researchers than all Mexican government research organizations together, and many undertake frontier research.

Policies for the Private Sector

Despite some successful innovation, Mexican business is not very active in R&D (Mexico, Foro consultivo científico y tecnológico, 2008). By 2005, only 1100 companies executed R&D, and fewer than 1000 had formal R&D units. Also, not many manufacturers were conducting R&D, as we can see in their low technological intensity (Table 6.10). In 2005, business financed about 35 per cent of GERD. Most R&D performers are large, foreign-controlled firms.

Mexico has implemented a series of incentives to increase R&D in

*Table 6.10   Mexico and OECD, manufacturing: technological intensity
and R&D/value added, 1999*

Industrial classification by technological intensity	OECD	Mexico
Pharmaceutical products	22.3%	0.35%
Office machinery	25.8%	0.11%
TV, radio, and communication equipment	17.9%	0.04%
Medical instruments, optical and precision, and others	24.6%	0.15%
Machinery and electrical equipment	9.1%	0.49%
Motor vehicles	13.3%	0.44%
Chemical products (excluding pharmaceutical)	8.3%	0.79%
Other transportation equipment	8.7%	0.18%
Other machinery and equipment	5.8%	0.02%
Rubber and plastic products	3.1%	1.04%
Coal, oil products, and nuclear energy	2.7%	0.18%
Non-metal mineral products	1.9%	0.29%
Primary metals and metal products	1.9%	1.1%
Other manufacturing	1.3%	1.29%
Wood, paper, printing, and editing	1%	1.37%
Food, beverages, and tobacco	1.1%	0.11%
Textiles, garment, leather, and fur	0.8%	0.21%
Total manufacturing	7.20%	0.45%

Source: Mexico, Foro Consultivo (2006a), p. 10.

the private sector – most important, a program of tax credits, which
was abandoned in 2009. The system allowed deduction of 30 per cent of
expenditures and investments in R&D, including training of personnel.
The credit was applicable to taxes on both profits and assets. While in
most industrial countries, such as Canada, the private sector can request
unlimited tax credits for R&D, Mexico set a maximum total amount –
U.S.$450 million in 2006. Tax credits do not encourage smaller firms,
because of the transaction costs in filling forms for a small credit. First,
this fixed amount tends even further to bias the incentive in favour of
large enterprises. These were already conducting R&D and have the
personnel to fill the forms and inquire about the incentive. Second, sizeable companies can more easily lobby for larger credits. If a system has
no ceiling, increasing numbers of SMEs will request the incentive. The
Mexican approach discouraged additionality: larger enterprises will
simply reduce their disbursements and shift 30 per cent of their R&D
costs to the state. In Mexico, bigger companies took the lion's share of
the tax credits. Between 2001 and 2004, a mere ten firms had obtained
over 35 per cent of them (Mexico, Foro consultivo, 2006a: 29). During

the same period only 505 enterprises obtained tax credits, against over 19 500 in Canada. Also, large foreign subsidiaries already familiar with the stimulus (such as Delphi, Du Pont, General Motors, HP, Nemak, and Volkswagen) and sizeable Mexican firms (Hylsa, Vitro) had obtained most of the incentives. Foreign companies received about 70 per cent of the funds, and local ones the balance. To increase R&D by existing firms of all sizes, domestic and foreign, Mexico needed to abolish the ceilings on tax credits.

In the meantime, Mexico has been unable to create a venture-capital industry (Mexico, Foro consultivo 2006a: 34–5). By 2005/6, Mexico had U.S.$2 billion in venture capital and an annual flow of $350 million and lagged far behind industrial nations and even other large countries in Latin America. It had no fiscal incentives for venture capital similar to Canada's, no direct public subsidies (like Israel's Yozma plan), and no public-sector firms (like the Business Development Bank of Canada or Brazil's Banco Nacional de Desenvolvimento).

With little involvement by the private sector in research and innovation, links between industry and academe and between industry and public research laboratories are not as strong as they may be in Europe or elsewhere in North America. Industry does not demand science and technology.

Finally, and maybe as important as all the considerations above, Mexico has not developed vertical policies for specific sectors of future relevance – those that will replace the aging oil and gas or textile industries. If economic development requires creation of new sectors (Saviotti and Pyka, 2004), then Mexico has been neglecting its future.

Conclusion on Mexico

Mexico is one of the world's largest economies and has made progress in incorporating science, technology, and innovation in the economy. However, its investment in this field is lagging, its policies are modest in both numbers and scope, especially as the country will soon run out of oil and gas, and its traditional industries face strong competition from South East Asia, both in world and in domestic markets. It seems evident that Mexico needs a much stronger tax credit for R&D without ceilings (like the Canadian one); requires other programs to complement this one, in order to produce more scientists and engineers (e.g., targeted fellowship programs for specific disciplines); should stimulate demand for them in the private sector by different means (venture-capital programs, direct subsidies for R&D in small firms such as IRAP, and incentives for firms to hire university graduates); and ought to strengthen links between academe and industry. Perhaps Mexico should imitate Singapore and hire high-level academics from overseas or copy Taiwan and launch new types of government laboratories to incubate high-tech firms, such as that island's ITRI. Windfall profits from oil and gas might support these and other initiatives. Mexican oil seems to have a ten-year future; increasing investments in STI will be much more difficult after the end of oil.

6.7   THE PHILIPPINES

In Asia in the late 1940s, only Japan had a bigger economy than the Philippines. Today, in a rapid-growing region that is increasing its human capital base and its investment in STI, the Philippines seems to lag far behind. As in Argentina, 30 per cent of people lived in poverty in 2007; the GDP per capita was U.S.$3300 (PPP), and the country boasted one of the worst rankings in corruption in *Transparency International*.

The Economy

The Philippines shares with most of Latin America the dubious honour of having been a colony of Spain – from 1565 until the American invasion of 1898, after which it was a U.S. protectorate until 1946. Economic development has been slow since 1946 in comparison with the exploding population. In 1962, its per-capita income was comparable to Taiwan's and represented 25 per cent of Japan's; in 1986, it was one-seventh of Taiwan's and 3 per cent of Japan's (Boyce, 1993). Between 1965 and 1998, per-capita GDP growth was actually negative (Gylfason and Zoega, 2006). The two decades 1965–85 saw the so-called green revolution: President Ferdinand Marcos launched an ambitious program to increase production of rice. In 1985, the last year of his government, the country imported over 500000 tons of rice. Drought, soil degradation, storms, peasants' debt (which kept them from buying fertilizers and pesticides), and macro-economic crisis and corruption severely limited the agricultural revolution.

In the 1980s and 1990s, with economic liberalization and opening of the domestic market, foreign direct investment poured in. The Philippines attracted a few large electronics companies such as Intel, Lexmark, Texas Instruments, and Toshiba, all exporting products from the country. In addition, business process outsourcing (BPO) has been growing but has not yet become a major export industry. In recent years, under President Arroyo, economic liberalization and infrastructure investment have pushed economic growth over 5 per cent a year, without transforming the economy. In 2005, the Philippines had gross exports of U.S.$34 billion in high-tech manufactures (basically electronic products) out of some U.S.$50 billion in total exports; however, imports by these same industries represented over U.S.$27 billion, for a net balance of some U.S.$7 billion.

There are several common explanations for this slow growth: little or no productivity growth (Chen, 1997); strong macro-economic fluctuations (Patalinghug, 2000); a strategy of relying on natural resources (Gylfason and Zoega, 2006); and high and increasing income inequality (Aghion et al., 1999). After a review of the literature, Chen (1997) concludes that an investment-driven economy could not become productive enough. When investment (particularly of the foreign direct variety) diminished, economic growth tended to halt. Besides, natural resources are a fixed factor of production (and in many cases a declining one) and severely restrict growth. Also, their abundance tends to weaken incentives to invest in human capital and encourages powerful groups to seek rent (Gylfason and Zoega, 2006). Aghion et al. (1999) emphasize that, despite its similarities with Taiwan, the Philippines (the more unequal society) grew more slowly. When one adds in the explanations above, one finds a pattern of reliance on natural resources, which induces little investment in human capital and reinforces rent-seeking by national elites. Low levels of education inhibit assimilation of foreign technology, to say nothing of development of new technology.

The National System of Innovation

The Philippines has at best an embryonic national system of innovation. Indicators abound: a GERD:GDP ratio of 0.11 per cent in 2003–4, down from 0.22 per cent in 1994 and 0.14 per cent in 2002. Output indicators are in line with such a low level of investments: two articles in science and engineering per million people in 2005, less than 50 patents per year in the United States between 2001 and 2005, and low expenditure on human capital and education. In 2002, the Philippines had 89 R&D scientists and engineers per million inhabitants (de la Peña, 2006), against 10 200 in Japan, 6400 in South Korea, and 4600 in Singapore.

The Public Sector

In 1958, the Philippines established a National Science and Development Board (NSDB) to conceive and implement policies and institutions to do with science and technology (Patalinghug, 2003); in 1982 the NSDB became the National Science and Technology Authority (NSTA). In 1987, the government created out of the NSTA the Department of Science and Technology (DOST), which set up several agencies:

- The Advanced Science and Technology Institute (ASTI) to conduct R&D in high technology;
- The Industrial Technology Development Institute (ITDI) to conduct R&D in manufacturing, minerals, and energy;
- The Science Education Institute (SEI) to plan development of science and engineering education;
- The Science and Technology Information Institute (STII) to collect data on science and technology;
- The Technology Application and Promotion Institute (TAPI) to commercialize technology.

In 1990, DOST implemented a ten-year Science and Technology Master Plan (STMP) to increase R&D investments, the number of researchers, and, most important, private-sector involvement in innovation. STMP enumerated a series of high-priority sectors. In 1993, DOST announced the Science and Technology Agenda for National Development (STAND) as the successor to STMP and picked new sectors for national technological development. Box 6.2 compares the two lists.

These priorities suffered two major setbacks. First, the Philippine government did not invest enough funds, All the rapid-growing countries in the previous chapter and the present-day catchers-up (China and South Korea) are substantially increasing their investments in technology and innovation in their priority list. Without funds, such sets of priorities appear more to be 'wish lists' than real priorities. Second, the lists contain almost every industrial sector. Picking some sectors means *not* picking others. No country – except maybe China or the United States – can select almost every industrial activity as a priority. If the lists contain 'energy,' then it would be crucial to decide what sort (nuclear, ocean, solar, thermal, wind). If 'transportation' is a priority, then 'roads, railways, air, fluvial, or ocean' would be more precise. From the many emerging technologies, Singapore picked 'electronics' and 'bio-pharmaceuticals,' not nanotechnologies or photovoltaic or space technologies.

In 1999, the Medium-Term Plan of DOST for 1999–2004 formulated again new goals and added to the number of agencies and institutes that DOST oversees. The present organization of DOST includes several organizations (see Box 6.3).

Patalinghug (2003) suggests that the public sector, which represents over 70 per cent of the country's GERD, lacks sufficient resources, incentives, personnel, and/or organizational suppleness to conduct R&D.

BOX 6.2   PHILIPPINES: PRIORITY INDUSTRIES

STMP priority sectors
1. Agriculture
2. Aquaculture and marine fisheries
3. Forestry and national resources
4. Metals and engineering
5. Textile industry
6. Mining and minerals
7. Process industry
8. Food and feed industry
9. Energy
10. Transportation
11. Construction industry
12. Information technology
13. Electronics, instrumentation, and control
14. Emerging technologies
15. Pharmaceutical

STAND priority list
A. **Export winners**
1. Computer software
2. Fashion accessories
3. Marine products
4. Fruits
5. Gifts, toys, and houseware
6. Furniture
7. Metals fabrication
B. **Basic domestic needs**
1. Food
2. Housing
3. Health and nutrition
4. Clothing
5. Environment
6. Energy
7. Transport
8. Telecommunications
9. Defence
10. Manpower
11. Disaster/hazard mitigation
C. **Support industries**
1. Packaging
2. Metals
3. Chemicals
D. **Coconut industry**
1. Production
2. Processing
3. Development of new products

Sources: Science and Technology Master Plan (Manila, 1990); DOST: Science and Technology Agenda for National Development (Manila, 1993).

Universities

Tertiary education is a post-war, post-independence phenomenon. In 1946, there were only 46 000 post-secondary students; by 1985, there were 1.5 million (James, 1991). There were 2.4 million as of 2005/6. The University

---

BOX 6.3   PHILIPPINE STI ORGANIZATIONS

Sectoral planning councils
Advanced Science and
    Technology R&D
Agriculture, Forest and
    Nature R&D
Aquatic Marine R&D
Health R&D
Industry and Energy R&D

R&D institutes
Advanced Science and
    Technology Institute
    (ASTI)
Food and Nutrition Research
    Institute
Industrial Technology
    Development Institute
    (ITDI)
Metals Industry R&D Centre
Philippines Nuclear
    Research Institute
Philippines Textile Research
    Institute

Advisory bodies
National Academy of
    Science and Technology
National Research Council
    of the Philippines

S&T service institutes
Atmospheric, Geophysical
    and Astronomical Services
    Administration
National Computer Centre
Philippines Science High
    School
Science and Technology
    Information Institute
Science Education Institute
Technology Application and
    Promotion Institute

---

of the Philippines, with seven constituent universities and twelve campuses, dominates the nation's university system. Operating since 1908, it enrols 50 000 students. In addition, there are over 1600 colleges and universities, many of them confessional and Christian. About 180 higher education institutions were public, and 1465 were private (Inocentes, 2006). The Philippines is one of the few countries in South East Asia where higher education is mostly in private hands. By 2003–4, two thirds of students were attending private institutions (Manasan et al., 2008). The system undertakes very little research (Teixeira and Amaral, 2001).

Total university enrolment for the last five years has been stable, at about 2.4 million. Some 26 per cent of these students are in agricultural sciences, engineering, mathematics and computer science, natural science, and technology. About 74 000 of them graduated in 2004 in these scientific and engineering fields. It is difficult to say where they work afterwards.

According to U.S. figures, however, in 2003, close to 132 000 immigrants of Filipino origin with university degrees were residents of the United States. Two-thirds of them had obtained their highest degree abroad (NSF, 2008).

In the Philippines, spending on education is fairly low, at 3.1 per cent of GDP in 2003–4, according to UNESCO (UNESCO, 2005b). In addition, the country 'has one of the lowest public expenditures on education at 0.4% of GDP, the amounts devoted to education have been contracting over the 1999–2005 period, and the quality of education is variable' (Manasan et al., 2008). Besides, government covers about 50 per cent (or 2.5 per cent of GDP) of the cost of education, with the private sector handling the rest. Analysing the Philippines, James (1991) suggests that in an environment where there is little research and where diplomas are valuable per se, students will buy the cheapest educational services and diplomas. In such private organizations, professors with PhDs are uncommon, cheaper disciplines with little research (such as business administration, law, and social sciences) are overwhelming, and classes are large. Her analysis applies equally to Argentina, where most private universities cater to these less expensive fields.

With little academic R&D and almost no private-sector R&D taking place, technology transfer from university to industry or even collaboration is scarce (Patalinghug, 2003).

Even more serious, many educated Filipinos could not find a job commensurate with their education and either migrated or took positions where their skills were not particularly helpful (Rodriguez, 1998). By shortly after 2000, there were some 2.8 million of them working abroad, including 2.2 million permanent migrants to the United States.

Public Policies

The Philippines introduced in the post-war period only a few policy incentives to increase R&D in the private sector. In addition, these few policies are not co-ordinated or strong enough to induce private sector R&D. Also, public universities may not receive private-sector contributions with profit-making goals. Two incentives appear to be central: tax incentives and direct subsidies.

In 1998, the Philippines introduced a tax incentive for R&D. Corporations and individuals can claim a reduction of tax on benefits, which are currently at 32 per cent to 35 per cent of eligible expenditures. Corporate tax rates may be reduced by up to 10 per cent; yet the law does not define R&D, and there are no available figures about the number of companies that have taken advantage of the law.

The other incentive is a grant on investments, which appeared in 1990, and the Board of Investments (BOI) administers it. Companies may be eligible for certain benefits and incentives if they invest in one of the Investment Priorities Plans (IPP). In 2008, such 'sectors' were agriculture and agribusiness, constructive and direct exports, engineered projects, infrastructure, R&D, and strategic investments (*Manila Times*, Feb. 26, 2008). Even if they are not in these industries, they can still receive incentives such as tax holidays if at least 50 per cent of their production is for exports (but 70 per cent, in the case of foreign-controlled firms). Over the period 1990–97, however, only 11 companies claimed the BOI incentives for R&D (Cororaton, 1999).

The Private Sector

R&D in Filipino industry has been dismal, most probably because of the lack of suitable incentives, but also because trained university researchers are so scarce. By the mid-1990s there were only 152 researchers in industry per million inhabitants. Government departments conduct little R&D, private-sector incentives are few and not co-ordinated, and universities carry out almost no R&D. In addition, there are few graduate students in science and technology who could help the private sector find, adopt, adapt, and master foreign technology.

Also, in the absence of major and permanent incentives for R&D, but taking advantage of favourable tax treatment, foreign companies have since the mid-1980s invested in manufacturing plants but do not conduct R&D. Similarly, few domestic firms are able to capture spillovers from foreign high-tech firms because they themselves do not conduct R&D or innovative activities. If spillovers from foreign direct investment (FDI) increase with the level of domestic competition in host countries (Blomström and Kokko, 1998), the Filipino private sector is not able to take advantage of inward FDI in manufacturing or services. Also, multinational corporations tend to move R&D activities to developing countries only when the supply of skilled labour there is strong, which is not the case in the Philippines. Figures from the U.S. NSF (2008) confirm that the Philippines is not a destination of expatriate R&D by U.S. multinationals.

Conclusion on the Philippines

The Philippines has sometimes tended to engender 'stationary bandits,' to use Mancur Olsen's concept, which Kushida already applied to it (2003). These are long-term politicians who maximize their own interests through a monopoly of power and legitimate violence, a commitment to respect private property, and promotion of some type of economic development. Marcos, who governed 1965–86 and whom *Transparency International* called the second most corrupt head of state ever, was the best example of the stationary bandit. According to some observers, the system has not substantially changed, and each new president, like counterparts in Argentina and Mexico, gives thousands of positions to friends and supporters. 'During the first two years the new officials will be pre-occupied with familiarizing themselves with their new job, start appointing their clients, friends and family members appointed to government positions and assuring loyalty from government employees' (Van de Loo, 2004: 265).

The country did not lack administrative structures, priority lists, and plans for science and technology. It suffered, however, from very low public commitment to STI, academic research, and public and private R&D. All these commitments have been absent in the entire story of the Philippines, under both Spanish and American rule, as well as since independence in 1946. Investments in R&D have been low, and policy incentives for the private sector basically non-existent.

Public commitment to education is as paper-thin as that to science and technology and helps explain the continuous downgrading of the country in an increasingly prosperous region.

CONCLUSION TO THE CHAPTER

Van de Loo's (2004) statement above may apply to most Latin American countries, as well as to the other nations in this chapter. In such countries the state is not an organization providing services to the general public, but something that politicians use to recognize and reimburse favours from political supporters, families, and friends. Such a system is the contrary of a professional, meritocratic bureaucracy, such as those existing in most industrial nations. The clientele bureaucracy of many developing countries is unable to design, implement, and evaluate public policy for STI (or any kind of policy). Policies are mostly declarations of intentions, but public funds to make these goals real do not appear.

The building of an NSI requires long-term public-sector commitments to invest in education, academic research, and public and private R&D. Such commitments have been lacking throughout the history of the Philippines. Investments in R&D have been low, and policy incentives for the private sector almost non-existent. Construction of an NSI also requires many policies at the national, regional, and local levels: policies to stimulate research by academic and public laboratories (such as transparent research councils and foundations, like the U.S. NSF, the Academy of Finland, and the European Science Foundation); to create incentives for venture-capital firms (such as Israel's Yozma Program); to nurture industry–university co-operation (such as Europe's 7th Program); to insert young professional engineers and scientists into firms; to stimulate private innovative activities through effective tax credits for R&D, loans, and subsidies (such as Canada's tax credits, Technology Partnerships, and IRAP); to attract foreign talent and R&D laboratories (such as Singapore's), and to allow SMEs to explore university and government laboratory technology (such as the Americans' SBIR and STTR). All these policies need investment, the right sequence of implementation, and regular evaluation by outsiders.

These countries seem trapped in a low-growth vicious circle involving corrupt governments, inefficient public bureaucracies, and inadequate investment in education, science, and technology. The private sector has almost no incentive to conduct R&D or to innovate. The public sector and higher education perform just as poorly in these areas. Under such conditions, domestic technological capabilities are stagnant, if not receding, and such countries cannot use technology, the 'lever of riches' (Mokyr, 1990).

Government intervention is essential, but even it will fail unless several conditions are met. The Filipino economist Epictetus Patalinghug (2000: 43–4) summarizes these conditions:

- A competent and honest civil service – performance-based standards of success;
- Government's ability to discipline big business;
- A stable macro-economic environment – consistent government policy.

The countries in this chapter do not meet these conditions of success. The low-growth trap in which they find themselves derives from such a loop of self-reinforcing obstacles to further and quicker development.

NOTES

1. The Human Capital Index is 'a composite of the adult literacy rate and the combined primary, secondary and tertiary ratio, with two thirds of the weight given to the adult literacy rate, and one third to gross enrolment ratio' (UN, 2004).
2. 'Human capital utilization' is the percentage of human capital actually employed. 'Human capital endowment' is the investment in schools, universities, and adult education.
3. The UK had a professional government since the 1840s, and the United States since the 1870s. Italy and Spain had not.
4. www.nrc.sci.eg

7. Regional systems of innovation: four cases[1]

Regional policy for science, technology, and innovation (STI) would be impossible in the absence of a national approach to innovation. Subnational units such as provinces, states or municipal governments do not have the legislative and financial resources needed to invest in such a risky area of activity. However, a national approach may not be enough to promote innovation. For several reasons, including historical accumulations of human capital in specific regions and deficiencies elsewhere, national policies may benefit some cities, metropolitan areas, or provinces. In this sense, construction of a national system of innovation (NSI) must precede the building of regional institutions. This is why regional STI policies and other regional institutions are now part of the full panoply of initiatives taking place in all OECD countries.

This chapter aims to explain the rationale for development of regional STI initiatives, policies, and programs, as well as the roles therein of science-based agencies, departments, and other organizations. Also, the chapter assesses the performance of such institutions in those endeavours.

Since the 1990s, regional agglomerations of industries and technologies have come to influence and shape STI policy. Several factors concur to explain such a trend:

- After over a half-century of national STI policy in OECD countries, it has become evident that only a few regions in each member country have taken advantage of such policy. In Canada, for example, Montreal and Toronto census metropolitan areas (CMAs), with 27 cent of the Canadian population, represent over half of business expenditure on R&D (BERD). Also, well over 75 per cent of Canada's BERD takes place in a few CMAs where half of the nation's people live (Niosi and Bourassa, 2008). The same phenomenon occurs in other countries, including the United States (Feldman and Audretsch, 1999). Both national and regional authorities in most OECD countries now seek to extend the benefits of technological innovation to other regions and reinforce regions already starting to undertake these new technologies or industries (OECD, 1999b, 2001, 2007c).

- The rise of science-based industries such as biotechnology, fuel cell and hydrogen technologies, and nanotechnology, which involve universities and public R&D laboratories, has made it evident that strengthening universities and public laboratories in specific technologies can help to attract private-sector investment, incubate new firms, and create high-skill and highly paid jobs in regions (Zucker et al., 1998).
- In Japan, North America, and western Europe, but also in most of Latin America, traditional labour- and capital-intensive industries are facing strong competition from emerging economies such as those of China and India, and their market shares are declining. Science-based industries have some protection from such competition from developing countries, because they require highly skilled workers and sophisticated policy institutions. These high-tech activities, which may replace dying industries, typically display a distinct geographical agglomeration around such knowledge-producing organizations as universities and public R&D laboratories.
- Finally, since Solow's seminal work (Solow, 1956), it became clear that technology is the main factor behind economic development. For over 50 years, they have tried to pinpoint the relevant technological factors, such as human capital in science and technology, R&D expenditures, and intellectual capital in terms of patents and scientific and engineering publications. In the last 20 years, thanks to the work of Freeman (1987, 1995, 2002), Lundvall (1988, 1992), and Nelson (1993, 2005b), attention has concentrated on institutions that produce, store, and transfer scientific and technological knowledge. Other authors have shown that the positive effects (knowledge spillovers) of such institutions are mostly local and regional (Jaffe et al., 1993). The concept of NSI gave birth to that of regional systems of innovation (RSIs).

7.1   DEFINING RSIS

Economists have used several concepts to characterize regional agglomerations of firms. Industrial districts and growth poles were among the first to capture the imagination of scientists and policy-makers. Clusters, innovative milieux, and RSIs followed them.

Industrial Districts

Alfred Marshall (1920) was perhaps the first social scientist to notice geographical agglomeration of companies in the same industry. He attributed the phenomenon to local accumulation of knowledge (knowledge externalities), formation of a specialized labour pool, and attraction of support and supplier industries. He coined the term 'industrial district' but did not mention supporting organizations such as universities and public R&D laboratories. As Goodman (1989: 21) observes, an industrial district is 'essentially a territorial system of small and medium sized firms.' The concept has become widespread in Italy, where dozens of authors have found numerous specialized industrial districts, particularly in the north (Bagnasco, 1977; Piore and Sabel, 1984; Brusco, 1986; Becattini, 1990; Belussi, Gottardi, and Rullani, 2003; Lazerson and Lorenzoni, 1999).

Growth Poles

In France, Perroux (1970) introduced the concept of growth poles to indicate such geographical agglomerations of industry that take place through the activities of one or a few large companies. These firms may be large system integrators (such as automobile and aerospace manufacturers) that attract suppliers of parts and components, or they may be producers of essential inputs (such as steel and petrochemical companies) that attract downstream manufacturers. His ideas became popular in western Europe, where governments tried to build automobile, chemical, or aerospace poles by attracting (often subsidizing) large corporations to specific regions. In Perroux poles, regional trade of parts, materials, and components linked firms together, and Wassily Leontieff's input–output analysis proved useful for studying them.

Clusters

In the 1990s, however, Paul Krugman (1991), among others, revived interest in the geographic component of industry.

Local Knowledge Spillovers

Krugman firmly established regional economics as a special field of enquiry and insisted that 'the geographic concentration of production is clear evidence of the pervasive influence of some kind of increasing returns' (1991: 5). Under such conditions, regions may implement policies to nurture increasing returns in some industries in specific locations.[2] Krugman analysis provided theoretical justification for regional STI policies. Krugman espoused the economic vision of Myrdal (1957), Kaldor (1970), and others: he saw a world of cumulative causation and multiple equilibria. If a region (or a country) became a leader in a new industry, increasing returns could allow them to remain so, just as increasing returns allow such companies as IBM, Intel, and Microsoft to dominate their industries. Knowledge externalities (benefits that some economic agents bestow on others without using the market mechanism) formed a central part of the increasing-return mechanism within regions.

Yet Krugman did not believe that it was possible to measure those knowledge spillovers. His dictum 'knowledge flows . . . are invisible; they leave no paper trail' (1991: 53) unleashed a flurry of studies, as many authors sought to measure those externalities. Jaffe et al. (1993) were among the first. They used information from the United States Patent and Trademark Office (USPTO) to show that patent citations come disproportionately from the same regions as the inventors. Other authors studied the mobility of inventors among firms within regions, as well as through local social ties (Breschi et al., 2005). This approach also used patent information to trace knowledge flows: the names of inventors appear in patents, and when they move between companies their knowledge travels with them. Both approaches proved quite useful.

Regional Systems of Innovation

Interest in regional industry and innovation came from quite a different strand. Douglass North suggested that institutions were the key factor in economic growth (North, 1981, 1990). Some authors, including North, focused on property institutions and the rule of law; others championed institutions for science, technology, and innovation (STI). Christopher Freeman (1987, 1988), Bengt-Ake Lundvall (1988, 1992), and Richard Nelson (1988, 1993, 2005a) managed to join the technology tradition in economics and the institutional approach and emphasized the quality of such institutions as universities, government R&D laboratories, and STI policies that produce human capital, create demand for such capital, generate new scientific and technical knowledge, and modify firms' behaviour through incentives for R&D. They jointly produced the concept of national system of innovation (NSI) – 'the network of institutions in the public and private sectors whose activities and interactions initiate, import, modify and diffuse new technologies' (Freeman, 1987: 1).

The NSI has incubated the concept of RSI. Cooke originally coined the concept (1992, 2001), with a similar underpinning to that of NSI: an RSI is a set of companies and institutions that interact in the production of science and technology in particular industries. 'Regions which possess the full panoply of innovation organisations set in an institutional milieu, where systemic linkage and interactive communication among the innovation actors is normal, approach the designation of regional innovation systems' (Cooke and Morgan, 1998: 71).

Howells (1999) stresses that NSIs are not homogeneous and that innovative activity is highly uneven within nations, in terms not only of specialization but of intensity as well. In all industrial nations, strong disparities persist between regions (e.g., in the United States, California or New York versus Mississippi or North Dakota). In other words, NSIs are not homogeneous entities.

Niosi (2001) uses the RSI concept but adds that in an RSI – unlike in an NSI – the geographical contour is often vague. Authors refer to RSIs sometimes as cities, sometimes as metropolitan areas and in several cases as sub-national administrative units (länder, provinces, states); writers occasionally invoke such hazy geographical territories as Route 128 and Silicon Valley. Niosi (2005) and Niosi and Bourassa (2008) apply the concept to Canada and use the CMA[3] as their unit of analysis. They find that a few CMAs (Toronto, Montreal, Ottawa, Vancouver, Calgary, Edmonton, Hamilton, and Quebec in descending size order) concentrate most of the country's industrial R&D. Also, the larger the region, the broader is the span of its innovation activities. The most specialized RSIs were Calgary, where oil and gas R&D dominates, and Ottawa, where telecommunications equipment, semi-conductors, and software dwarfed all other R&D.

An RSI is usually a set of interrelated clusters (Tödtling and Trippl, 2005: 1206), where public research institutions and organizations play a key role. RSIs are thus easier to find in CMAs than in smaller, more specialized cities.

Innovative Clusters

Michael Porter jumped on the new approach. His industrial clusters are reminiscent of Marshall's industrial districts. Clusters are 'geographical concentrations of interconnected companies, specialised suppliers, service providers, firms in related industries and associated institutions . . . in particular fields, that compete but also cooperate' (Porter, 1998: 197).

Porter suggested that clusters enhance productivity by attracting or creating common support industries, training programs, infrastructure, and business services. Local rivalry also helps to increase productivity. Clusters make it easier for firms to compare performance among competitors, monitor supplier costs, and attract specialized labour.

Porter (2000) argues that clusters make business innovation easier. Sometimes sophisticated customers are part of the cluster, and interaction between user and producer helps orient the producer's innovative activities. Innovators can also obtain skilled personnel and suppliers more quickly. And constant competitive pressure, which the cluster generates, forces companies to innovate.

In Porter's theory, governments provide support, and facilitate innovative activity. They do not pick clusters or start them from scratch. Porter and Takeuchi (1999) criticize Japanese government laboratories for being not able to forestall the country's difficulties in the 1990s. For them, academic research is more open, more flexible, and more likely to transfer results to industry through graduates, publications, and spin-offs. In his *Clusters of Innovation Report* (2001), Porter also acknowledges the role of government centers in clusters but does not describe it.

Clusters are also more conducive to formation of new businesses because gaps in products and services are more evident in clusters and abundant labour and suppliers lower barriers to entry.

The Birth and Evolution of Clusters

The evolution of clusters and industrial districts has captured the attention of scholars since Alfred Marshall. He noted that some industrial districts emerge close to concentrations of large market demand for specific products (i.e., large cities), some near natural resources or transportation facilities, and a few by historical accident. He also observed that such districts may disappear when demand for their products declines or when the supply of their industry fails. 'A district which is dependent on only one industry is liable to extreme depression. This evil again is in a great measure avoided by those large towns, or industrial districts in which several distinct industries are strongly developed' (Marshall, 1920: 227). In present-day terms, Marshall would prefer an RSI hosting several interrelated clusters, rather than a specialized agglomeration.

Perroux poles come into being when one or a few large corporations invest in a particular location, with their supply effects downstream and their demand effects upstream. They may decline when their most dynamic, large firms decline or die.

Markusen (1996) explores the idea that clusters are not always agglomerations of small and medium-size firms (SMEs). She suggests at least three other types of clusters: the hub-and-spoke cluster around large firms, the satellite industrial platform consisting of subsidiaries of foreign multinational corporations, and the state-centred district, where a government organization anchors the regional economy. Markusen finds the smaller-firm industrial district dominant in northern Italy, and the hub-and-spoke type in the United States. These agglomerations display little co-operation among large firms, little venture capital, and export markets for final products.

Developing Markusen's ideas, Agrawal and Cockburn (2003) suggest that large, local R&D-intensive firms anchor many clusters. Such enterprises capture knowledge from university research and public laboratories and may spin off or attract other SMEs in the same area. This type of cluster thus differs from the SME variant and the hub and spoke.

Feldman (2003) shows that in biotechnology research universities give birth to large clusters of small firms. The university creates positive knowledge externalities for those enterprises. Such biotechnology clusters recall Markusen's state-centred agglomerations, but the public-sector anchor provided mainly demand for services. Feldman sees the biotechnology anchor as generating knowledge spillovers that make local private sector R&D cheaper. She also notes that U.S. biotechnology clusters tend to specialize further over time. Her finding also echoed Zucker et al. (1998), who observed that U.S. biotech enterprises are usually near research universities with 'star' scientists on staff.

Universities are not the only public-sector anchor tenants. According to Niosi and Bas (2001), Canada's NRC biotechnology laboratories attracted or spun off new biotech firms nearby. Similarly, Feldman and Francis (2003) find that the large biotechnology cluster in Maryland, around Washington, DC, may be a response to the anchoring effects of eight large government facilities. 'These government laboratories anchor the biotech industry in the Capital region through personnel movements, technology licensing and government sponsored cooperative research agreements' (ibid: 71).

Other authors see agglomerations emerging when a large parent organization spins off new firms close by (Klepper, 2005, 2007). Klepper's work complements the anchor-tenant model of Markusen (1996), Agrawal and Cockburn (2003), and Feldman (2003). Also, Klepper remarks that the spin-offs (i.e., firms that former employees of the incumbent corporation set up) inherit the routines of the parent company, thus becoming more efficient than would be an independent start-up in the same industry and territory. In addition, superior firms have more spin-offs, which tend to locate near the parent organization because, as many authors have remarked, labour is the least geographically mobile of all production factors. Larger R&D-active companies are usually superior firms and so produce more knowledge and tend to incubate more superior spin-offs.

Critique of Clusters Concepts and Theories

The above literature review pinpoints advantages of the cluster concept. Martin and Sunley (2003), however, argue that the idea is popular but vague. Their main target is Porter's theory and definition. They find that

Porter's definition can accommodate any geographical agglomeration of firms, as it does not indicate what are industries or related industries (what level of aggregation makes a group of companies a cluster), how many firms make up a cluster, or the geographical limits of clusters.

Martin and Sunley also dispute Porter's assertion that demand for clusters' products exists within the clusters themselves. Like Markusen and others, they contend that some clusters concentrate on exports and do not respond to local demand. In addition, the types of connections (commercial, financial, personal, technology transfer, knowledge spillovers) among the firms in Porter's cluster are not evident and visible either. Without clear industrial or geographical boundaries, or a precise definition of links among firms, anything can constitute a cluster. Martin and Sunley cite such clusters in Porter's works as large as the California agribusiness cluster and the Massachusetts medical-devices agglomeration, and others as small as the media district in lower Manhattan. Martin and Sunley discover the same confusion in a long list of authors who receive fewer citations.

They also dispute the competitiveness of clusters, which Porter strongly proposes. Are competitive clusters more productive? How can we apply the term 'competitiveness' to regions when its original meaning refers to firms?[4] In addition, local knowledge spillovers are hard to measure, particularly those involving tacit knowledge. Why would local knowledge flows be more important than knowledge flows that take place within a large firm with plants in many locations? Finally, economists often analyze clusters in isolation from national and international policies and economic trends. If a large firm that anchors a cluster goes bankrupt because of international competition, how does it affect tacit knowledge, its local flows, and other supposed advantages of the cluster?

Performance Measures

Performance indicators for cluster success often help in policy and academic analysis. They usually include such dimensions as

- Patents and intellectual property that academic, government, and private sector R&D create
- Human resources in science and technology as percentage of workforce
- Business R&D expenditure (BERD) as a proportion of sales in the region
- Public R&D expenditures in the region
- Number of spin-off companies in the cluster emerging from government institutes, universities, and existing companies – business

start-ups in the region – performance of firms within the cluster in comparison with those elsewhere
- Growth of employment in cluster-related organizations
- Average salary in the region – venture capital that new technology-based firms attract to the cluster
- New academic programs and research centers in the cluster
- Star scientists that these higher-education organizations attract
- Large corporate organizations that invest in the region (Hollanders, 2006; Lord Sainsbury, 2007).

Cluster Life Cycles

Clusters evolve through industry-specific phases: emergence, development, maturation, and decline. First, emergence: In such industries as aerospace, biopharmaceuticals, and software, emergence involves, respectively, installation of an anchor organization, such as a large systems integrator; a research university or public R&D laboratory; or a large software developer (Andersson et al., 2004; Maskell and Malmberg, 2007; Menzel and Fornahl, 2007).

Second, development: the cluster attracts new companies and other organizations, or the anchor spins them off. Co-operation among organizations increases. New ideas, projects, products, and services appear, involving various agents.

Third, maturation: the cluster has attained a critical mass and grows not by attracting new firms, but from inside, via formation of new firms, development of new products, and the like.

Fourth, transformation: new industrial sectors emerge from previous ones, as with Montreal and Toronto's attracting aircraft producers in the 1920s on the basis of their skills in welding and metal fabrication, which they acquired building railway cars. In a few cases the cluster may die out because of international competition, as happened with shoe production in Montreal and Toronto.

Despite some vagueness, and many debates, the cluster and related concepts have stimulated design and implementation of national and sub-national policy in OECD countries.[5] Many countries – but not the United States – have put in place nation-wide cluster policies; aims, instruments, and procedures vary substantially, however, and there is no one unified plan. Some nations have tried to stimulate laggard regions, others to reinforce winning ones, and still others to diversify older industrial areas into high-tech activities. In addition, sub-national public administrations have often put forward their own policy schemes. Some of them target a specific industry or set of technologies, and others a specific metropolitan area, while others aim at developing 'high-tech' industry without concentrating in a particular sector. The next three sections review some of these national and regional strategies in the United States, in the European Union, and in Asia and Australia. The fifth section considers rationales for government intervention, paricularly in the light of the case studies in this chapter.

7.2   THE UNITED STATES

In the United States, there is no national policy on clusters, but many states have devised their own regional strategies. According to the OECD (2007a), 41 out of 50 U.S. states offer regional financial support for life sciences and biotechnology. Many states have conducted their own analysis of their industrial strengths and weaknesses within particular regions, using different definitions and methods, and have arrived at their own strategic plans (Bergman and Feser, 1999). In many cases, Porter's consulting company has been working on analysis and diagnostics and on policy design and monitoring.

Since the 1990s, with the help of the National Institute of Standards and Technology (NIST), all states have created extension centers of public technology (Shapira, 2001). These institutions provide training and basic technology services such as quality control, standards, and measurement. In addition, the large national R&D laboratories exist in many states, and some have, among their missions, production of new technology and its transfer to industry. Most often, such transfers operate under a Cooperative R&D Agreement (CRADA), a legal formula that Washington created in 1986 and whereby a government laboratory and a private company agree to work together on a technical project. The firm provides funds, personnel, equipment, and facilities, and the federal agency other similar resources but not funds. Public laboratories can have similar arrangements with consortia of companies, such as the U.S. Advanced Battery Consortium and the American Textile Industry Association.

North Carolina

Bergman and Feser (1999) identify clusters for North Carolina using input–output techniques and propose policies for each cluster. Many clusters were in decline (apparel, tobacco products, textiles, and wood products). Others were emerging, most notably in the Research Triangle Park,[6] such as information technology and instruments, chemicals and plastics, printing and publishing. But these new clusters had many fewer jobs than the declining ones. Policies included training and assistance in developing entrepreneurs (North Carolina Board of Science and Technology, 2000). As well, regions within the state have devised their own plans, including the Research Triangle Region (RTR). In 2001, the RTR commissioned Michael Porter to conduct a study and created a task force[7] to implement his recommendations. The RTR is now focusing on eight 'areas of opportunity': advanced medical care, agricultural bio-technology, analytical instrumentation, biological agents and infectious diseases, informatics, nanoscale technologies, pervasive computing, and pharmaceuticals. The task force developed an action blueprint, which included increased networking among the region's economic agents, creation of new businesses, and development of high-tech industries across the region outside the original Research Triangle Park (Research Triangle Region Task Force, 2004).[8] The park itself hosts several national laboratories, such as those for the Centers for Disease Control, the Environmental Protection Agency (its Air Quality Modelling Group laboratory), and the National Institute of Health (NIH) National Institute for Environmental Science (one of the NIH's 27 labs). Among the state institutions, the most important is the Research Triangle Institute, with over 2600 employees and activity in several fields; the most notable federal-backed non-profit R&D institute is the Semiconductor Research Corporation.

Georgia

In 1990, Georgia reacted to its lacklustre economic performance when the private sector launched the creation of the Georgia Research Alliance (GRA), an initiative that uses universities as research hubs for clusters. Business leaders, academics, and government officials make up the GRA, which implements state policy. Georgia did not target one specific sector or technology, but any high-tech projects with potential benefit for the state. Groups of professionals from university and industry selected these projects (OECD, 2007b). Primary policy instruments are entrepreneur-ship (incubation of new firms), funding innovation (mainly collabora-tive R&D), and attraction of world-class researchers and students. The state has provided $400 million since 1990 for academic research, and the leverage effect of such funds was 1 to 5: the state collected over $1 billion in federal research funds and another $1 billion in private R&D investments. The GRA manages several programs. A technology transfer program pays for commercialization of academic research. The Eminent Scholar Program (ESP) attracts distinguished researchers from around the globe. The GRA also manages a venture-capital fund and a fund for academic research, which support industry–university collaborative projects. The ESP is permanent and has spent some $27 million a year since 1990.

Unlike the situation in North Carolina, there is no specific regional agenda within Georgia. The GRA monitors attraction of eminent scholars, research funding, business incubation, and the like (GRA, 2007).[9] Georgia hosts several federal research institutes, the most important of which depend on the Department of Defense (DOD). DOD laboratories receive 88 per cent of all federal research funds that go to Georgia each year. Other institutes depend on the federal departments of Agriculture and of Energy, the federal Environmental Protection Agency, and the National Aeronautics and Space Administration.

Maryland

The legislature created Maryland's Technology Development Corporation (TEDCO) in 1998 to capitalize on the presence of many large government laboratories (Food and Drug Administration, National Aeronautics and Space Administration, National Institutes of Health, National Institute for Standards and Technology, National Ocean and Atmospheric Administration, Naval Surface Warfare Center, and Patuxtent River Naval Warfare Center) and universities (e.g., Johns Hopkins and the University of Maryland) in the state and the nearby District of Columbia and to promote creation of high-tech firms through commercialization of public technology. Its inspiration was the Ben Franklin Technology Partnerships program, which Pennsylvania started in 1986 to promote high-tech industries in that state. A 15-member board from industry, university, non-profits, and the public sector governs TEDCO.

With a similar aim, Maryland created several seed funds, such as the Maryland Technology Transfer Fund (MTTF), to defray some of the costs of R&D to move technology towards commercialization from public laboratories and universities to new firms. The MTTF calculates that for each dollar it has invested in an early-stage company, the new businesses have attracted $32 from other sources (TEDCO, 2008). Since 1998, the MTTF has invested $6.3 million in 108 companies. The Incubator Development Fund has helped create incubators in universities across the state to help launch new firms. In 2006, the legislature created the Stem Cell Research Fund, which TEDCO operates and which receives $18 million a year for biotech firms and university research.

TEDCO does not support any particular high-tech sector, but some foci have emerged – most notably biotechnology. The state now hosts the third largest concentration of biotech firms in the country. The other sectors of particular interest are communications, engineering, and software.

7.3 EUROPEAN UNION

In the European Union, regions are becoming the cornerstone of STI policy. This section considers France's Sophia Antipolis cluster, Finland, Scotland, the United Kingdom, the Netherlands, Denmark, and the Basque Country in Spain.

France – Sophia Antipolis

In France, the Sophia Antipolis cluster is an early case in point. The initiative of Senator Pierre Lafitte launched it in 1968, with the aim of creating a French Silicon Valley. After 40 years, the park hosts some 1300 high-tech firms, which employ about 30 000 people. The region is home to eight post-secondary institutions, including the CERAM Business School, the École des mines de Paris à Sophia and the Institut Eurecom (two other engineering schools), and the Polytech Nice – Sophia (the Polytechnic School of the Université de Nice). The region's 20 government laboratories include the CNRS-UNSA-IPMC (Institut de Pharmacologie Moléculaire et Cellulaire), the CNRS-UNSA-I3S (Laboratoire d'Informatique, Signaux et Systèmes de Sophia Antipolis), INRA (Institut national de recherche agronomique), and INRIA (Institut national de recherche en informatique et en automatique). The region has attracted companies in several areas of endeavor. Electronics represents 25 per cent of companies and 50 per cent of jobs, in such firms as Amadeus, Bouygues Telecom, France Telecom, IBM, Siemens, and Texas Instruments. The second major sector is life sciences and biotechnology (which includes Agro, Allergan Europe, Dow, and Rhône-Poulenc), as well as a government R&D laboratory (Institut de Pharmacologie Moléculaire et Cellulaire), an affiliate of the CNRS. The third and emerging sector is earth sciences and environment, with 250 jobs and several SMEs and public laboratories.

According to Longhi (1999), Sophia Antipolis has been more successful at attracting investment and firms from outside the region than at generating them through spin-offs. He sees INRIA as a major exception, having launched many new technology spin-offs. He also finds increasing specialization in information and communication technologies and electronics, despite efforts to diversify in life sciences and environment. Barlatier and Thomas (2007) conclude that only the telecom sector, within ICT, has become strong and self-sustaining.

Finland

In 1994, this Nordic country became one of the first European nations to launch a cluster policy, in response to the serious economic recession of the early 1990s, after the dismembering of the Soviet Union, its main trade partner. At the same time, Finland was also one of the first countries in the world to regionalize its science, technology, and innovation policy, as well as to launch a national system of innovation. National and regional systems developed together and over the years became very much integrated.

In 1993, the national industrial policy defined nine clusters – environmental technologies, energy, food products, forest products, logistics, new media, telecommunications, transportation, and working life. The government's aim was to increase networking and co-operation 'between technology investors, research institutes, companies specialising in technology transfer, centers of technology and regional centers for expertise' (Murto et al., 2006: 89). In 1998, it approved 14 regional centers and two national ones. Also, it decided that new clusters would not concentrate solely on technology. A 2001 study led to a regional and national debate in 2003 on what clusters to develop, and new regional centers of expertise emerged. Helsinki, for instance, has nurtured seven regional or national clusters: active materials, digital media, gene technology, logistics, medical and welfare technologies, microsystems, and software. In 2008, Finland had 13 national clusters (or centers) of expertise and 21 regional clusters.

Government laboratories are key players in all clusters, as providers of advanced technology for existing and newly incubated firms, networking, and training institutions. Such laboratories are often anchors of their clusters. VTT – the central national laboratory – is the main technology centre, with 2750 employees, more than 950 patents and patent applications at the beginning of 2008, and 5730 customers (over 3200 of them Finnish companies), as well as 60 spin-off companies. An assessment of VTT in 1993 suggested that it had to focus more on customers; a reorganization produced nine independent research institutes. In 2006, VTT reshaped itself to align better with the national clusters (ibid. 90–107).

Finnish cluster programs receive money from relevant ministries, from Tekes (the national agency supporting R&D), and from the Academy of Sciences (Pentikäinen, 2000). A national committee under Professor Y. Neuvo continually monitors the clusters, prepares an annual evaluation, and proposes funding to Tekes, which also supports programs in innovation and technology.

Scotland

Scotland occupies the northern part of the United Kingdom, with a population of 5.1 million and 78 700 sq. km. The regional government developed a cluster policy in the 1990s through a government organization, Scottish Enterprise (SE). SE launched the policy in 1997, after a thorough examination of existing clusters by Monitor – Michael Porter's consulting firm. Scotland initially developed four major clusters, in biotechnology, food and drink, oil and gas, and semi-conductors. The strategy aimed principally to attract foreign direct investment (FDI) into Scotland.

One of the most successful clusters is the so-called Silicon Glen. It originated in the 1940s with the Ferranti electronics plant in Edinburgh; IBM followed suit in 1953. Many other companies located in the triangle region between Dundee, Inverclyde, and Edinburgh; they included Hughes Aircraft (1960) for germanium and silicon diodes, Elliott Automation (1966), and later DEC, General Instruments, Motorola, NEC, Signetics, and Sun. This most famous Scottish cluster based itself not on home-grown R&D or spin-offs but on manufacturing by foreign firms.

The world economic crisis in 2000 led to a number of plant closures and lay-offs, and Scotland turned to software promotion with some success: Adobe, Amazon, Microsoft, and Oracle set up shop to develop software in Scotland. The government has attracted foreign companies through tax breaks but not stimulated emergence of local ones through academic or public-sector R&D. Public technology is a responsibility of SE, particularly in agriculture, environment, fisheries, forestry, land use, and veterinary sciences.

In 1999, new clusters in creative industries, forestry, opto-electronics, and tourism followed the original ones. But the early emphasis on developing clusters through foreign manufacturing remained. It had brought few backward linkages (towards suppliers), led to few spin-offs, and always depended on international flows of capital and technology.

In 2001, Scotland launched Smart Successful Scotland, which emphasized domestic entrepreneurship, networking, and human capital. In 2003, SE started the fund ITI Scotland to bridge the gap between academic or public sector inventions and commercialization. Up to July 2008, ITI had invested 135 million pounds in energy, life sciences, and media programs. It is too early to judge the impact of the program on existing clusters. It is difficult to figure out precisely what would have happened in the absence of those initiatives. In 2005, the government evaluated the cluster strategy. Some clusters seemed to have gained critical mass, to the detriment of focus. That was the case, for example, of the Creative Industries cluster, where one finds everything from architecture to film, mass media, music, publishing, and radio. The Silicon Glen cluster was trying to redefine itself with the help of ITI.

The United Kingdom

The British government has no national cluster policy under that name but encourages regional economic development through Regional Development Agencies (RDAs), which it founded in 1999. The RDA 'started by trying to imitate the relatively successful FDI strategies of the existing RDA in Scotland' (OECD, 2007a: 56). Originally, there were nine RDAs, including the North West Regional Development Agency (NWDA). The Competitiveness White Paper of 1998 had nurtured ideas about clusters, and a 2001 paper identified 14 existing clusters. The British Competitiveness paper drew inspiration from Michael Porter's studies, as well as from similar experiences in Scotland and elsewhere in Europe.

The British government intervened to promote economic development, particularly in regions where the decline of traditional industries was exacerbating high unemployment. Government laboratories support existing clusters throughout Britain, yet industries lead the clusters, which may well prove able to prosper by themselves, with funding from the departments of Communities and Local Government; Education and Skills; Environment, Food and Rural Affairs; and Trade and Industry.

Government institutes play different roles in various clusters. They are not critical actors in the Food and Drink cluster but central in the biomedical one. Patenting, licencing, and incubating spin-offs are not parts of their mandate, but networking is a key mission. Conversely, Lord Sainsbury's (2007) *Review of Government's Science and Innovation Policies* portrayed research universities as the main anchors of high-tech clusters in Britain:

> 'Clusters of excellence with universities at their core are increasingly attracting multinational businesses who are seeking to recruit, to invest in research, and to find solutions to the business product, process and management issues they face. Capacity and infrastructure in universities for business collaboration has continued' (p. 57).

> 'Most RDAs have also developed science cities, based in the concept that clusters of knowledge-intensive firms tend to form around large research universities' (p. 139).

> 'High technology clusters have been forming in the UK around our world-class research universities. This supports the theory that universities are one of the driving forces behind the formation of clusters . . . A cluster grows out of the research excellence of a university' (p. 143).

Sainsbury also describes clusters around government laboratories, such as the Daresbury and Harwell Science and Innovation campus, where several public R&D laboratories attract and spin off firms (p.142). His report indicates, however, that the majority of high-quality spin-offs emerge from research universities. They carry out the bulk of technology transfers and can bring research personnel to new firms. Their patenting and licencing activity attracts venture capital to the region. The document cites the cases of Cambridge, Oxford, and Manchester as large research universities spinning out new technology firms and anchoring high-tech clusters.

The Netherlands

Under the inspiration of Michael Porter and using input–output analysis, Dutch national policy started in 1991 and included technology dimensions (and subsidies) but also co-operation and networking, competition policy, technology forecasts, and other policy methods. The Ministry of Economic Affairs (MEA) identified 12 existing clusters, including agro-food, chemicals, commercial services, construction, energy, furniture, glass, health, media, metal-electro, and transportation and communication. The clusters are nation-wide in this small country. The idea of building on existing industries pervades the Dutch policy and is in line with Porter's theory. In 1997, a white paper led to a new cluster policy, which included aluminum (Antheum), ECP.nl (electronic commerce), EMTV (electro-magnetic power technology), life sciences, and water. Several clusters (including construction) remained the same. In 2003, the MEA launched its innovation policy with five additional key sectors: chemicals, creative industries, flowers and food, high-tech systems and materials, and water. Clusters remain nation-wide.

Government subsidies, networking, incubation of new firms, and studies are among the policy instruments whereby national authorities support clusters. However, government is continually evaluating and adapting policy. It has moved from cluster policy to regional policy to innovative regional policy.

The role of public technology institutes depends on the cluster. In the food and nutrition Delta cluster, it is crucial. In other sectors (e.g., chemicals, ICT), private firms, such as Philips Electronics, the largest electronics firm in the European Union, play a central role. Yet the institutes' record in patenting, licencing, and launching new spin-offs is variable and receives little mention.

Denmark

Denmark adopted a cluster policy late in 1990, following Michael Porter's Ten-Nation Study, which included that country. The first generation of public policies (1990–92) favoured regional networking among firms, universities, and government laboratories. In 1994, the government launched a 'mega-clusters' approach, centring on biotechnology and health, building construction, environment, food products, ICT, transportation and communication, and tourism. In the late 1990s, it turned to aluminum processing, biotechnology, and industrial design; its new program, Clusters of Competence, identified 29 such clusters. In 2000–1, it decided to leave the 17 regions free to choose their own sectors and clusters to expand and transferred resources to them to develop clusters in their own way. In 2003, it launched an Action Plan for Public–Private Partnerships on Innovation, in order to reinforce co-operation between private firms, government research institutes, and universities. Its Action Plan for Regional High-tech Development of 2004 encompassed creation of Regional Centres of Expertise and of Regional Knowledge Pilots.

During the last decade, the government has receded and left regions to conduct their own cluster policies (Engelstoft et al., 2006). Porter analysis deeply impressed Denmark: clusters are critical masses of inter-related companies, and government documents make reference to public research institutions providing technology to them. For instance, the nascent sensor-technology cluster emerged around the Risoe Danish Nuclear Research Centre, a few companies, five public technology-service centers, and three research universities.[10] The new bio-informatics cluster is 'mushrooming' out of private-sector enterprises and public research organizations. Public research organizations thus seem central to emerging technology-based clusters, through technology transfer and spin off of new firms. Table 7.1 identifies national and regional clusters as well as existing and emerging ones.

The Basque Region in Spain

The Basque Autonomous Community occupies north central Spain. With 2.2 million inhabitants, it contains 5 per cent of the Spanish population but produces 6 per cent of its GDP, 8 per cent of its industrial GDP, and 10 per cent of its exports. The region was host to traditional steel, naval construction, and mechanical industries that were declining after 1945. To consolidate existing industries and start new industrial sectors, the regional government hired Porter's Monitor Company and

Table 7.1   Denmark, 29 clusters of competences, early 2000s

	National	Regional
Existing	Thermal technology	Mobile/satellite
	Technical appliances for	communications
	disabled	Business tourism
	Pork meat	Stainless steel
	Dairy products	Horticulture
	Water environment	Health care
	Fur	Textile/clothing
	Seed growing	Offshore industry
	Power electronics	Furniture
	Hearing aids	Transport
	Wind technology	
	Maritime industry	
Emerging	Organic food	Movies/TV production
	Children's play and learning	Food network
	Waste management	PR/communication
	Sensor technology	Pervasive computing
	Bio-informatics	

Source: Ministry of Trade and Industry, *A new economy and its new clusters.*

proposed a list of clusters in 1991 and a new list in 1995. In the end, the region selected 11 clusters, including aerospace, automotive, environment, household appliances, machinery, and telecommunications. Government laboratories and academic programs existed in some of these fields, and the region revamped them or created new ones to help establish the cluster (Santisteban, 2003 and 2006; OECD, 2007a and 2007b). Table 7.2 summarizes adoption of the cluster strategy in sectors of the Basque industry.

Government institutes sell services at cost to private-sector firms, which act as a form of subsidy. The Basque authorities have combined all government institutes into two major ones: Tecnalia and IK4. Tecnalia is the merger of Azti, European Software Institute, Fatronik, Inasmel, Labeln, Nelker, and Robotiker. It employs 1325 people (of whom 162 have PhDs) and operates in such areas as building, energy, food, machinery, materials, and robotics. It has obtained on average 26 patents a year since its inception and has spun off about 47 companies. Similarly, IK4 is the merger of seven R&D centers, employs 1300 people, and operates in aerospace, agro-food, appliances, chemicals, electronics, and transportation.

Table 7.2   Evolution of Basque clusters

Industry	Year
Appliances	1992
Machinery	1992
Automotive	1993
Bilbao Port	1994
ICT	1994
Environment	1995
Energy	1996
Aeronautics	1997
Shipbuilding	1997
Paper	1998
Audiovisual	2004

7.4   ASIA AND AUSTRALIA

Industrial and emerging Asian countries and Australia have their own cluster policies, which tend to differ from both European and North American ones. Japan has tended to rely on technology service centers to support SMEs outside large metropolitan areas. Taiwan has used large national research institutes as incubators of high-tech clusters. In Australia, the Commonwealth (national) government, the states of Queensland and South Australia, and several industries have launched notable cluster policies.

Japan

The literature on Japanese clusters has focused on agglomerations of industrial SMEs, very much in the Marshall and Porter traditions (Gonda and Kakizaki, 2001; Yamawaki, 2001). Economists often describe clusters of cotton fabrics, hand tools, kitchenware, and silk garments. A few of these clusters are of the hub-and-spoke type, where smaller companies congregate because of demand from a large assembler in automobiles, construction machinery, or aircraft. Government research and technology centers helped bring into being or reinforced clusters. The government set up 41 such centers 1894–1926, 46 of them 1927–45, and 57 more 1946–64 (Yamawaki, 2001: 11). These 'publicly strengthened industrial districts' offered technological guidance and consulting, testing and inspection, R&D, and seminars and dissemination of information on the latest technologies and products. But the government has also created new clusters to avoid excessive concentration in a few megalopolises (Gonda and Kakizaki, 2001). More recently, since 2001, the Ministry of Economy, Trade and Industry (METI) has promoted creation of clusters through the Industrial Cluster Project. It is now implementing 18 regional projects involving over 10 000 SMEs and 290 universities and industrial colleges. In fiscal year 2008, it allocated over 12.8 billion Yen to the Cluster Project, which aims to develop new technologies such as advanced manufacturing, biotechnology, energy, and semi-conductors (Japan, METI, 2008).[11]

Taiwan

Since 1973, Taiwan has based its cluster policy on creation of six science parks to assist in development of high-technology clusters. The Science Parks are under the authority of the National Research Council.

The Hsinchu Science Park, which started in 1980, is the most famous. Its specialty is the semi-conductor industry, and its powerhouse is the non-profit, government-backed Industrial Technology Research Institute (ITRI) of Taiwan, which we met above. ITRI has spun off over 140 of the more than 400 high-tech companies, in many niches of ICT, that occupy the park (Chu et al., 2006; Hu et al., 2005; Hung and Chu, 2006).[12]

Australia

The Australian government started to assess regional development policies in 1993 and 1994. A federal taskforce analyzed the actual and potential development of the main regions of the country. In 1994, the McKinsey Report suggested organizing economic development policies around clusters. However, the change of government in 1996 led to abandonment of all policy debates on clusters. In 2000, however, following a study by Professor Jane Marceau (1999), a federal government conference and several reports emphasized the need for cluster policies.

In the meantime, two states organized initiatives: Queensland and South Australia, as well as the city of Adelaide in this state. Adelaide has followed a cluster policy since the mid-1990s, in order to fight very high unemployment. Learning from the Japanese Technopolis, the city launched a Multi-Function Polis (MFP) project, which involved the planning of defense, spatial, and water clusters. At the same time, Cairns, in Queensland, started a similar initiative around its revamped airport, with the goal of increasing FDI and tourism. A tourism cluster has developed, as well as an educational one, and a few others are in the making. Other regions in Australia have followed a similar path. Australia, like the United States, has let regions develop clusters from the bottom up (Enright and Roberts, 2001).

Parallel to these regional clusters, Roberts and Enright (2004) find industry in Australia leading the emergence of more national clusters in such fields as education, fishing, and wine.

7.5   RATIONALES FOR GOVERNMENT INTERVENTION

In the OECD, almost all national governments have launched clusters policies – 'specific governmental efforts to support clusters' (Commission of the European Communities, 2008: 7) – with a view to creating new industries, particularly high-tech ones, to fill the void that the decline of labour-intensive industries has created. Such policies have varied from country to country in terms of their role vis-à-vis other policies for science, technology, and innovation (STI), their funding mechanisms, the total investment they receive, and the organizations participating. Some of the initiatives targeted revitalization of older and declining cities, others planting of new technology seeds in smaller, more specialized towns. However, despite their differences, almost all of them involved some type of partnership between academe, government R&D laboratories, and industry, and most aimed at developing high-tech clusters in such sectors as aerospace, biotechnology, fuel cells, information and communication technologies, life sciences, machinery, nanotechnology, and robotics. Also, they included plans for either attracting external resources, such as human capital, private direct investment, and R&D funding, or creating new ones through training, incubation of spin-off companies, or R&D. Finally, they all proposed networking and partnerships among economic agents in the region.

Clusters are like 'reduced scale national innovation systems' (OECD, 1999b: 7). The rationale for policy intervention in systems of innovation is addressing failures (Niosi, 2002), which may include system inertia (regional or national) to the building of new knowledge-intensive sectors that derive not from natural resources or physical capital, but from human capital and intellectual property. Systems of innovation depend on the complementary character of policy interventions (Mohnen and Röller, 2005). In matters relating to markets for human capital (as probably in all types of markets), Say's Law, which postulates that supply creates its own demand, does not apply. Regional and national economies may find themselves in a 'low-skill' equilibrium, producing and demanding little human capital. Entire countries in Africa, Asia, and Latin America seem to have no way out of vicious circles; in the OECD countries, including Canada, some provinces and states are in that predicament. Regional policy aims at breaking such stagnation. Also, production of knowledge creates knowledge externalities and increasing returns that foster economic development (Romer, 1986). Knowledge is costly to produce and easy to reproduce and thus can serve many more agents than the original investors. And regional knowledge is probably easier to transfer in its region of origin, if it has enough absorptive capacity. Finally, clusters increase interaction and learning, and new theories about innovation put forward interactive models (with multiple flows of knowledge, people, and funding) instead of linear ones (where ideas and people move from university to government laboratories and thence to industry). Interaction, for instance, is necessary to create new firms, transfer public technology, and obtain venture capital for new businesses.

Analysts have used various methods to evaluate such policies, as well as structures and evolution of clusters: cost–benefit analysis, input–output analysis, more qualitative case studies, and narrative stories (deBresson and Hu, 1999; Diez, 2001). Evaluation is difficult, however. Such clusters are not islands, and their success or failure may depend on external demand for their products or competition from other clusters. Yet new technologies may face unexpected difficulties, as they tend to evolve rapidly into new areas of knowledge. Biotechnology is no longer simply genetic engineering but also combinatorial chemistry, genomics, and proteomics, applications and markets for which remain unclear (Pisano, 2006). The many applications of nanotechnologies, as well as the market response to such novelties, are still evolving. Evaluation is also difficult because official statistics are often at the national level, sometimes cover states or provinces, seldom address metropolitan areas, and never refer to such regional units as the M-10 corridor, Route 128, or Silicon Valley. Input–output analysis presents similar drawbacks. In addition, no country in the OECD, except the United States, has created a database of innovations; one can trace the regional roots of inventions through patents, but patent figures do not provide details on where the patents find use or commercialization.

Besides the numerous national policies, the European Union (EU) has put forward supranational policies for regional and cluster development. The Innovating Regions in Europe (IRE) project started in the mid-1990s with four regions. At the end of 2008, it encompassed 235 regions in 32 countries. The EU provides funding for development of clusters and for Benchmarking Projects, Regional Innovation Policy Impact Assessments, Thematic Networks of Regions, and Trans-regional Innovation Projects. In addition, the multi-billion-Euro Framework Programs favours regional clusters in the EU.[13]

Are these policies successful? There are so many of them in OECD countries that a final decision is not available. Also one can ask 'successful in what sense?' The answer may be: more employment, more production and exports, and better salaries and skills. OECD and other studies tend to be cautious about these cluster policies. The simple identification of existing clusters and concentration of public investment in them may increase path dependence[14] and lock-in[15] effects in sectors that may not be competitive in the long run. Inter-organizational networking may not be easy and may take time, as universities, government laboratories, and industry tend to live with different routines that are not always compatible (Boekholt and Thuriaux, 1999). Also, absorptive capacity is important. Clusters may be difficult to expand in smaller metropolitan areas, where financial and entrepreneurial skills are in short supply (Glasmeier, 2000: 367). Fairly high levels of pre-existing economic activity may be necessary for the cluster to take hold in a region. Organizational inertia may be stronger than national planners initially estimate, and such inertia may affect local universities that focus on undergraduate programs, local firms with traditional products and services, and local financial institutions that manage commercial and mortgage loans but not more risky funding.

In evaluating the success or failure of cluster policies, another major hurdle is the debate about specialized versus diversified regions. Two bodies of thought diverge on whether specialization or diversification is better. The specialization school derives from Marshall, Arrow, and Romer (the MAR approach). It contends that specialization brings focus to the region and increases intra-industry knowledge spillovers. The opposite, diversification school – the 'Jane Jacobs' – affirms that the most economically valuable spillovers are inter-industry or agglomeration externalities, and so large agglomerations have the edge in terms of innovation outputs (Werke and Athreye, 2004).

The debate has continued for decades without a clear winner. The analysis of Canadian regions using Statistics Canada's special tabulations of industrial R&D (independent variable) by census metropolitan areas did not find a definitive answer. Larger agglomerations have more diversity in innovation than specialized ones. Yet by using patents as indicators of innovativeness (dependent variable), one cannot show that large, diverse regions show more innovation once their population is taken into consideration. The reason is that the propensity to patent varies enormously among industries. It is very high in biotechnology, chemicals, pharmaceuticals, and telecommunications equipment and very low in aerospace, finance, and software (Niosi and Bourassa, 2008). Regions specializing in a high-patenting sector (e.g., Ottawa-Hull) appear very innovative, while those including R&D-intensive industrial laboratories in aerospace and software, such as Montreal and Toronto, look less so.

The policy implications of the MAR–Jacobs debate are evident: should governments favour specialized or diversified clusters? The state of our knowledge precludes a definitive response. Several tentative classifications of national cluster policies have emerged. Table 7.3 presents that of Roeland and den Hertog (1999), which looks at systemic failures that the policy response addresses and names the countries that focus on each type of strategy.

The Role of Government Institutes/Laboratories

In these cluster policies and initiatives, government laboratories have received four types of roles:

- Industrial extension: Government laboratories can supply basic industrial knowledge to private firms, particularly SMEs, such as certification, just-in-time systems, metrology, quality control, technological and strategic foresight, and other managerial practices concerning adoption of technology. In Canada, the Alberta Research Council and Quebec's Centre de recherche industrielle du Québec (CRIQ), for example, conduct this type of activity. In the United States, the Manufacturing Extension Partnerships program at National Institute for Standards and Technology (NIST) also promotes this activity through some 70 centers in all 50 states (Shapira, 2001).
- Advanced R&D: Public R&D laboratories can conduct contract R&D for firms and transfer technology that stems from their internal R&D projects. VTT labs in Finland and NIH facilities in Maryland are good examples of this role.
- Networking: Laboratories help build networks, creating trust and co-operation within the cluster. The Finnish technology centre – namely VTT – includes global networking among its missions. The British laboratories have a similar mandate.
- Spinning off firms: Public laboratories may actually create the cluster by spinning off new technology-based firms out of their own R&D activities and personnel. Taiwan's ITRI is the paradigmatic case.

In most countries, government laboratories provide one or two of these services to private firms and the cluster economy. A few laboratories, such as Taiwan's ITRI, are active in all these fields.

As to the significance of these laboratories in the clusters, appreciation

Table 7.3   Systemic and cluster-based policy responses in OECD countries

Systemic and market failure	Policy response	Countries' focus in cluster-based policy-making
Inefficient functioning of markets	• Competition policy and regulatory reform	• Most countries
Informational failures	• Technology foresight • Strategic market information and strategic cluster studies	• Netherlands, Sweden • Canada, Denmark, Finland, Netherlands, U.S.A.
Limited interaction between actors in innovation systems	• Broker and networking agencies and schemes • Provision of platforms for constructive dialogue • Facilitating co-operation in networks	• Australia, Canada, Denmark, Netherlands • Austria, Denmark, Finland, Germany, Netherlands, Sweden, U.K., U.S.A. • Belgium, Finland, Netherlands, U.K., U.S.A.
Institutional mismatches between public knowledge infrastructure and market needs	• Joint industry-research centres of excellence • Facilitating joint industry-research co-operation • Human-capital development • Technology-transfer programmes	• Belgium, Denmark, Finland, Netherlands, Spain, Sweden, Switzerland • Finland, Spain, Sweden • Denmark, Sweden • Spain, Switzerland
Missing demand	• Public procurement policy	• Austria, Denmark, Netherlands, Sweden
Government failure	• Privatization • Rationalize business • Horizontal policy-making • Public consultancy • Reduce government interference	• Most countries • Canada • Canada, Denmark, Finland • Canada, Netherlands • Canada, U.K., U.S.A.

of them varies among nations and even among clusters. In a study of 12 clusters in six European countries, Borrás and Tsagdis (2008) find that industry ranked them ninth (among 11 types of institutions), after banks and venture-capital firms, universities and higher education organizations, chambers of commerce, sector associations, certification laboratories, service centers, consulting firms, and others. They wonder 'whether the number of these centers, and their quality and resources, are good enough to support firms and innovation in the clusters studied' (ibid.: 248). Yet they note extensive variety among the responses: in some, the facilities were an anchor of the cluster; in others, they were secondary.

Also, the roles and missions of government laboratories vary widely within the same country and also between countries. U.S. government laboratories have many missions, ranging from pure science to defense and development of civilian technology (Crow and Bozeman, 1998). Not all these mandates include technology transfer to the private sector or creation of new technology-based firms. The same is true in Canada (Niosi, 2000a). In both countries, but also in others, 'one-size-fits-all' strategies do not work. The mission of technology transfer or spinning off new firms will not easily accommodate super-colliders or atomic energy laboratories. Conversely, R&D projects in biotechnology laboratories are closer to industrial activities and can both transfer technology and incubate new firms.

This literature review and brief survey confirm such range in missions and effectiveness. In Finland and Taiwan, as well as in Maryland and in the Basque Country, government facilities anchor clusters. They provide technology and R&D services to industrial and emerging technology-based companies and spin off new enterprises in the cluster, to which they transfer their initial technology. No consulting firm or private service company could provide such knowledge to companies in the cluster. At the opposite end, in other clusters such as Sophia Antipolis, most of the public centers are simply basic research organizations, which produce scientific articles.

Public laboratories usually display some characteristic strengths and weaknesses vis-à-vis their closest institutional cousins. Among their strengths, they can form larger R&D teams than academic institutions. In an academic department, teaching requires the presence of different sub-disciplines. A physics department, employing perhaps 20–30 professors, cannot employ more than a few nuclear scientists. In comparison, Atomic Energy of Canada has over 5000 scientists, engineers, and technicians working on nuclear physics and engineering.

Also, academics have several duties: teaching, research, and administration. In a public R&D laboratory, employees do only research, thus having the potential to produce more R&D than their counterparts in universities.

The main comparative weaknesses come from the fact that government facilities do not have students, although they can help train students through, for instance, internship programs. Academic institutions can more easily transfer their knowledge to industry through their graduates, many of whom link universities with private firms. It is also easier for academic institutions to create spin-off firms because entire laboratories can work part or full time with new technology-based firms. Typically, more new biotechnology enterprises spin off from post-secondary institutions than from public R&D laboratories. In Canada, 86 per cent of biotechnology spin-offs come from universities, and 6 per cent from public R&D laboratories (Statistics Canada, 2002: 13).

The role of government facilities may evolve through the life cycle of the cluster. They may become an anchor in high-tech clusters, where they may remain among the main knowledge producers, as in biotechnology and nanotechnologies, fuel cells, and hydrogen technology. They may support new forms of technology in the development phase through technology transfer and provision of laboratory services. They can also conduct networking at this stage. In the transformation-or-decline stage they may lead in introduction of new technologies to rejuvenate existing clusters or incubate new ones in the regional system of innovation.

In early 2000, the Canadian federal government developed cluster policies (using the National Research Council, or NRC, as the delivery mechanism) that are closer to the Finnish and Taiwanese policies, as well as those of some U.S. states, including Maryland. The approach involves 'adding high-technology clusters to the existing industrial structures' rather than following Porter's perspective of consolidating existing industries. For that purpose, the NRC created or upgraded 11 regional R&D laboratories.[16] Their missions, depending on the cluster initiative, include generating and transferring new technology, networking both within the cluster and between the cluster and out-of-cluster agents, spinning off firms, and providing technical services for private firms.

The government implanted initiatives where there was local expertise and sought to reinforce the local industrial tissue. Despite its being a recent initiative (not yet 10 years old), some results are already evident in the form of new companies, transfer of new technologies, new projects, new partnerships, and attraction of human capital. Also, many of the new laboratories were on a university campus, which may increase their impact on the academic community.

The scanty literature on clusters in developing countries puts the accent on agriculture, cattle raising, fishing, and other natural resources. A study of a dozen Latin American clusters for the Inter-American Development Bank looks at apples, grapes, mangoes, and metalworking (Brazil), salmon (Chile), furniture and software (Mexico), and milk and dairy (Nicaragua) (Pietrobelli and Rabellotti, 2004). This choice is not fortuitous: Latin

America has for decades concentrated on developing natural resources. The regional investment in science and technology is almost non-existent, and there is little public support for innovation. In a collection of papers, Cassiolato and Lastres (1999: 771) conclude that governments have shown little interest in regional innovation and regional policies for science and technology.

Besides the aerospace cluster in San José (Brazil), close to São Paulo, few software clusters seem to emerge in cities such as Buenos Aires, Mexico City, Montevideo, Rio de Janeiro, San José (Costa Rica), and São Paolo. However, such clusters emerge spontaneously, as large multinational corporations seek to outsource modules and services to low-cost labour in developing countries. Software giants do not come exclusively from North America or western Europe, but increasingly from India (Niosi and Tschang, 2009). The case of Montevideo (capital of Uruguay) is paradigmatic: a regional system of innovation (RSI) serving local clients grew out of a large initial investment in 2002 by TCS, the multinational software service subsidiary of the Tata Group. Mexican clusters may follow the Uruguayan path: local clusters of small and medium-size domestic firms serving the regional market and the entry of powerful multinationals outsourcing processes and subsystems to Latin America and Europe. Guadalajara (Mexico) is also emblematic. The cluster there attracted TCS, which opened a new center in the city, the second largest in the country.

Costa Rica is different, because its software and semi-conductor cluster around the capital of San José flowed from government efforts beginning in the 1990s to transform its economic activity and exports by attracting Intel, seeking foreign direct investment, and upgrading the labour force (Rodriguez-Clare, 2001). But such cases remain exceptions in Latin America, where governments neglect building of regional institutions for STI even more than they do national infrastructure.

Conclusion and Policy Implications

Industrial districts have been part of the economic literature for over a century. Today, the concepts of clusters and RSIs have somewhat replaced industrial districts, partly because they focus on knowledge-producing non-economic institutions such as research universities and government R&D laboratories, while the industrial district is purely an agglomeration of small and medium-size enterprises (SMEs). The literature emphasizes that clusters have become increasingly important and visible because of the growing relevance of knowledge-intensive industries in wealthy economies. Consequently, both national and regional governments have implemented strategies to develop such clusters.

All OECD members have applied cluster initiatives and policies, most often at the national level, but sometimes in states or provinces. The motives for such policies include systemic failures in coping with the rapid rise of new industries and technologies and desire to renovate old industrial regions in decline or spur large metropolitan areas with a fragmented industrial base and no critical mass in particular industries. Andersson et al. (2004) enumerate the potential benefits of clusters:

- Exploitation of local natural resources
- Lower transaction costs, particularly for transfer of knowledge
- Economies of scale and scope
- Availability of supply
- More efficient markets for information – interplay with local customers in some particular type of cluster.

Tödtling and Trippl (2005) describe application of cluster initiatives and policies to many types of regions and their deficiencies. Peripheral regions, old industrial areas, and fragmented metropolitan areas present assets and rigidities that cluster policies have tried to address. Such system failures include underdeveloped institutions (e.g., few universities or few research universities), overspecialization in traditional, 'sunset' industries and obsolete technologies, and missing or inappropriate interaction among agents such as university, industry, and public laboratories. Besides, the solutions that policies advance may range from adding resources to existing clusters to creating new clusters (sectors) in the region. Tödtling and Trippl (2005) suggest deficiencies by type of region (Table 7.4).

Other classifications of regions respond to the dynamics and composition of the cluster. The industrial district and Porter's cluster concept make reference to agglomerations of small and medium-size firms. Porter stresses local demand and virtually ignores knowledge-producing public research organizations. The work of Markusen, Agrawal and Cockburn, and of Feldman offers a different picture: a large private firm or a public-sector institution (e.g., university or government laboratory) anchors the cluster, whose demand is not local but global (Markusen's 'hub-and-spoke' cluster). Such a cluster is of particular relevance to agglomerations where government R&D institutes may represent the anchor. In aerospace and automobile manufacturing, as well as in biotechnology and nanotechnology, this type of anchor should be prevalent. Conversely, the traditional 'industrial district' is a self-organizing agglomeration of firms, which move to be near their counterparts in similar industries. Northern Italy hosts many of these specialized districts in different sectors; no anchor exists in these districts.

In light of this review it may be said that the role of government

Table 7.4   Problem areas and deficiencies of RSIs, by type of region

	Deficiencies		
Problem areas	Peripheral regions	Old industrial regions	Fragmented metropolitan regions
Cluster characteristics	Clusters often missing or weakly developed	Often specialized in mature industries	Many industries but high-profile clusters missing
	SME dominance	Large-firm dominance	Large firms and SMEs present
Innovation activities	Low level of R&D; incremental and process innovation	Mature technological trajectories	R&D in headquarters of large firms; product innovation and new-firm formation low
Universities/ public research organizations (PROs)	Few or low profile	Often oriented to traditional industries and technologies	Many and high-quality but often weak industry links
Education/ training	Emphasis on low- to medium-level skills	Emphasis on technical skills; managerial and modern skills missing	Large variety of educational institutions
Knowledge transfer	Some services available but 'thin' structure	Many services but weakly co-ordinated	High density of services, mostly commercial
Networks	Few in the region because of weak clustering and institutional structure	Often characterized by technological and political lock-ins	Market links dominate; often few clusters and little innovation-related networking

Source: Tödtling and Trippl (2005).

laboratories varies according to the following perspectives. In Porter's neo-Marshallian theory of competitive clusters, government R&D institutes are contingent: they may or may not contribute to the cluster. Existing private industry leads the cluster; government plays a networking role. The regions and nations that followed these prescriptions are more likely to try to consolidate existing industries. In the more proactive Maryland TEDCO and Pennsylvania Ben Franklin approaches, government promotes creation of new sectors, using available technologies and human capital, rather than available companies and industries. Government laboratories and universities represent the 'anchor tenants' of new sectors: they provide technology and new entrepreneurs.

The more general conclusions of this chapter are as follows:

First, any evaluation of cluster policy has to fit the characteristics of the technology, region, and goals of the cluster strategy. Thus one could expect short- to medium-term results in fields close to market, such as aluminum and information technology. But it would be unreasonable to expect short-term results from such technical fields as fuel cells and nanotechnology, where market commercialization will take years.

Second, also, custom-made performance indicators have to take various elements into consideration: history and initial resources and absorptive capacity, missions of the cluster policy, funds that the policy earmarks for the cluster, and future visions about the cluster. For instance, an input–output analysis of the region makes sense only if the new cluster is to obtain demand from regional agents. Patent indicators will be useful, depending on the 'patent propensity' of the sector (e.g., it will be low in a software-industry cluster, high in biotechnology or nanotechnology). The rate of formation of new firms will be a good indicator of success in biotechnology and less so in aerospace.

Third, any evaluation must take into account the cluster's level of resources. If the region lacks a well-developed pool of scientists and engineers, then it may be possible to determine success by capacity to attract high-level scholars ('star' scientists) to the region.

Precise measurement of the success of a cluster strategy is a difficult task, and it depends on the initial set of resources the cluster hosted and on the industries and technologies it aimed at developing, the private and public investment, and external conditions such as product demand and speed of technological change in the sector. All indicators must be industry-specific and suit the characteristics of the agglomeration(s) under analysis.

Fifth, policy approaches differ widely. Michael Porter represents one approach, which focuses on markets: 'Successful regions leverage their unique mix of assets to build specialised clusters. Successful regions do not pick winners, but build on their inherited assets (e.g. geography, climate, population, research centers, companies, governmental organizations), to create specialised economies that both differ from other regions and offer comparative advantages to local companies' (Porter et al., 2001: xiii).

In this policy perspective, regions must increase competitiveness and productivity in the sectors they already possess. The British regional development agencies and the Basque Country Competitiveness Framework reflect this approach. Britain's regions have built on financial services, food and drink, and textiles and more recently have added a set of more modern sectors; the Basque Country has developed clusters in automobiles, Bilbao Port, household appliances, and shipbuilding. Porter's consulting company, which has advised these clusters, always starts with a thorough analysis of existing industry and proposes incentives to consolidate it. In this approach, government R&D laboratories are contingent.

At the opposite end, one finds the Finnish, Taiwanese, or Maryland TEDCO high-technology approach: the launch of entirely new sectors, such as biotechnology, communications and software, engineering, and nanotechnology, whether or not companies already exist in the area. The approach derives not from industries that exist, but from new technologies that emerge from government R&D laboratories and universities within the region. The TEDCO way is more similar to Finland's initiatives and Canada's cluster policies. In this perspective, government laboratories are central components of clusters. Table 7.5 summarizes the advantages and disadvantages of each type of policy.

Table 7.5   Market and high-tech-oriented policy approaches: advantages and disadvantages

	Market-oriented policy approaches (e.g. Michael Porter)	High-tech-oriented policy perspective (e.g. Maryland's TEDCO)
Advantages	Close to existing industrial capabilities	Krugman-type early entrance advantage
	Easier to understand and absorb by existing industries	More protection from low-wage emerging nations
	Less costly	Economic diversification: may nurture entire new sectors
	Less risky	Favours co-operation between university, government labs, and industry
Disadvantages	May keep traditional industry on artificial life support	More risky (e.g., moving into non-established areas)
	Less protection from imports from emerging countries	More costly
	Less prone to co-operative agreements with academe and government labs	More difficult to understand and absorb by existing industry

Finally, the role of government laboratories varies widely from country to country and also from one cluster to the others within the same region or country. The Dutch experience in this sense is paradigmatic. When clusters consist mainly of SMEs (e.g., food and flowers) with little technology and scanty R&D and foresight capabilities, government laboratories represent a major anchor of the cluster. Conversely, when large firms exist and hold together the cluster (e.g., Philips in the Dutch ICT cluster), then government institutes play a more modest role.

Also, laboratories' roles depend on their missions. In Sophia Antipolis, most of them do scientific research. They share areas with industry but do not often interact with it. They are very different from the NRC Canada, Finnish, or Taiwanese research institutes, which produce technology for industry, incubate new firms, and provide technical services to private enterprises.

NOTES

1. The National Research Council of Canada (NRC) commissioned this study in the framework of the evaluation of NRC's Cluster Initiatives Portfolio.
2. Increasing returns is the law that governs new, R&D-intensive industries, such as aerospace, biotechnology, and software. It is the tendency to reduce unit costs of products through larger production runs. Because of high upfront R&D costs, companies in technology-based industries try to increase the scale of production in order to distribute those initial costs over the largest possible volume of products. The corollary is that they expand as much as possible and early entrants enjoy an advantage over latecomers. Increasing returns generate positive feedback loops: the more the firm grows, the more it becomes difficult to dislodge from the top (Arthur, 1996).
3. CMAs are agglomerations with a population of 100 000 and over.
4. 'The U.S. President's Commission on Competitiveness defines competitiveness as "the ability to sell goods and services under free and fair market conditions while maintaining and increasing living standards over the long run"' (Neill, 1999). Conversely, Krugman (1994) argues that the very concept of competitiveness is loose and tends to obscure issues and should give way to productivity.
5. In this chapter, the concept of policy is narrower than that of initiatives. Private-sector associations, public laboratories, and even universities (e.g., Albany Nanotech) or individuals (Sophia Antipolis) can launch cluster initiatives. Only public-sector actors can implement policy (Andersson et al., 2004: 52) but they can launch initiatives.
6. The Research Triangle Park is circumscribed by the cities of Chapel Hill, Durham, and Raleigh. The park includes 7000 acres (28 sq. km.) in Durham and Wake counties.
7. Former governor Hunt chaired the 37-member task force, which included 20 members from industry, 7 from universities, 4 from government laboratories, and 6 from government and other organizations.
8. www.researchtriangle.org
9. www.gra.org
10. Danish Ministry of Trade and Industry, *A New Economy and Its New Clusters* www.ebst.dk/publikationer/rapporter/gb_klynge/efspup0202/kap2.htm#2.5
11. www.cluster.gr.jp
12. www.itri.org.tw

13. www.innovating-regions.org
14. Path-dependent processes are those where any state of the system depends on previous states; in other words, the process evolves on the basis of its own history. Increasing returns are a paradigmatic case of path dependence.
15. Lock-in is a situation where a system enters into a trapping region, a stable equilibrium. Gunnar Myrdal describes long-term underdevelopment as such a situation: poor countries' populations have little schooling and suffer from bad health, therefore they cannot pay for education that would help them to escape from poverty: the vicious circle of poverty feeds on itself.
16. They are the Vancouver Institute for Fuel Cell Fuel Innovation (2006), the Edmonton National Institute for Nanotechnology (NINT, 2001), the Saskatoon Plants for Health and Wellness Lab (the existing Plant Biotechnology Institute, which diversified into nutraceuticals and functional foods), Regina's Centre for Sustainable Infrastructure (2004), the Winnipeg Biomedical Technologies Lab (1992), Ottawa's Photonics Lab (2005), the Saguenay Aluminum Technology Centre (2002), the Fredericton–Moncton Information Technology Institute (2003), the Halifax Biomedical Magnetic Resonance Research Laboratory (2008), the Charlottetown Institute for Nutrisciences and Health (2006), and the St John's Institute for Ocean Technology (2003).

8. Conclusion: Putting it together

Neoclassical economics emphasized the advantages of being late: backward countries could obtain existing technology from wealthier nations and catch up with them rapidly. In the real world, however, latecomers suffer from a number of disadvantages, many of them institutional. It is sometimes possible to licence, transfer, or imitate technologies, but it is not easy to imitate mores, organizations, best practices, and public policies. Besides, national specificities (natural resources, culture, geographical location, sector choice) mean that at best catching-up countries can take some inspiration from industrial nations, old or new. Yet national idiosyncrasies make imitation impossible.

In the nineteenth and early twentieth centuries, each would-be catcher up developed its own institutions: Germany invented its multi-function banks, France and Italy their state enterprises, and Japan its conglomerate *zaibatsu*. In the late twentieth century, South Korea took the example of Japanese conglomerates to establish its national *chaebols*; Canada and Finland created their own mix of science, technology, and innovation (STI) policies and picked specific sectors to nurture their economic development. Singapore chose two industrial sectors (electronics and biopharmaceuticals) and developed specialized human capital through an aggressive policy of importing capital, corporations, and skilled labour.

In contrast, the developing countries we saw in Chapter 6 did not choose industries, technologies, or sectors and made only timid movements to create their own STI institutions. They not only set up few institutions; they conceived them poorly, seldom evaluated them, and when they did assess them it was through local organizations – sometimes too close to bring the necessary critical viewpoint. This conclusion recalls the main theoretical issues of the book and their policy implications.

This conclusion returns to theory, under the light of the chapters above. It reviews the question of why STI policy exists at all, outlines the obstacles that newcomers are facing, shows how they might overcome these hurdles, and points out the daunting, long-term nature of the task.

8.1 WHY STI POLICY?

The rationales for the implementation of STI policy are several, depending on the theoretical framework. In the neoclassical tradition, which assumes that economic agents possess perfect or quasi-perfect knowledge, market failures and externalities are the key explanations. Market failures include first and foremost financial ones: innovation activities are complex, long-term, and opaque and face risk and uncertainty. Thus financiers tend to reduce their support to these activities to a minimum, causing under-investment in public- and private-sector STI. This explanation barely holds: if private financiers keep themselves aloof from science and technology, why would governments risk public monies on their promotion? Also, market failures presuppose that markets are inherently efficient, that few of them fail, that their collapses are always harmful, and that STI policies aim only to reduce failures while in fact they may implement them to attain social goods such as defense and health.

Externalities, a concept that derives from Arrow's work (1962), provides a more sound theoretical support to STI policy. They are the only type of market failure that has resisted a thorough analysis. Private investors are aware that they will be unable to recuperate positive returns on their investment because the production of knowledge is much more costly than its reproduction. Imitators and consumers would then receive windfall profits from the original innovator. Governments thus may choose to subsidize technological innovation with public funds, because taxpayers would be recipients of a large share of the resulting benefits.

In the evolutionary, innovation system and institutional approaches, government intervention may create entire sets of institutions that markets do not provide, such as universities, government laboratories, intellectual-property regimes, and incentives for private firms. These currents underline the fact that markets are never perfect and never lack regulation; the institutions that frame these markets may be prone to failure, and markets may systematically fall short in producing some socially desirable goods, including education, health, and knowledge. Governments thus intervene to remediate these system failures.

How do Governments Intervene?

Several parallel strands of literature analyze the relationships between policy, growth, and catching up. Many empirical works explain 'the residual' by measuring the role of human capital (Becker and Murphy, 1990), R&D expenditures (Romer, 1990; Aghion and Howitt, 1992; Aghion et al., 1999), and other technology-related metric variables. The results were somewhat disappointing: all these variables are co-linear, and none shows a significant relationship with economic growth.

The evolutionary, institutional, and innovation-systems theory of growth (in the works of Carlsson, Freeman, Lundvall, Malerba, Nelson, Niosi, and others) puts the accent on institutions and their interaction. Institutions – more specifically those for STI – explain growth. Institutions neither are perfectly efficient nor move towards optimality (David, 1994). They are path dependent and may, like technology, lock themselves in traps with inefficient incentives. The evaluation and redesign of such institutions thus become crucial.

In this book, the key institutions fall into four types: mores, organizations, routines, and policies. They divide the 'big bag' of institutions (Nelson, 2005a) into more homogeneous groups with different origins, trajectories, and practical and theoretical implications.

Mores are customary ways of thinking and acting, sometimes under the influence of religion, sometimes of ancient laws. They include the role of women in education and the labour force (King and Hill, 1993), the languages that people speak, and public attitudes towards science and technology. People respect mores because of social pressures that materialize through threats of social exclusion or religious punishment. Also, customs structure action through guilt and disapprobation (Shevell, 2002). They evolve slowly under the constraint of law (e.g., Ataturk's Turkey curtailing religious activities or modifying the alphabet), education, and other factors. Governments thus may intervene by modifying mores that inhibit absorption of science and technology.

Organizations are social units that human beings construct purposely to seek specific goals (Aldrich, 1999). Most often, participation in them is voluntary, even if they are hierarchical and tend to have authorities and internal rules. Because they tend to search for some degree of efficiency and effectiveness, they use routines for recruitment, production, sales, research, and other functions. Innovative firms, universities, government laboratories, venture-capital firms, and other relevant organizations are central to national, regional, and sectoral systems of innovation and thus to economic development. Yet organizations develop inertia – resistance to change – over the course of their lives. Organizations are modular institutions and are most often decomposable into other second- and third-level organizations such as academic departments, corporate divisions, army regiments, and bank establishments. Yet at their lower level of disaggregation, they consist of routines.

Government policies (or lack thereof) affect the behaviour of all the main organizations in national systems of innovation (NSI). STI policies may create (or not) incentives for firms to conduct in-house R&D – activity that increases their absorptive capacity and allows them to purchase or imitate learning about existing technologies (Mowery and Nelson, 1999: 8) and related best practices such as benchmarking, continuous improvement, and quality control. In developing countries, governments may conceive of firms as black boxes, the performance of which they leave to the market; thus policy incentives are either non-existent or ineffective at altering behaviour. In addition, those STI policies may affect other organizations: they may induce universities, for example, to conduct R&D and transfer, through different channels, their research results to industry and society, moving beyond their teaching mission. In developing countries, academic mental models, rules, regulations, and salaries are unable to foster those activities. Public authorities need to intervene to nurture organizational change. The same reasoning applies to government laboratories, financial institutions, and government organizations.

Routines are repetitive patterns of action within organizations (Cohen et al., 1996). They allow organizational learning and change and underlie organizational competencies. Organizational change may be architectural (entire redesign) or modular: most often it consists of the addition, modification, or elimination of routines. Examples include companies adding an R&D planning activity or incorporating project management into quality control, universities implementing new rules of academic hiring, or government laboratories developing new rules for technology transfer. Because routines are by definition inertial, authorities should promote adoption of socially beneficial ones. Such an approach is different from the black-box perspective of neoclassical economics, where perfectly rational economic agents know better than governments what is good for them.

Laws or policies are rules of conduct that national or regional authorities impose. They evolve under the legislative action of governments, judicial rulings, or popular pressure. Policies structure human behaviour through legal sanctions and sometimes through incentives. Some policies aim at inducing organizational change in firms, such as government procurement regulations that give priority to companies with some level of quality control (e.g., ISO 9000), or at fostering some routines through direct subsidies or tax credits (e.g., inducements to invest in particular industries or regions or to conduct R&D).

OECD governments usually implement such policies after observing other countries' interventions and taking into consideration the previous direction of their STI rules and regulations, previous investments, as well as existing assets and the outcomes they desire.

STI policies are complementary and 'super-modular' (Mohnen and Röller, 2005). In addition, they need some kind of organizational and customary support.[1] No science policy would be effective in a country where religious beliefs create obstacles to the production and diffusion of scientific knowledge. No technology and innovation policy can become effective if organizations (universities, public laboratories, and, above all, private firms) do not include routines favouring innovation.

Thus economic development is akin to the diffusion of policies, organizations, routines, and customs that allow scientific, technological, and organizational innovation. Teubal (1996) presents economic development as a process wherein R&D activities penetrate organizations, allowing extensive collective learning and producing multiple knowledge externalities.

These externalities often diffuse across borders. National and international diffusion of policy is a well-known phenomenon. Such policy diffusion is more frequent among geographically and culturally close states and nations. The Humboldt-type research university started in Germany and then spread to English-speaking countries, while teaching-only, Bologna-type universities have emerged in Latin Europe and Latin America. Also, there is a large institutional convergence between Canada and the United States, but not, because of strong cultural differences, between the United States and Mexico.

Yet institutional inefficiencies and system failures occur everywhere (Niosi, 2002). There is no natural selective pressure towards increasingly better institutions. Selection and improvement are the result of consciously designed policies, not of markets. 'Clever, modern Panglossians have come up with the proposition that the increasing likelihood that laws resulting in inefficient resource use will be exposed to economically motivated litigation, thereby creating "selective pressure" to remould property laws in ways that tend to render it more efficient. . . . and that some beneficent "invisible hand" thus guides the evolution of legal institutions affecting economic performance' (David, 1993: 22).

8.2   OBSTACLES TO CATCHING UP

Traditional economics has pinpointed the advantages of latecomers: they would need only to absorb science, technology, and related institutions in order to catch up and converge with rich nations. Because agents are perfectly rational, either they adopt best technologies, practices, and organizational forms from the start, or they rapidly adopt or imitate them from the original innovators.

Evolutionary economics, in contrast, in an effort to explain why convergence is at best regional (continental or sub-continental) and not global, has stressed the difficulties of catching up. It emphasizes the strength of barriers to economic development, including international intellectual-property arrangements, such as the Trade-Related Aspects of Intellectual Property Rights (TRIPS) agreements, and growing obstacles to developing countries experimenting with existing technology. The same agreements sometimes threaten access to life-saving drugs and push up drug prices (Kumar, 2003).

Barriers also include efforts by rich countries to impose free trade on developing nations while protecting their own industries through subsidies, some of them agricultural, and non-tariff obstacles, as with textiles and clothes: quotas (1950–74), the International Multifibre Arrangement (1974–94), and the Agreement on Textiles and Clothing (1995–2004), which for several decades kept textiles and clothes from developing countries out of rich nations' markets. Also, in the post-war period, rich countries developed a long list of STI policies. These seldom receive coverage in any academic curriculum, yet they belong to the realm of public administration and represent institutional novelties that developing countries seldom understand or discuss.

Organizational and Institutional Inertia: Why Are All Developing Countries Not Catching Up?

Successful South East Asian countries are creating a variety of routes to economic development that is unfamiliar to Africa, Latin America, and other parts of Asia. If OECD members often imitate each other's national STI policies, few developing countries do so. The reasons are many, and I enumerate eight below:

- The long term: Development is a long-term endeavour, but in democracies most politicians focus on the short term, favouring policies that produce results that voters can appreciate. Therefore democratic governments tend to concentrate on immediate problems and issues. South East Asian countries tend to have stable governments, and permanent professional bureaucracies add to the stability and reduce the number of drastic changes in policy. In addition, economic success furthers political stability. Many nations in Africa and Latin America have experienced political convulsions and military coups, including radical shifts in policy vis-à-vis economic development.
- Opportunity costs: Investing in education, technology transfer, or R&D tax credits or subsidies, all of which offer long-term returns, displaces spending on health, housing, and other pressing needs of poor countries. Education, R&D, and technology would

also challenge areas of investment with higher and faster political returns, such as highway construction and cash subsidies for the poor or the unemployed, such as those in Argentina, Brazil, Mexico, and Venezuela (Marshall, 2004).

- An orphan subject: STI policy is an orphan subject. Economists give it only marginal attention, even though their colleagues discovered 50 years ago the links between economic development and technology. Political scientists focus more on elections, polls, political identity, and international relations. Management scientists may study business firms rather than the institutional conditions that make some enterprises more innovative than others.

- The curse of natural resources: A nation's plethora of natural resources can hurt economic development through several channels. In the 'Dutch disease,' booms in natural resources increase the price of resources and exchange rates, thus inhibiting manufacturing and exports of sophisticated services. Rent seeking affects both producers, which tend to neglect high-value added products and invest in resources, which bring quick profits, and governments, which tax those profits. A sudden bonanza creates a sense of security and tends to obscure the need for bureaucratic efficiency and institutional quality. Governments invest in developing natural resources and forget about human resources and institutions. In addition, the lobbies for natural resources in developing (and in wealthy) countries support free trade and oppose subsidies for domestic technology-intensive firms or R&D activities. Natural resources usually create demand for poorly educated labour. 'Natural capital appears to crowd out human capital' (Gylfason, 2001: 847).

- Inefficient bureaucracies: Developing countries tend to have inefficient public-sector bureaucracies, unable to design, evaluate, modify, and fund STI policies. The United Kingdom created a professional bureaucracy in the 1840s, and the United States in the 1880s, yet most industrializing nations still do not have one; each new government reshuffles the bureaucracy, which prevents organizational learning.

An efficient and merit-based public bureaucracy is a condition for catching up. Civil servants apply the laws that the legislative power presents but do so with latitude, because neither the executive nor the legislative branches can foresee all contingencies. Besides, in most OECD countries, the executive usually drafts laws with the help of the professional bureaucracy, which consists of specialists. Civil services in North America, Japan, and western Europe thus play central roles in governance.

The task of creating professional and efficient bureaucracies seems out of reach for much of Latin America and Africa. Typically, in those countries each incoming government appoints hundreds if not thousands of new public employees, often in all ranks below minister. Low pay, the scarcity of private-sector job opportunities, and lack of incentives for performance help explain those corrupt bureaucracies. Because the new, ephemeral bureaucracies have only a few years to milk the public purse, they tend to exploit all possible opportunities and have little time for or interest in organizational learning, policy design, and evaluation. The state is thus more predatory than developmental.

- Causal ambiguity: Each set of STI policies is different: Canada has R&D tax credits as the backbone of its STI policies, but Finland has no such credits, while the United States has weak ones. If there is no 'one-size-fits-all' solution, what should industrializing governments do? We know that each of the 'tigers' of South East Asia has produced its own set of policies, by imitation, trial, and error. South Korea copied Japan's *zaibatsu*, its large domestic corporations, its government laboratories, and its 'flying geese' method of choosing sectors but mostly excluded foreign direct investment (FDI). It has embodied its STI policies in some 90 laws that it has adopted since 1967. In contrast, Taiwan incubated its local small and medium-size firms in its public laboratories, while inviting foreign direct investors in selected sectors. China opened its economy to a massive influx of FDI while modernizing its universities and changing the practices of its public laboratories. For developing countries, devising a set of STI policies can thus be a daunting prospect.

- Corruption: Corruption is widespread among industrializing states, and the 'principal–agent problem' is central. The principal (the taxpayer) lacks information about what the agents (politicians and civil servants) are doing. Agents are usually keen to hide information from principals.

  In the most common type of corruption, politicians or bureaucrats request bribes from companies to approve government contracts or provide public services.[2] Less common, but more harmful, firms bribe legislators, policy-makers, or even judges to influence laws, regulations, rules, and contracts (Hellman and Kaufman, 2001).[3]

  Politicians and civil servants in most developing countries are keener to become rich quickly than to learn about STI policies. Cases of corruption that reach the prosecution stage in Africa and Latin America usually appear in the press, and this sometimes happens in Asia. Also, if Transparency International's rankings are accurate, then most African, Latin American, and Asian countries are fairly corrupt. But, of course, the issue of 'who guards the guardians?' (World Bank, 2003) remains key.

- Tragedy of the commons: Last but not least, if market economies are plagued with 'tragedy of the commons' problems such as overuse of natural resources, they are also beset by similar problems of building common goods. STI institutions and human capital are common goods. But politicians are not interested in building these goods that require long periods before they produce results, because they are elected for short terms. They are thus biased in favour of those public goods that can be completed during their mandates such as roads and bridges. In other words, the political personnel of democracies that is unfavourable to reforestation or preservation of fish stocks, is for the same reasons not inclined to building common good political institutions (Dietz et al., 2003).

8.3   OVERCOMING OBSTACLES

These obstacles are not new. They have been present in all wealthy and all industrializing countries. Various policies and organizational initiatives have overcome them in many nations.

Creating a Separate Ministry or Agency for Science, Technology, and Innovation

It is necessary to establish a government department caring for long-term growth and to provide it with an adequate budget. Economic development and catching up are decades-long tasks, and such a department should make long-term growth its chief goal. Countries that have caught up have nurtured one such agency.

In 1967, South Korea created the Ministry of Science and Technology (MOST); Singapore set up A*Star to guide long-term economic development. China has also created such a department. Boxes 8.1 and Boxes 8.2 summarize the mandates of such departments.

Taiwan set up its National Science Council in 1959 and later mandated it to design and apply STI policies; review, control, and evaluate government plans in, survey activity in, and recruit personnel for science and technology; fund research projects; and develop science parks. Its 2007 budget was U.S.$1.293 billion for academic research, science parks, and other missions.

BOX 8.1   MISSIONS OF CHINA'S MINISTRY OF SCIENCE AND TECHNOLOGY (MOST)

1. MOST takes the lead in drawing up development plans and policies for science and technology (S&T), drafting related laws, regulations, and department rules, and guaranteeing implementation.

2. MOST is responsible for drafting the National Basic Research Program, the National High-Tech R&D Program, and the S&T Enabling Program. It aims to serve socio-economic growth by co-ordinating basic research, frontier technology research, and research on social services, key technology, and common technology.

3. MOST teams up with other organizations in demonstrating, assessing, and accepting schemes and in making policy for special projects in S&T, and it provides advice on major changes.

4. MOST compiles and implements plans on national laboratories, innovative bases, national S&T programs, and research conditions so as to promote construction of infrastructure and sharing of resources.

5. MOST formulates and supervises S&T plans according to policies, drafts policies on high-tech commercialization with other departments, and guides the national high-tech industrial development zones.

6. MOST draws up policies and measures on enhancing rural and social progress with S&T to improve the livelihood of the people.

7. MOST issues policies to encourage the synergy of enterprises, universities, and research institutes, promotes application and demonstration of scientific discoveries and technological inventions, and works to improve the innovation capacity of enterprises.

8. MOST makes proposals on institutional reform and supervises establishment and restructuring of research institutes.

9. MOST is responsible for budgeting, final accounting, and supervising of S&T funds. It also, with relevant departments, proposes major policies and measures on rational allocation of S&T resources.

10. MOST is responsible for appraising the National S&T Award, drawing plans on S&T talents, team-building, and making proposals on policies.
11. MOST drafts plans and policies on science popularization, technology markets, and S&T intermediaries. It is also responsible for issuing confidential measures and managing S&T assessment and statistics.
12. MOST draws up policies on S&T co-operation and exchange through bilateral and multilateral channels, guides relevant departments and local governments in international interaction, appoints and supervises S&T diplomats, and facilitates aid to and from China.
13. MOST undertakes other tasks assigned by the State Council.

Note: Missions are numbered by MOST.

Source: China: MOST.

BOX 8.2   MAIN FUNCTIONS OF SOUTH KOREA'S MINISTRY OF SCIENCE AND TECHNOLOGY (MOST)

1. To provide technology forecasting to set up basic policy for science and technology development and promotion.
2. To pursue national technological self-reliance in the safe use of nuclear energy.
3. To execute national programs for development of core technologies, future-oriented technologies, 'big science,' and multidisciplinary technologies, including aerospace, ocean, and nuclear energy.
4. To support basic and applied R&D by government, university, and private-sector R&D laboratories.
5. To build a policy for R&D investment, human resources, information, and international co-operation in science and technology.
6. To promote public understanding of science and technology and so on.

Source: South Korea: MOST.

Argentina's Ministry for Science, Technology and Productive Innovation started with an annual budget of U.S.$450 million; by 2008 it was receiving $1 billion per year, but that amount included the budgets for public laboratories and academic research.

Addressing Opportunity Costs

Subsidizing innovation and investing in education may seem to displace urgent spending in health and housing. But investing in education and subsidizing R&D in fast-growing companies that employ new graduates can help solve health and housing problems in developing countries. Education and employment for graduates will generate revenues for people requiring health care and housing.

Orphan STI Policy Issues

Developing countries do not need to wait until economics, political science, or management science incorporate these themes into their curricula. It would be much better (and faster) to create government think tanks like the Office of Science and Technology Policy, which the United States established in 1976 to 'serve as a source of scientific and technological analysis for the President with respect to major policies, plans and programs of the Federal Government' (ostp.gov). In Canada, the Science Council (1966–94) and later the National Advisory Board on Science and Technology (NABST) have shared a similar mandate, as has, in Switzerland, the Council for Science and Technology. Such organizations are usually multi-disciplinary units, where social and natural scientists work with engineers and policy-makers.

Curing Diseases in Natural Resources

Several governments have established funds to avoid the 'Dutch disease' and to preserve natural resources for future generations – for example, the Alberta Heritage Fund in Canada, Chile's Cooper Fund, Norway's Oil Fund, and Taiwan's National Stabilization Fund. At the very opposite end of the spectrum, Argentina, Mexico, Venezuela, and many other developing countries have been spending their way towards extinction of their natural resources. Norway's Government Pension Fund Global is a model organization, and the largest in Europe, with total assets of U.S.$373 billion at the end of 2007. Of course, such funds may become new sources of corruption unless ethical guidelines and adequate transparency are the rule.[4] But they can also serve to strengthen education and prepare people for the future, after the natural resources disappear, give way to substitutes, or suffer from declining prices.

From Inefficient to Efficient Bureaucracies

In developing states, it is difficult, but not impossible, to change the public sector from the principle 'to the victor belong the spoils' to recruitment on the basis of merit. In the United States, this transition to recruitment for merit occurred progressively after introduction of the Civil Service Reform Act of 1883. Over the years, the program came to cover the entire federal civil service. Later the Hatch Act, 1939, prohibited public employees from active involvement in politics in order to ensure a non-partisan bureaucracy. In 1978, the Civil Service Reform Act established an Office of Personnel Management and a Merit System Protection Board.

Also, information-disclosure acts have guaranteed more transparent bureaucracies. The United States adopted the Information Disclosure Act in 1966, which allowed citizens to scrutinize government files. Sweden enacted similar legislation in 1949, Finland in 1951, Denmark and Norway in 1970, and France in 1971. In 1983, Canada passed the Access to Information Act. By the mid-1990s, some 12 OECD countries had approved similar laws, which seem to alter the political culture.

Periodic evaluation of government departments, research institutes, universities, and other public institutions, including policies, also helps to increase their efficiency, particularly if independent third parties do the assessment and if their findings become public, as happens in many OECD countries.

Yet governments recruiting personnel on the basis of merit and seeking transparency in the public service need also to offer competitive salaries, similar to those that the private sector pays for equivalent education and productivity.

Reducing Causal Ambiguity

There are no miracle cures for 'causal ambiguity.' The appropriate combination of policies and institutions is highly idiosyncratic. Yet some constant elements serve to reduce uncertainty and risk in policy-making.

First, it seems useful to review foreign practices, present and past. How did Canada and the United States move from 'to the victor belong the spoils' to efficient bureaucracies? How did they create universities that recruit abroad and on merit, instead of hiring friends and relatives? How did traditional universities change from teaching to teaching plus research plus incubation of technology-based companies? How did government induce its own laboratories to conduct not only agricultural and industrial extension but also R&D and technology transfer with other countries? What obstacles surfaced when North American and Nordic governments proposed and enacted information-disclosure laws? The institutional culs-de sac that developing countries face today appeared decades ago in other countries, and solutions were applied.

Second, it may be useful for government to avoid massive changes. It might do well instead to test the waters – perhaps in new organizations, such as a ministry of science and technology, new research universities, or new government laboratories – especially if it wants these institutions to operate under rules (and salaries) that it plans to diffuse through the entire system. Best practices diffuse slowly (Niosi, 1999), whether in government or industry.

Third, some level of tinkering, trial and error, and reshuffling is unavoidable. But it is easier to change things in new institutions than in old ones, which labour under the burden of decades of organizational inertia and long-standing inferior practices.

Fighting Corruption

The policies above (hiring for merit, disclosing information, paying competitive salaries) should reduce corruption in the civil service. Employees receiving competitive pay based on merit are normally keen to keep their positions. Information disclosure enables citizens to detect illegal payments and contracts and other unlawful transactions. Also, agencies and commissions can inquire about and increase accountability. Yet these bodies must have good staffs, adequate finances, and the authority to request and process information. These latter conditions are difficult to fulfil in countries with few highly educated lawyers, economists, managers, and other specialists. Also, old ways of doing things die hard. They will not disappear overnight. And mobilizing the losers may be a difficult and costly endeavour.

8.4   A LONG TERM PROPOSITION

It takes decades to build national, regional, or sectoral systems of innovation. The outcomes of such efforts are path dependent and respond strongly to existing attitudes, organizations, practices, and policies. According to Niosi (2000a), Canada took between 25 and 40 years to construct a national system of innovation (NSI), depending on where one drew the start and finish lines. Governments have to create both the supply and the

Table 8.1   Creating supply and demand for human capital

Supply	Demand
Fellowships	Tax credits for industrial R&D
Loan-grants	Subsidies for SMEs' R&D
Skilled immigrants	Venture-capital policies
University research funding councils	Reimbursable loans for industrial R&D
Fiscal exemptions for foreign researchers	Public R&D laboratories
Accelerated immigration for foreign students	Joint university–industry R&D centres

demand for human capital, avoiding the poverty trap of both supply and demand of unskilled labour. These institutions take decades to start up and begin running efficiently. Table 8.1 summarizes the policies.

Finding the right combination of industrial policies as well as horizontal and vertical technology policies is also crucial. While there are no magic formulas for successful sets of technology policies, some general lessons seem to emerge from both wealthy and developing countries. Let us start with the area that has shown the least progress: the private sector's demand for personnel.

Tax Credits for R&D

A national system of tax credits could be a good start for building such a system. To begin with, tax credits for R&D, without limits as to the number of firms able to claim them or total amounts firms can claim (as in Canada) is the kind of horizontal policy that can induce both domestic and foreign companies to conduct in-house R&D. To avoid the difficulties that the United States experienced, government should make the policy permanent and not tie it to incremental expenditures. Learning from Mexico's problems, it should not limit the number of eligible companies or sectors or the total amounts available, so that firms of any size from any industry and country of control could benefit. Starting this way may silence criticisms about 'picking winners' that usually surface with both industrial and vertical technology policies. As well, the policy can be easy both to implement and to evaluate. Finally, no civil servant needs to decide which claimant receives the credit, thus reducing the chances of favouritism (or worse).

Experience shows, however, that the number of companies applying would increase slowly, as firms learn to use the incentive. In Canada, the number grew from under a hundred in 1977 to a thousand in the early 1980s to about 7000 in the early 1990s to almost 20 000 in 2004–5 (Niosi, 2000a: 196, IRAP). Also, the national government continually improved the credits, and provinces implemented their own and other measures to support in-house R&D (including provincial tax credits). In Chile, the new credit disbursed only U.S.$200 000 to two firms in its first year of operation (2008). As almost all OECD countries as well as the BRIC group of nations already have tax credits, such measures will probably generate little controversy. The Achilles' heel of the system would be verifying, by random sampling or otherwise, effective application of the tax credits to R&D.

Direct Subsidies for SMEs

Direct subsidies for small and medium-size firms (SMEs) could be a second national measure. Again, this policy requires no consideration of any priority in industry or sector, but would-be adopters should be aware that several different systems exist.

The U.S. Small Business Innovation Research program (SBIR), launched in 1982, aims at transfer of public technology to existing or new SMEs. The subsidy supports development of such technology, including proof of concept and supplementary R&D to take it closer to the market. Such a system is relevant only in a country where universities and public laboratories produce numerous new technologies and where it is easy to create or upgrade SMEs to develop them. The model thus may not be the most convenient for developing countries, where universities and public laboratories may produce little new technology and SMEs may possess little absorptive capacity. The Japanese SBIR, which started in 1998, takes fewer risks than the U.S. system but also favours new technology-based firms. Similarly, in 1999, the Japan Science and Technology Corporation launched, through its Science and Technology Agency, a U.S.$800 000 Pre-Venture Program allocating non-reimbursable funds to new technology firms.

Canada's Industrial Research Assistance Program (IRAP) has no bias in favour of high-tech firms, and allocates funds to SMEs with sound business plans in any sector. Its total budget is over $150 million per year. But even such a low-profile program may be difficult to implement in developing countries. If we judge by the experience of Chile, with CORFO and its many programs, and of Uruguay, with its PDTI program, even the less corrupt and wealthier Latin American countries may lack managers to run such endeavours efficiently. Yet their experience can prove instructive for other developing countries planning similar efforts.

Venture Capital

Some countries such as Argentina, Brazil, and Chile have created venture-capital programs. With so few companies there conducting R&D and so few avenues existing for venture capitalists either in the stock market or with other firms, such programs may seem premature. Venture capital requires abundant technology managers, experienced financial experts, and several channels (stock exchanges, large industrial firms, and experienced managers with access to credit ready to support a buyback scheme). Such resources are not abundant even in such OECD countries as Canada, Japan, and those in western Europe. Developing countries have none.

Human Capital

The building of a pool of human capital in developing countries faces major obstacles. These include low salaries, scarce research funds, language barriers, and mental models in academics and policy-makers, according to which university teaching and research are luxury services that the country cannot afford. The result is that the human-capital pool in Africa and Latin America, but also in parts of Asia, grows slowly, if at all.

Creating New Institutions for Human Capital

It is easier to create new academic and public R&D institutions than to reform old ones. Besides, it is not possible to reform an academic system from top to bottom. Chile has modified part of its university system by adding new institutions and changing some of the existing ones. The number of universities grew from 8 in 1980 to 23 in 1986, 60 in 1990, and 61 in 2006. At the same time, total enrolment rose from 108 000 in 1980 to 473 000 in 2006 (Katz and Contreras, 2009). Yet creation of new universities with practices similar to those of the older ones does not improve the situation, as the case of Argentina clearly shows.

Paying Higher Academic Salaries

A study of academic salaries in 15 countries shows Argentina, Colombia, and India paying entry-level university professors on average about U.S.$1000 or less (in PPP) per month, and Malaysia and South Africa slightly over $2000. At the other end of the spectrum, Australia and Canada were paying over $4500 per month (Rumbley et al., 2008). Under the lower-end conditions, it may not be easy to attract the best talent, even among local people born in developing countries with graduate degrees from OECD countries. However, some nations have solved the problem. Both Israel and Singapore, but also some Chinese universities, are attracting foreign scholars with higher salaries and special conditions. Some universities in Chile (particularly public ones such as Universidad de Chile, Católica, and private ones, such as Universidad Adolfo Ibáñez) are now paying foreigners high salaries and attracting instructors from North America.[5] Several universities are also conducting R&D, together with a few other post-secondary institutions: five public ones spend 80 per cent of all R&D money for higher education.

Hiring International Scholars and Networking with Them

Endogamy is a curse of higher education in developing countries but also in European universities: institutions tend to hire instructors from among their own graduates, which may reduce productivity by reshuffling a reduced set of ideas (Aghion et al., 2007).

In South East Asia, governments have repatriated many national students graduating abroad and added foreign PhDs with suitable qualifications. In many developing countries, such efforts are not regular, so that a brain drain results. Some nations have implemented 'brain gain' measures to subsidize links between their professionals working abroad and those who have stayed home, in hopes that such networks could facilitate transfer of knowledge.

Transforming Organizations

Government laboratories, universities, and other public and private bodies producing or diffusing science and technology may change dramatically with the addition of R&D activities (either specific routines or modular organizations). Public laboratories for industrial or agricultural extension may incorporate R&D laboratories by attracting highly skilled personnel. Similarly, universities can develop advanced graduate programs. Incubators, government laboratories, and universities may incorporate routines for technology transfer. Private firms may add R&D facilities.

Because of inertia and path dependence, contracts and mental models will inhibit adoption of advanced activities and hence transformation of organizations. Contracts freeze public bodies and are difficult to change. Firms have developed ways of acquiring technology (usually physical technologies and related training activities) from other organizations without producing it in-house. As well, R&D activities differ greatly from traditional routines that characterize operations. The latter are fast and

Table 8.2   Operations versus R&D routines

Operation routines	R&D routines
Repetitive	Always different
Fast	Slow
Clear roles of personnel	Opaque roles of personnel
Many data	Few data
Continual improvement	Sporadic improvement
Permanent control	Periodic control
Safety and confidence	Risk and uncertainty

repetitive, safe, and continually improving, with well-defined roles and transparent outcomes. R&D involves risk and uncertainty, slow processes, and opaque outcomes; in addition, roles are sometimes obscure (who developed the idea?).

It is not by chance that companies, universities, and government laboratories hesitate in adding R&D activities. Thus firms prefer to concentrate on repetitively producing goods and services, higher-education institutions on teaching, and government laboratories on producing extension activities. This is why in OECD countries actual performers of industrial R&D form such a small percentage of firms, post-secondary institutions with graduate programs (in which R&D takes place) are relatively scarce, and few public laboratories conduct R&D.

In addition, transfer of public technology to the private sector, whether from universities or from government research bodies, poses delicate questions. Why and how to transfer this technology? Are multiple or exclusive licences preferable? How much should the licence cost? What protection should the technology receive: a patent, copyright, or secrecy? Who owns the technology: the inventor, the public organization, or some other person or body? How to assume the cost of the protection, and how to divide returns between inventors and public organizations?

OECD countries have put together a variety of responses to these questions, and debates still rage about best practices on all these issues. In these matters, as in all others, the policy implication is that developing countries have to devote resources to studying and understanding other nations' experiences and ought only then to build their own solutions, during years of trial and error, designing solutions and evaluating them. There are no 'one-size-fits-all' sets of best practices and no clear-cut optimal solutions, only satisfying local ones.

Such a conclusion is perfectly in keeping with the micro-foundations of this work, which I base on behavioral, evolutionary, and institutional economics. We did not find one best possible set of STI institutions, but several appropriate ones, with a pattern of institutional imitation among geographically and culturally close countries and a few cases of institutional 'saltation' from western Europe and North America to South East Asia.

NOTES

1. Hodgson (2009) emphasizes the difference between custom and law. Hayek (1973) holds the opposite view, according to which custom is the essence of law.
2. In 2008, the U.S. Department of Justice found Siemens AG, a German corporation, guilty of agreeing to pay U.S.$450 million to officials in Argentina, Bangladesh, Iraq, and Venezuela to obtain government contracts (U.S. Department of Justice, 2008).
3. A 1999 study by the International Monetary Fund and the European Bank for Reconstruction and Development of some 4000 firms in 22 countries in central and eastern Europe found various levels of 'state capture' (Hellman and Kaufman, 2001). Azerbaijan, Moldova, Russia, and Ukraine led, with over 30 per cent of enterprises complicitous.
4. 'Transparency refers to both the degree of openness of the state's decision-making processes and the extent of disclosure of the interactions that could influence those decisions' (Hellman and Kaufman, 2001).
5. www.aquevedo.wordpress.com/2009/06/23/cuanto-pagan-las-universidades-chilenas/

References

Aboites, J., and M. Cimoli (2002), 'Intellectual property rights and national innovation systems: some lessons from the Mexican experience', *Revue d'économie industrielle*, **99**, 15–233.

Abramovitz, M. (1986), 'Catching up, forging ahead and falling behind', *Journal of Economic History*, **46**, 385–406.

Abramovitz, M. (1989), *Thinking about growth*, Cambridge: Cambridge University Press.

Achiladellis, B. and N. Antonakis (2001), 'The dynamics of technological innovation: the case of the pharmaceutical industry', *Research Policy*, **30**, 535–88.

Adler, E. (1987), *The power of ideology: the quest for technological autonomy in Argentina and Brazil*, Berkeley: University of California Press.

Aghion, P., E. Caroli, and C. García-Peñalosa (1999), 'Inequality and economic growth: the perspective of the new growth theories', *Journal of Economic Literature*, **37**(4), 1615–60.

Aghion, P., M. Dewatripont, C. Hoxby, A. Mas-Collell, and A. Sapir (2007), 'Why reform Europe's universities?', Brussels, *Bruegel Policy Brief*, Issue 2007/4.

Aghion, P., M. Dewatripont, C. Hoxby, A. Mas-Collell, and A. Sapir (2009), *The governance and performance of research universities*, Cambridge, MA, NBER WP 14851.

Aghion, P., and P. Howitt (1992), 'A model of growth through creative destruction', *Econometrica*, **60**, 323–51.

Aghion, P., and P. Howitt (2005), 'Appropriate growth policy: a unifying framework', Joseph Schumpeter Lecture.

Agrawal, A., and I. Cockburn (2003), 'The anchor tenant hypothesis: exploring the role of large, local, R&D intensive firms in regional innovation systems', *International Journal of Industrial Organization*, **21**, 1227–53.

Aidt, T.S. (2003), 'Economic analysis of corruption', *Economic Journal*, **113**, 632–52.

Akamatsu, K. (1962), 'A historical pattern of economic growth in developing countries', *Developing Economies*, **1**(1), 3–25.

Alcorta, L., and W. Peres (1998), 'Innovation systems and technological specialization in Latin America and the Caribbean', *Research Policy*, **26**, 857–81.

Aldrich, H. (1999), *Organizations evolving*, London: Sage.

Alic, J. (2008), 'A weakness in diffusion: U.S. technology and science policy after World War II', *Technology in Society*, **30**, 17–29.

Altinok, N., and H. Murseli (2007), 'International database on human capital quality', *Economic Letters*, **96**, 237–44.

Amable, B., R. Barré, and R. Boyer (1997), *Les systèmes d'innovation à l'ère de la globalisation*, Paris: Economica.

Amir, S. (2007), 'Nationalistic rhetoric and technological development: the Indonesian aircraft industry in the New Order regime', *Technology in Society*, **29**, 283–93.

Amsden, A. (1991), 'Diffusion of development: the late-industrializing model and greater East Asia', *American Economic Review*, **81**(2), 282–86.

Amsden, A.H. (1989), *Asia's next giant: South Korea and late industrialization*, New York, Oxford: Oxford University Press.

Amsden, A. (2001), *The rise of the rest: challenges to the West from late-industrializing economies*, Oxford: Oxford University Press.

Anchordoguy, M. (1989), *Computers Inc.: Japan's challenge to IBM*, Cambridge, MA: Harvard University Press.

Anderson, P.W., K. Arrow, and D. Pines (eds) (1988), *The economy as an evolving complex system*, Boulder, CO: Westview Press.

Andersson, T., S. Schwaag Serger, J. Sörvik, and E. Wise Hansson (2004), *The cluster policies Whitebook*, Malmo, Sweden: IKED.

Anwar, M.A. and A.B. Abu Bakar (1997), 'Current state of science and technology in the Muslim world', *Scientometrics*, **40**(1), 23–44.

Aoki, M. (2007), 'Endogenizing institutions and institutional changes', *Journal of Institutional Economics*, **3**(1), 1–31.

Archibugi, D., and M. Pianta (1992), 'Specialization and size of technological activities in industrial countries: analysis of patent data', *Research Policy*, **21**, 79–93.

Arrow, K. (1962), 'Economic welfare and the allocation of resources for invention', in *The rate and direction of economic activity: economic and social facts*, Princeton, NJ: Princeton University Press, pp. 609–25.

Arthur, W.B. (1994), *Increasing returns and path dependence in the economy*, Ann Arbor: University of Michigan Press.

Arthur, W.B. (1996), 'Increasing returns and the new world of business', *Harvard Business Review*, July/August.

Arthur, W.B., S.N. Durlauf, and D.A. Lane (1997), *The economy as an evolving complex system II*, Reading, MA: Perseus.

Asheim, B., and M. Gertler (2005), 'The geography of innovation: regional innovation systems', in J. Fagerberg, D.C. Mowery, and R.R. Nelson (eds), *The Oxford handbook of innovation*, Oxford: Oxford University Press, pp. 291–317.

Atkinson, R.C., and W. Blanpied (2008), 'Research universities: core of the US science and technology system', *Technology in Society*, **30**, 30–48.

Axelrod, R., and M. Cohen (2000), *Harnessing complexity: organizational implications of a scientific frontier*, New York: Basic Books.

Bae, J., and C. Rowley (2004), 'Macro and micro approaches in human resource development: context and content in South Korea', *Journal of World Business*, **39**(4), 349–61.

Bagnasco, A. (1977), *Tre Italia: la problematica territoriale dello sviluppo italiano*, Bologna: Il Mulino.

Baldwin, J., W. Chandler, C. Le, and T. Papailiadis (1994), *Strategies for success: a profile of growing small and medium sized enterprises in Canada*, Ottawa, Statistics Canada, Cat. 61–523.

Balzat, M., and H. Hanusch (2004), 'Recent trends in the research on national innovation systems', *Journal of Evolutionary Economics*, **14**(2), 197–210.

Barkley Rosser, J., Jr. (ed.) (2003), *Complexity in economics*, Cheltenham, UK: Edward Elgar Publishing.

Barlatier, J.-P., and C. Thomas (2007), 'Savoir collectif et développement de capacités réseau', *Revue française de gestion*, **170**, 173–90.

Barro, R. (1991), 'Economic growth in a cross section of countries', *Quarterly Journal of Economics*, **106**(2), 407–43.

Basalla, G. (1988), *The evolution of technology*, Cambridge: Cambridge University Press.

Beasley, W. (1995), *Japan encounters the barbarian*, New Haven, CT: Yale University Press.

Beaudry, C. (2006), 'Enterprise in orbit: the supply of communication satellites', *Economics of Innovation and New Technology*, **15**(7), 679–700.

Becattini, G. (1990), 'The Marshallian industrial district as a socio-economic notion', in F. Pyke, G. Becattini, and W. Sengenberger (eds), *Industrial districts and interfirm cooperation in Italy*, Geneva: International Institute for Labour Studies, 37–51.

Becker, G., and K.M. Murphy (1990), 'Human capital, fertility and economic growth', *Journal of Political Economy*, **98**(5), S12–S37.

Beinhocker, E. (2006), *The origin of wealth: evolution, complexity and radical remaking of economics*, Boston, MA: Harvard Business School Press.

Belal, A., and I. Springel (2006), 'Research in Egyptian universities: the role of research in higher education', UNESCO Forum on Higher Education, Research, and Knowledge, Paris, Nov. 29–Dec. 1.

Belussi, F., G. Gottardi, and E. Rullani (eds) (2003), *The technological evolution of industrial districts*, Boston: Kluwer.

Benhabib, J., and M. Siegel (1994), 'The role of human capital in economic development: evidence from aggregate cost-country data', *Journal of Monetary Economics*, **34**, 143–73.

Benhabib, J., and M. Siegel (2002), 'Human capital and technology diffusion', Discussion Paper, New York University, Department of Economics.

Bergman, E.M., and E.J. Feser (1999), 'Industry clusters: a methodology and framework for regional development policy in the United States', in OECD, *Boosting innovation: the cluster approach*, Paris, pp. 243–68.

Bérubé, C., and P. Mohnen (2007), *Are firms that received R&D subsidies more innovative?* Maastricht, Netherlands: MERIT-UNU United Nations University.

Birch, A. (1997), 'Evaluation of the Danish GTS system', in OECD, *International conference on policy evaluation in innovation and technology*, Paris, Chapter 17.

Bisang, R. (1995), 'Libre mercado, intervenciones estatales e instituciones de ciencia y técnica en Argentina', *Redes*, **3**(2), 13–58.

Blomström, M., and A. Kokko (1998), 'Multinational corporations and spillovers', *Journal of Economic Surveys*, **12**(2), 1–31.

Bloom, D.E., and D. Canning (2000), 'The health and wealth of nations', *Science*, **287**(5456), 1207–9.

Bloom, N., R. Griffith, and J. Van Reenen (2002), 'Do tax credits work? Evidence from a panel of countries 1979–1997', *Journal of Public Economics*, **85**, 1–31.

Boekholt, P., and B. Thuriaux (1999), 'Public policies to facilitate clusters: background, rational and policy practices in international perspective', in OECD, *Boosting innovation: the cluster approach*, Paris: OECD Proceedings, pp. 381–412.

Borrás, S., and D. Tsagdis (2008), *Cluster policies in Europe: firms, institutions and governance*, Cheltenham, UK: Edward Elgar Publishing.

Boschma, R.A., and M. Sotarauta (2007), 'Economic policy from an evolutionary perspective: the case of Finland', *International Journal of Entrepreneurship and Innovation Management*, **7**(2–5), 156–74.

Boyce, J. (1993), *The Philippines: the political economy of growth and impoverishment in the Marcos era*, Honolulu, University of Hawaii Press.

Bozeman, B. (2000), 'Technology transfer and public policy: a review of research and theory', *Research Policy*, **29**, 627–55.

Braun, M., and R. Di Tella (2004), 'Inflation, inflation variability and corruption', *Economics and Politics*, **16**(1), 77–101.

Breschi, S., F. Lissoni, and F. Montobbio (2005), 'The geography of knowledge spillovers: conceptual issues and measurement problems', in S. Breschi and F. Malerba (eds), *Clusters, networks and innovation*, New York: Oxford University Press, pp. 343–78.

Breschi, S., and F. Malerba (1997), 'Sectoral innovation systems: technological regimes, Schumpeterian dynamics, and spatial boundaries', in C. Edquist (ed.), *Systems of innovation*, London: Pinter, pp. 130–56.

Brock, W.-A., and D. Colander (2000), 'Complexity and policy', in D. Colander (ed.), *The complexity vision and the teaching of economics*, Cheltenham, UK, Edward Elgar Publishing, pp. 73–96.

Brusco, S. (1986), 'Small firms and industrial districts: the experience of Italy', in D. Keeble and E. Wever (eds), *New firms and regional development in Europe*, London: Croom Helm, 184–202.

Bruton, H.J. (1998), 'A reconsideration of import substitution', *Journal of Economic Perspectives*, **36**(2), 903–36.

Bush, V. (1945), *Science, the Endless Frontier, A report to the President of the United States*, Washington, DC: US government Printing Office.

Caminati, M. (2006), 'Knowledge growth, complexity and the returns to R&D', *Journal of Evolutionary Economics*, **16**, 207–29.

Canadian Biotechnology Advisory Committee (2001), *Brief history of the Canadian patent system*, Ottawa, available at www.cbac-cccb.ca/epic/site/cbac-cccb.nsf/en/ah00405e.html#historicl

Capron, H., and Bruno van Pottelsberghe de la Potterie (1997), 'Public support for business R&D: a survey and some new quantitative evidence', in OECD, *International conference on policy evaluation in innovation and technology*, Paris, Chapter 10.

Cardoso, E., and J. Fishlow (1992), 'Latin American economic development, 1950–1980', *Journal of Latin American Studies*, **24**, 197–218.

Carew, R. (2001), 'Institutional arrangements and public agricultural research in Canada', *Review of Agricultural Economics*, **23**(1), 82–101.

Carroll, G. (1994), 'A sociological view on why firms differ', in R.P. Rumelt, D. Schendel, and D.J. Teece (eds), *Fundamental issues in strategy*, Boston, MA: Harvard Business School Press, 271–90.

Carullo, J.C. (1999), *Políticas públicas y el sistema nacional de innovación: el caso argentino*, Quilmes, Universidad de Quilmas. www.innred.net/iber/Eventos/1999/C99_003.htm

Cassiolato, J., P. Bernardes, and H. Lastres (2002), *Innovation systems in the south: a case study of Embraer*, Vienna, UNCTAD DITE.

Cassiolato, J., and H. Lastres (1999), 'Inovação, globalização e as novas politicas de desenvolvimento industrial e tecnológico', in J. Cassiolato and H. Lastres (eds), *Globalização e inovação localizada*, Brasilia: IEL.

Chandler, A. (1962), *Strategy and structure*, Boston, MA: MIT Press.

Chandler, A. (1977), *The visible hand*, Cambridge, MA: Belknap Press.

Chandler, A.D. (2001), *Inventing the electronic century*, New York: Free Press.

Chang, H.-J. (2003), *Kicking away the ladder: development strategy in historical perspective*, London: Anthem.

Chang, P.-L., and H.-Y. Shih (2004), 'The innovation systems of Taiwan and China: a comparative analysis', *Technovation*, **24**, 529–39.

Chen, E. (1997), 'The total factor productivity debate: determinants of economic growth in South East Asia', *Asian Pacific Economic Literature*, **11**(1), 18–38.

Chiang, J.-T. (1999), 'Defense conversion and systems architecture: challenges to Taiwan's aircraft industry', *Technology in Society*, **21**, 263–74.

Chong, A., and C. Calderón (2000), 'Causality and feedback between institutional measures and economic growth', *Economics and Politics*, **12**(1), 69–81.

Chu, P.-Y., Y.L. Lin, H.H. Hsiung, and T.Z. Liu (2006), 'Intellectual capital: an empirical study of ITRI', *Technological Forecasting and Social Change*, **73**, 886–902.

Chudnovsky, D., and A. Lopez (2007), *The elusive quest for growth in Argentina*, New York: Palgrave Macmillan.

Chudnovsky, D., J. Niosi, and N. Bercovich (2000), 'Sistemas nacionales de innovación, procesos de aprendizaje y política tecnológica: una comparación de Canadá y Argentina', *Desarrollo Económico*, **40**(158), 213–52.

Chung, S. (2002), 'Building a national innovation system through regional innovation systems', *Technovation*, **22**, 485–91.

Cimoli, M. (ed.) (2000), *Developing innovation systems: Mexico in the global context*, London: Continuum/Pinter.

Clark, C. (1940), *The conditions of economic progress*, London: Macmillan.

Clark, N., and C. Juma (1987), *Long-run economics: an evolutionary approach to economic change*, London: Pinter.

Cohen, M.D., R. Burkhart, G. Dosi, M. Egidi, L. Marengo, M. Warglien, and S. Winter (1996), 'Routines and other recurring patterns of organisations: contemporary research issues', *Industrial and Corporate Change*, **5**(3), 653–99.

Cohen, W., and D.A. Levinthal (1989), 'Innovation and learning: the two faces of R&D', *Economic Journal*, **99**(397), 569–96.

Cohen, W., and D. Levinthal (1990), 'Absorptive capacity: a new perspective on learning and innovation', *Administrative Science Quarterly*, **35**, 128–52.

Commission of the European Communities (2008), *The concept of clusters and cluster policies and their role for competitiveness and innovation: main statistical results and lessons learned*, Brussels, COM (2008) 652.

Cook, B.J. (1999), 'Egyptian higher education: inconsistent cognition', PhD thesis, Faculty of Oriental Studies, University of Oxford.

Cooke, P. (1992), 'Regional innovation systems: competitive regulation in the new Europe', *Geoforum*, **23**, 365–92.

Cooke, P. (1996), 'Regional innovation systems: an evolutionary approach', in H. Baraczyk, P. Cooke, and R. Heidenreich (eds), *Regional innovation systems*, London: University of London Press.

Cooke, P. (2001), 'Regional innovation systems, clusters and the knowledge economy', *Industrial and Corporate Change*, **10**(4), 945–74.

Cooke, P., M. Gomez Uranga, and G. Etxebarria (1997), 'Regional innovation systems: institutional and organizational dimensions', *Research Policy*, **26**, 475–91.

Cooke, P., and K. Morgan (1998), *The associational economy: firms, regions and innovation*, Oxford: Oxford University Press.

Cororaton, C.B. (1999), 'R&D gaps in the Philippines', *Journal of Philippine Development*, **4826**(2), 47–66.

Correa, C. (1998), 'Argentina's national system of innovation', *International Journal of Technology Management*, **15**(6–7), 721–60.

Cowen, T. (ed.) (1988), *The theory of market failure*, Fairfax, VA: George Mason University Press.

Crawford, S. and E. Ostrom (1995), 'A grammar of institutions', *American Political Science Review*, **89**(3), 582–600.

Crow, M., and B. Bozeman (1998), *Limited by design: U.S. laboratories in the national innovation system*, New York: Columbia University Press.

Cummings, B. (1984), 'The origins and development of the Northeast Asian political economy: industrial sectors, product cycles and political consequences', *International Organization*, **38**(1), 1–40.

Czarnitzki, D., P. Hanel, and J. Rosa (2004), *Evaluating the impact of R&D tax credits on innovation: a micro-econometric study of Canadian firms*, Centre for European Economic Research, Discussion Paper 04–77.

David, P. (2000), 'Path dependence, its critics and the search for historical economics', in P. Garrouste and S. Ioannides (eds), *Evolution and path dependence in economic ideas*, Cheltenham, UK, Edward Elgar Publishing.

David, P.A. (1993), 'Intellectual property institutions and the panda's thumb: patents, copyrights and trade secrets in economic theory and history', in M. Wallerstein, M. Mogee, and R. Schoen (eds), *Global dimensions of intellectual property rights in science and technology*, Washington, DC: National Academy Press, pp. 19–61.

David, P.A. (1994), 'Why are institutions the carriers of history? Path dependence and the evolution of conventions, organizations and institutions', *Structural Change and Economic Dynamics*, **5**(2), 205–20.

Davis, J.P., K.M. Eisenhardt, and C.B. Bingham (2007), 'Developing theory through simulation methods', *Academy of Management Review*, **32**(2), 480–99.

DeBresson, C., and X. Hu (1999), 'Identifying clusters of innovative activity: a new approach and toolbox', in OECD, *Boosting innovation: the cluster approach*, Paris, OECD Proceedings.

De Britto, C., and L. de Mello (2006), 'Boosting innovation performance in Brazil', Paris, OECD Working Papers No. 532.

De la Mothe, J., and G. Paquet (eds) (1998), *Local and regional systems of innovation*, Boston, MA: Kluwer.

De la Peña, F. (2006), *National innovation systems, policy frameworks and programs for the Philippines*, Manila: DOST.

Del Monte, A., and E. Papagni (2003), 'R&D and the growth of firms: empirical analysis of a panel of Italian firms', *Research Policy*, **32**, 1003–14.

Deyo, F.C. (1987), *The political economy of the new Asian industrialism*, Ithaca, NY, and London: Cornell University Press.

Diez, M.A. (2001), 'The evaluation of regional innovation and cluster policies: towards a participatory approach', *European Planning Studies*, **9**(7), 907–24.

Dietz, T., E. Ostrom, and P.C. Stern (2003), 'The struggle to govern the commons', *Science*, **302**(5652), 1907–12.

Dobson, I.R., and S. Hölttä (2001), 'The internationalisation of university education: Australia and Finland compared', *Tertiary Education and Management*, **7**, 243–54.

Dohse, D. (2000), 'Technology policy and the regions – the case of the BioRegio contest', *Research Policy*, **29**, 1111–33.

Doloreux, D., and S. Parto (2005), 'Regional innovation systems: current discourse and unresolved issues', *Technovation*, **27**, 133–53.

Dossani, R., and M. Kenney (2002), 'Creating an environment for venture capital in India', *World Development*, **30**(2), 227–53.

Dunning, J.H. (1998), 'Location and the multinational enterprise: a neglected factor?', *Journal of International Business Studies*, **29**(1), 45–66.

Ederer, P. (2006), *Innovation at work: the European human capital index*, Brussels, Lisbon Council.

Edgington, D., and R. Hayter (2000), 'Foreign direct investment and the flying geese model: Japanese electronics firms in the Asia-Pacific', *Environment and Planning A*, **32**, 281–304.

Edquist, C. (1997), 'Systems of innovation approaches   their emergence and characteristics', in C. Edquist (ed.), *Systems of innovation*, London: Pinter, 1–35.

Edquist, C. (2005), 'Systems of innovation', in J. Fagerberg, D.C. Mowery, and R.R. Nelson (eds), *The Oxford Handbook of Innovation*, Oxford: Oxford University Press, pp. 181–208.

Engelstoft, S., C. Jensen-Butler, I. Smith, and L. Winther (2006), 'Industrial clusters in Denmark: theory and empirical evidence', *Papers in Regional Science*, **85**(1), 73–97.

Enright, M.-J., and B.H. Roberts (2001), 'Regional clustering in Australia', *Australian Journal of Management*, **26**, 65–84.

Ergas, H. (1987), 'The importance of technology policy', in P. Dasgupta and P. Stoneman (eds), *Economic policy and technological performance*, Cambridge: Cambridge University Press, pp. 51–96.

Eriksson, S. (1995), 'Global shift in the aircraft industry', PhD thesis, Gothenburg University.

European Commission (1992, 1996, 2001), *Community innovation survey*, Brussels.

Fagerberg, J., and M. Godinho (2003), 'Innovation and catching up', in J. Fagerberg, D.C. Mowery, and R.R. Nelson (eds), *The Oxford handbook of innovation*, Oxford: Oxford University Press, 514–42.

Fagerberg, J., and M. Srholec (2005), 'Catching up: what are the critical factors for success?', Oslo: Background paper for the UNIDO World Industrial Development Report 2005.

Falk, M. (2004), 'What drives business R&D intensity across OECD countries?', Presentation to DRUID, Aalborg University.

Falk, M. (2007), 'What determines patents per capita in OECD countries?', *Problems and Perspectives in Management*, **5**(2), 4–18.

Feldman, E. (1985), *Concorde and dissent: explaining high-technology failures in Britain and France*, Cambridge: Cambridge University Press.

Feldman, M. (2003), 'The locational dynamics of the U.S. biotech industry: knowledge externalities and the anchor tenant hypothesis', *Industry and Innovation*, **10**(3), 311–28.

Feldman, M., and D. Audretsch (1999), 'Innovation in cities: science-based diversity, specialization and localized competition', *European Economic Review*, **43**, 409–29.

Feldman, M., and J. Francis (2003), 'Fortune favours the prepared region: the case of entrepreneurship and the capital region biotechnology cluster', *European Planning Studies*, **11**(7), 765–88.

Feller, I. (1999), 'The American university system as performer of basic and applied research', in L.M. Branscomb, F. Kodama, and R. Florida (eds), *Industrializing knowledge: university–industry linkages in Japan and the United States*, Boston, MA: MIT Press, pp. 65–101.

Finland (2003), *Knowledge, innovation and internationalization*, Helsinki: Science and Technology Council of Finland.

Finland Ministry of Education (2005), *OECD thematic review of tertiary education: country background report for Finland*, Helsinki.

Finlay, M.R. (1988), 'The German agricultural experimental stations and the beginnings of American agricultural research in the United States: past, present and future', *Agricultural History*, **62**(2), 41–50.

Fischer, M.M. (ed.) (2001), *Knowledge, complexity and innovation systems*, New York: Springer Verlag.

Fischer, M.M. (ed.) (2002), *Regional development reconsidered*, New York: Springer Verlag.

Fogel, R.W. (1990), *The conquest of high mortality and hunger in Europe and America: timing and mechanisms*, Cambridge, MA, NBER Working Paper Series on Historical Factors in Long-Run Growth, WP 16.

Fogel, R.W. (1999), 'Catching-up with the economy', *American Economic Review*, **89**(1), 1–21.

Foray, D. (2003), 'Higher education and universities in the knowledge economy of the industrialised world: a general framework', UNESCO Higher Education Forum, Paris.

Forrester, J. (1971), *World dynamics*, Cambridge: Wright Allen.

Frank, L. (2001), 'A biotech gambit in the desert', *Science*, **292**(5521), 1478.

Frantzen, D. (2000), 'R&D, human capital and international technology spillovers: a cross-country analysis', *Scandinavian Journal of Economics*, **102**(1), 57–75.

Freeman, C. (1987), *Technology policy and economic performance*, London: Pinter.

Freeman, C. (1988), 'Japan: a new national system of innovation?' in G. Dosi et al. (eds), *Technical change and economic theory*, London: Pinter, pp. 330–48.

Freeman, C. (1995), 'The national system of innovation in historical perspective', *Cambridge Journal of Economics*, **19**(1), 5–24.

Freeman, C. (1996), 'Catching-up and falling behind: the case of Asia and Latin America', in J. de la Mothe and G. Paquet (eds), *Evolutionary economics and the new international political economy*, London: Pinter, pp. 160–79.

Freeman, C. (2002), 'Continental, national and sub-national innovation systems – complementarity and economic growth', *Research Policy*, **31**, 191–231.

Frenken, K. (2006a), *Innovation, evolution and complexity theory*, Cheltenham, UK, Edward Elgar Publishing.

Frenken, K. (2006b), 'Technological innovation and complexity theory', *Economics of Innovation and New Technology*, **15**(2), 137–55.

Galli, R., and M. Teubal (1997), 'Paradigmatic shifts in national innovation systems', in C. Edquist (ed.), *Systems of innovation, technologies, institutions and organizations*, London: Pinter, 342–70.

Georghiou, L. (1997), 'Issues in the evaluation of innovation and technology policy', in OECD, *International conference on policy evaluation in innovation and technology*, Paris, Chapter 3.

Georgia Research Alliance (2007), *Annual report*, Atlanta.

Gil Valdivia, G., and S. Chacon Domínguez (2008), *La crisis del petróleo en México*, México, Foro Consultivo en Ciencia y Tecnología.

Glasmeier, A.K. (2000), 'Economic geography in practice: local economic development policy', in G.L. Clark et al. (eds), *The Oxford Handbook of Economic Geography*, Oxford: Oxford University Press, pp. 559–79.

Goh, A.L.S. (2005), 'Promoting innovation in aid of industrial development: the Singaporean experience', *International Journal of Public Sector Management*, **18**(3), 216–40.

Goldstein, A., and S. McGuire (2004), 'The political economy of strategic trade policy and the Brazil–Canada export subsidies saga', *World Economy*, **27**(4), 541–66.

Gonda, K., and F. Kakizaki (2001), 'Knowledge transfer in agglomerations: a regional approach to Japanese manufacturing clusters', in OECD, *Innovative clusters: drivers of national innovation systems*, Paris, 289–302.

Goodman, E. (1989), 'Introduction', in E. Goodman and J. Bamford (eds), *Small firms and industrial districts in Italy*, London: Routledge, 1–30.

Griliches, Z. (1997), 'Education, human capital and growth: a personal perspective', *Journal of Labour Economics*, **15**(1), S330–S344.

Guellec, D., and B. Van Pottelsberghe (2003), 'The impact of public R&D expenditure on business R&D', *Economics of Innovation and New Technology*, **12**(3), 225–43.

Gylfason, T. (2001), 'Natural resources, education and economic development', *European Economic Review*, **45**, 847–59.

Gylfason, T., and G. Zoega (2006), 'Natural resources and economic growth: the role of investment', *World Economy*, **29**(8), 1091–1116.

Hall, B. (1992), *R&D tax policy during the eighties: success or failure?*, Cambridge, MA: National Bureau of Economic Research, Working Paper 4240.

Hall, B. (2002), 'The financing of research and development', *Oxford Review of Economic Policy*, **18**(1), 35–52.

Hall, B., and J. Van Reenen (2000), 'How effective are fiscal incentives for R&D? A review of the evidence', *Research Policy*, 449–69.

Han, M.-Y. (1999), *From rice paddles to flat panel displays: an annotated chronology of Korea's science and technology*, Duke University, available at www.duke.edu/~myhan/kaf0401.html

Harris, J.-R. (1998), *Industrial espionage and technology transfer: Britain and France in the 18th century*, Aldershot, UK: Ashgate.

Hayek, F. (1973), *Law, legislation and liberty*, Vol. 1, London: Routledge.

Hays, S.P. (1996), 'Patterns of reinvention: the nature of evolution during policy diffusion', *Policy Studies Journal*, **24**(4), 551–66.

Hellman, J., and D. Kaufman (2001), 'Confronting the challenge of state capture in transition economies', *Finance and Development*, **38**(3) (IMF quarterly electronic magazine).

Hirschman, A. (1968), 'The political economy of import substituting industrialisation in Latin America', *Quarterly Journal of Economics*, **82**(1), 1–32.

Hodgson, G. (1993a), *Economics and evolution*, Ann Arbor: University of Michigan Press.

Hodgson, G. (ed.) (1993b), *Evolution and institutions*, Cheltenham, UK, Edward Elgar Publishing.

Hodgson, G. (1999), *Evolution and economics*, Cheltenham, UK, Edward Elgar Publishing.

Hodgson, G. (2001), *How economics forgot history: the problem of historical specificity in social science*, London: Routledge.

Hodgson, G. (2009), 'On the institutional foundations of law: the insufficient foundations of custom and private order', *Journal of Economic Issues*, **43**(1), 143–67.

Holland, S. (ed.) (1972), *The State as Entrepreneur. New Dimensions for Public Enterprise: the IRI State Shareholding Formula*, White Plains, NY: International Arts and Sciences Press.

Hollanders, H. (2006), *European regional innovation scoreboard (2006 RIS)*, Maastricht, Netherlands, MERIT.

Hong Kong University of Science and Technology (2002), *Changing education profile of Singapore population*, Conference on Chinese Population and Socio-economic Studies.

Honkapohja, S., and E. Koskela (1999), 'The economic crisis of the 1990's in Finland', *Economic Policy*, (14), 399–426.

Horgan, J. (1995), 'From complexity to perplexity', *Scientific American*, June, 104–9.

Howells, J. (1999), 'Regional systems of innovation', in D. Archibugi, J. Howells, and J. Michie (eds), *Innovation policy in a global economy*, Cambridge: Cambridge University Press, 67–93.

Hu, T.S., C.Y. Lin, and S.-L. Chang (2005), 'Technology-based regional development strategies and the emergence of regional communities: a case study of HSIP, Taiwan', *Technovation*, **25**, 367–80.

Hung, S.C., and Y.Y. Chu (2006), 'Stimulating new industries from emerging technologies: challenges for the public sector', *Technovation*, **26**, 104–10.

Inocentes, A. (2006), *The future of higher education in the Philippines: a presentation to the Asia–Pacific Forum on Education*, Beijing, November 14–17.

Invest Korea (2006), *R&D human resource development program*, Seoul.

Islam, N. (2003), 'What have we learnt from the convergence debate?', *Journal of Economic Surveys*, **17**(3), 309–63.

Jaffe, A., M. Trajtenberg, and R. Henderson (1993), 'Geographic localisation of knowledge spillovers as evidenced by patents', *Quarterly Journal of Economics*, **108**(3), 577–98.

Jaffe, A.-B. (2002), 'Building policy evaluation into the design of public research support programmes', *Oxford Review of Economic Policy*, **18**(1), 22–35.

Jain, A.K. (2001), 'Corruption: a review', *Journal of Economic Surveys*, **15**(1), 71–121.

James, E. (1991), 'Private higher education: the Philippines as a prototype', *Higher Education*, **21**, 189–206.

Jan, T.-S., and Y. Chen (2006), 'The R&D system for industrial development in Taiwan', *Technological Forecasting and Social Change*, **73**, 559–74.

Jankowski, J. (2001), 'A brief data-informed history of science and technology policy', in M.P. Feldman and A.N. Link (eds), *Innovation policy in the knowledge-based economy*, Boston, MA: Kluwer, 5–36.

Janszen, F.H., and G.H. Degenaars (1998), 'A dynamic simulation model between the structure and the process of national systems of innovation using computer simulation: the case of Dutch biotechnology', *Research Policy*, **27**, 37–54.

Japan, METI (2008), *Industrial cluster project*, Tokyo.

Jauhlainen, J.S. (2008), 'Regional and innovation policies in Finland – towards convergence and/or mismatch?' *Regional Studies*, **42**(7), 1–15.

Jensen, B.E. (2004), 'Clustering in Denmark and Danish cluster policy', Paper for the Nordic Cluster Gathering, August 15–16.

Jéquier, N. (1974), 'Computers,' in R. Vernon (ed.), *Big business and the state*, Cambridge, MA: Harvard University Press, 195–254.

Johnson, C. (1982), *MITI and the Japanese miracle. The growth of industrial policy, 1925–1975*, Tokyo: Tuttle & Co.

JTC (Jurong Town) Corporation (2007), *Biopolis @ one north*, Singapore.

Kaldor, N. (1970), 'The case for regional policies', *Scottish Journal of Political Economy*, **17**(3), 337–48.

Kasahara, S. (2004), *The flying geese paradigm: a critical study of its application in Asian regional development*, Vienna, UNCTAD Discussion Paper No. 169.

Katz, J. (2000), 'The dynamics of technological learning during the import substitution period and recent structural changes in the industrial sector in Argentina, Brazil and Mexico', in L. Kim and R.R. Nelson (eds), *Technology, learning and innovation*, Cambridge: Cambridge University Press, 307–34.

Katz, J., and C. Contreras (2009), *The dynamics of university behaviour in Chile*, Intelis and Department of Economics, University of Chile, Santiago.

Kelly, D., and T.-L. Amburgey (1991), 'Organizational inertia and momentum: a dynamic model of strategic change', *Academy of Management Journal*, **34**(3), 591–612.

Kim, L. (1997a), 'Technology policies and strategies for developing countries: lessons from Korea', *Technology Analysis and Strategic Management*, **10**(3), 311–24.

Kim, L. (1997b), *Imitation to innovation: the dynamics of Korea's technological learning*, Boston, MA: Harvard Business School Press.

Kim, L., and R.R. Nelson (eds) (2000), *Technology, learning and innovation: experiences of newly industrialized economies*, Cambridge: Cambridge University Press.

King, E., and M.A. Hill (1993), *Women's education in developing countries, barriers, benefits and policies*, Baltimore: Johns Hopkins University Press, World Bank Book.

Klaasen, G., A. Miketa, K. Larsen, and T. Sundqvist (2005), 'The impact of R&D on innovation for wind energy in Denmark, Germany, and the U.K.', *Ecological Economics*, **54**(1–3), 227–40.

Klepper, S. (1997), 'Industry life cycles', *Industrial and Corporate Change*, **6**(1), 145–81.

Klepper, S. (2005), 'Entry by spin-offs', *Management Science*, **51**(8), 1291–1306.

Klepper, S. (2007), 'Disagreements, spin-offs and the evolution of Detroit as the capital of the U.S. automobile industry', *Management Science*, **53**(4), 616–31.

Knack, S. (1996), 'Institutions and the convergence hypothesis: the cross-national evidence', *Public Choice* **87**, 207–28.

Kneller, R., and P. Stevens (2006), 'Frontier technology and absorptive capacity: evidence from OECD manufacturing industries', *Oxford Bulletin of Economics and Statistics*, **68**(1), 1–21.

Koenig, R. (2007), 'Egypt plans a shakeup of research programs', *Science*, **317**(5834), 30.

Kohtamäki, V., and A. Lyytinen (2004), 'Financial autonomy and challenges to being a regionally responsive higher education institution', *Tertiary Education and Management*, **10**, 319–38.

Kotilainen, H. (2005), *Implementation of the innovation policy: lessons from Finland*, Presentation to the meeting Linkages between Higher Education, Research and the Business Sector, Riga, Latvia.

Krueger, A.B., and M. Lindhal (2001), 'Education for growth: why and for whom?', *Journal of Economic Literature*, **39**(4), 1101–36.

Krugman, P. (1983), 'New theories of trade among industrial countries', *American Economic Review*, **73**(2), 343–7.

Krugman, P. (1991), *Geography and trade*, Cambridge, MA, MIT Press.

Krugman, P. (1994), 'Competitiveness: a dangerous obsession', *Foreign Affairs*, **73**(2), 29–44.

Kuhlmann, S. (1997), 'Evaluation as a medium of science and technology policy: recent developments in Germany and beyond', in OECD, *International conference on policy evaluation in innovation and technology*, Paris, Chapter 25.

Kumagai, S. (2008), 'A journey through the secret history of the flying geese model', IDE Discussion Paper, JETRO, Chiba, Japan.

Kumar, N. (2003), 'Intellectual property rights, technology and economic development', *Economic and Political Weekly*, **38**(3), 209–15 and 217–26.

Kuran, T. (1997), 'Islam and underdevelopment: an old puzzle revisited', *Journal of Institutional and Theoretical Economics*, **153**, 41–72.

Kuran, T. (2004), 'Why the Middle East is economically underdeveloped: historical mechanisms of institutional stagnation', *Journal of Economic Behavior and Organization*, **18**, 71–90.

Kushida, K. (2003), 'The political economy of the Philippines under Marcos', *Stanford Journal of East Asian Affairs*, **3**(1), 119–27.

Kwan, C.H. (2002), 'The rise of China and Asia's Flying Geese Pattern of Economic Development: An empirical analysis based on US import statistics', Tokyo: Nomura Research Institute, NRI Paper N. 52.

Lall, S. (2000), 'Technological change and industrialization in the Asian newly industrializing economies: achievements and challenges', in L. Kim and R.R. Nelson (eds), *Technology, learning and innovation: experiences of newly industrializing economies*, Cambridge: Cambridge University Press, 13–68.

Lall, S. (2004), *Reinventing industrial strategy: the role of government policy in building industrial competitiveness*, UNCTAD, Vienna, Discussion Paper Series, No. 24.

Lampinen, O. (2001), 'The use of experimentation in educational reform: the case of the Finnish polytechnic experiment 1992–1999', *Tertiary Education and Management*, **7**, 311–21.

Landes, D. (1969), *The unbound Prometheus: technological change and industrial development in western Europe from 1750 to the present*, Cambridge: Cambridge University Press.

Landes, D. (1972), *The Unbound Prometheus, Technological Change and Industrial Development in Western Europe from 1750 to the Present*, Cambridge, MA: Cambridge University Press.

Landes, D. (1999), *The wealth and poverty of nations: why some are so rich and some are so poor*, New York: Norton.

Lazerson, M., and G. Lorenzoni (1999), 'The firms that feed industrial districts: a return to the Italian source', *Industrial and Corporate Change*, **8**(2), 235–66.

Lazonick, W. (1994), 'Social organization and technological leadership', in W.J. Baumol, R.R. Nelson, and E.N. Wolf (eds), *Convergence of productivity: cross national studies and historical evidence*, Oxford: Oxford University Press, 164–93.

Lee, K., and C. Lim (2001), 'Technological regimes, catching up and leapfrogging: findings from the Korean industries', *Research Policy*, **30**(3), 459–84.

Lee, T.-L., and N. von Tunzelmann (2005), 'A dynamic analytic approach to national innovation systems: the IC industry in Taiwan', *Research Policy*, **34**, 425–40.

Leonard, D. (1996), 'The nature of core capabilities and core rigidities', in *Wellsprings of knowledge: building and sustaining the sources of innovation*, Boston, MA: Harvard Business School Press.

Li, H.-L., L.C. Xu, and H.-F. Zou (2000), 'Corruption, income distribution and growth', *Economics and Politics*, **12**(2), 155–82.

Lipsey, R., and K. Carlaw (1998), 'Technology policies in neo-classical and structuralist-evolutionary models', *STI Review*, **22**, 30–73.

Lipsey, R.G. (2002), 'Some implications of endogenous technical change for technology policy in developing countries', *Economics of Innovation and New Technology*, **11**(4–5), 321–51.

List, F. (1841), *Das Nationale System der politischen öekonomie* (English translation, London, Longmans, Green & Co., 1909).

Liu, J.-T, M.-W. Tsou, and J.K. Hammitt (1999), 'Export activity and productivity: evidence from the Taiwanese electronics industry', *Weltwirschaftliches Archiv*, **135**(4), 675–91.

Liu, X., and S. White (2001), 'Comparing innovation systems: A framework and application to China's transitional context', *Research Policy*, **30**, 1091–1114.

Loasby, B. (1999), *Knowledge, institutions and evolution in economics*, London: Routledge.

Longhi, C. (1999), 'Networks, collective learning and technology development in high-technology regions: the case of Sophia Antipolis', *Regional Studies*, **33**(4), 333–42.

Lorenz, E. (1994), 'Organizational inertia and competitive decline: the British cotton, shipbuilding and car industries, 1945–1975', *Industrial and Corporate Change*, **3**(2), 379–403.

Low, L. (1998), 'Science, technology and the state in Singapore: an overview, evaluation and comparison', *Journal of the Asia–Pacific Economy*, **3**(2), 183–206.

Lundvall, B.-A. (1988), 'Innovation as an interactive process: from user/producer interaction to the national system of innovation', in G. Dosi, C. Freeman, R.R. Nelson, G. Silverberg, and L. Soete (eds), *Technical change and economic theory*, London: Pinter, pp. 349–69.

Lundvall, B.-A. (ed.) (1992), *National innovation systems*, London: Pinter.

MacDonald, N. (1988), 'Henry Kaiser and the establishment of an automobile industry in Argentina', *Business History*, **30**(3), 329–45.

Malerba, F. (2005), 'Sectoral systems of innovation: a framework for linking innovation to the knowledge base, structure and dynamics of sectors', *Economics of Innovation and New Technology*, **14**(1), 63–82.

Malerba, F. (ed.) (2004), *Sectoral systems of innovation*, Cambridge: Cambridge University Press.

Manasan, R., J.S. Cuenca, and E.C. Villanueva Ruiz (2008), *Benefit incidence of public spending on education in the Philippines*, Malaki City: Philippine Institute for Development Studies, Discussion Paper Series 2008-08.

Mansfield, E. (1977), *The production and application of new industrial technology*, New York: Norton.

Marceau, J. (1999), 'The disappearing trick: clusters in the Australian economy', in J. Guinet (ed.), *Boosting innovation: the cluster approach*, OECD, Paris, 155–76.

March, J., and H. Simon (1993), *Organizations*, 2nd ed., Cambridge, MA: Blackwell.

Markusen, A. (1996), 'Sticky places in slippery space: a typology of industrial districts', *Economic Geography*, **72**(3), 293–313.

Marshall, A. (1920), *Principles of economics*, 8th ed., London: Macmillan.

Marshall, A. (2004), *Labour market policies and regulations in Argentina, Brazil and Mexico: programmes and impacts*, Buenos Aires, CONACYT and IDES, WP 2004/13, prepared for the ILO.

Martin, R., and P. Sunley (2003), 'Deconstructing clusters: chaotic concept or policy panacea', *Journal of Economic Geography*, **3**, 5–35.

Maskell, P., and A. Malmberg (2007), 'Myopia, knowledge development and cluster evolution', *Journal of Economic Geography*, **7**(5), 603–19.

Mauro, P. (1997), *Why worry about corruption?* Washington, DC: IMF Economic Issues.

Mauro, P. (2004), 'The persistence of corruption and slow economic growth', *IMF Staff Papers*, **51**(1) (electronic document).

Mayer, D. (2001), 'The long-term impact of health on economic growth in Latin America', *World Development*, **29**(6), 1025–33.

Mazzoleni, R. (2008), 'Catching up and academic institutions: a comparative study of past national experiences', *Journal of Development Studies*, **44**(5), 678–700.

McKelvey, M. (1991), 'How do national systems of innovation differ? A critical analysis of Porter, Freeman, Lundvall and Nelson', in G. Hodgson and E. Screpanti (eds), *Rethinking economics*, Cheltenham, UK, Edward Elgar Publishing, 117–37.

McKelvey, M. (1997), 'Using evolutionary theory to define systems of innovation', in C. Edquist (ed.), *Systems of innovation*, London: Pinter, 200–22.

Menzel, M.P., and D. Fornahl (2007), *Cluster life cycles – dimensions and rationales of cluster development*, Jena, Jena Economic Research Papers 2007, No. 006.

Metcalfe, J.S. (1995), 'Technology systems and technology policy in an evolutionary framework', *Cambridge Journal of Economics*, **19**, 25–46.

Metcalfe, J.S., and L. Georghiu (1997), *Equilibrium and evolutionary foundations of technology policy*, Manchester, CRIC Discussion Paper No. 3.

Mexico, Foro consultivo científico y tecnológico (2006a), *Diagnóstico de la política científica, tecnológica y de innovación en México, (2000–2006)*, Mexico DF.

Mexico, Foro consultivo científico y tecnológico (2006b), *Proyecto: bases para una política de estado en ciencia, tecnología e innovación en México*, Mexico DF.

Mexico, Foro consultivo científico y tecnológico (2008), *Promoviendo la innovación y el desarrollo tecnológico*, Mexico DF.

Mitchell, W. (1991), 'Dual clocks: entry order influences on incumbent and newcomer market share and survival when specialized assets retain their value', *Strategic Management Journal*, **12**(2), 85–100.

Mo, P.H. (2001), 'Corruption and economic growth', *Journal of Comparative Economics*, **29**, 66–79.

Mohnen, P., and L.H. Röller (2005), 'Complementarities in innovation policy', *European Economic Review*, **49**, 1431–50.

Mokyr, J. (1990), *The lever of riches: technological creativity and economic progress*, Oxford: Oxford University Press.

Motohashi, K., and X. Yun (2007), 'China's innovation system reform and growing industry and science linkages', *Research Policy* **36**(8), 1251–1260.

Moulaison, H.L. (2004), 'Minitel and France's legacy of democratic information access', *Government Information Quarterly*, **21**(91), 99–107.

Mowery, D. (1998), 'The changing structure of the U.S. national innovation system: implications for international conflict and cooperation in R&D policy', *Research Policy*, **27**(6), 639–54.

Mowery, D., and N. Rosenberg (1989), *Technology and the pursuit of economic growth*, Cambridge: Cambridge University Press.

Mowery, D. (ed.) (1996), *The international computer software industry*, Oxford: Oxford University Press.

Mowery, D., and R. Nelson (eds) (1999), *Sources of Industrial Leadership*, Cambridge, MA: Cambridge University Press.

Murto, E., M. Niemelä, and T. Laamanen (2006), *Finnish technology policy from the 1960s to the present day*, Helsinki, Ministry of Trade and Industry.

Myrdal, G. (1957), *Economic theory and underdeveloped regions*, London: Duckworth.

Mytelka, L., and K. Smith (2002), 'Policy learning and innovation theory: an interactive and co-evolving process', *Research Policy*, **31**, 1467–79.

National Science Foundation (NSF) (2006), *Science and Engineering indicators*. Washington, DC.

National Science Foundation (NSF) (2008), *Science and engineering indicators*, Washington, DC.

Neale, W.C. (1994), 'Institutions', in G.H. Hodgson, W. Samuels, and M.R. Tool (eds), *The Elgar companion to institutional and evolutionary economics*, Cheltenham, UK, Edward Elgar Publishing, 402–6.

Neill, R. (1999), 'Francis Bacon, John Rae and the economics of competitiveness: capital theory and trade policy', *American Journal of Economics and Sociology*, **58**(3), 385–98.

Nelson, R.-R. (1983), 'Government support of technical progress: lessons from history', *Journal of Policy Analysis and Management*, **2**(4), 499–514.

Nelson, R.-R. (1988), 'Institutions supporting technical change in the United States', in G. Dosi et al. (eds), *Technical change and economic theory*, London: Pinter, 312–329.

Nelson, R.R. (1994a), 'The co-evolution of technology, industrial structure and institutions', *Industrial and Corporate Change*, 3(1), 47–63.

Nelson, R.R. (1994b), 'Why do firms differ and how does it matter?' in R.P. Rumelt, D. Schendel, and D.J. Teece (eds), *Fundamental issues in strategy*, Boston, MA: Harvard Business School Press, 247–69.

Nelson, R.R. (1995), 'Recent evolutionary theorizing about economic change', *Journal of Economic Literature*, 33(1), 48–90.

Nelson, R.R. (2003), *Physical and social technologies and their evolution*, Pisa, Sant'Anna School of Advanced Studies, LEM Working Paper Series, 2003/09.

Nelson, R.R. (2005a), *Technology, institutions and economic growth*, Cambridge, MA: Harvard University Press.

Nelson, R.R., and E.S. Phelps (1966), 'Investment in humans, technological diffusion and economic growth', *American Economic Review Proceedings*, 56, 69–75.

Nelson, R.R., and N. Rosenberg (1994), 'American universities and technical advance in industry', *Research Policy*, 23(3), 323–48.

Nelson, R.R., and B. Sampat (2001), 'Making sense of institutions as a factor shaping economic performance', *Journal of Economic Behavior and Organization*, 44, 31–54.

Nelson, R.R., and S. Winter (1982), *An evolutionary theory of economic change*, Cambridge, MA: Belknap Press of Harvard University Press.

Nelson, R.R. (ed.) (1993), *National innovation systems*, New York: Oxford University Press.

Nelson, R.R. (ed.) (2005b), *The limits of market organization*, New York: Russell Sage Foundation.

Niosi, J. (1999), 'The diffusion of organizational routines', in J. Groenewegen et al. (eds), *Institutions and the evolution of capitalism*, Cheltenham, UK, Edward Elgar Publishing, pp. 109–22.

Niosi, J. (2000a), *Canada's national system of innovation*, Montreal: McGill-Queen's University Press.

Niosi, J. (2000b), 'Science-based industries: a new Schumpeterian taxonomy', *Technology in Society*, 22(3), 429–44.

Niosi, J. (2001), *Regional systems of innovation: an evolutionary approach*, Presentation to the Annual Congress of EAEPE, Sienna, Nov. 8–11.

Niosi, J. (2002), 'National systems of innovation are x-efficient (and x-effective): why some are slow learners', *Research Policy*, 31(2), 291–302.

Niosi, J. (2003), 'Alliances are not enough: explaining rapid growth in Canadian biotechnology', *Research Policy*, 32(5), 737–50.

Niosi, J. (2005), *Canada's regional innovation systems: the science-based industries*, Montreal: McGill-Queen's University Press.

Niosi, J., and M. Banik (2005), 'The evolution and performance of bio-technology regional systems of innovation', *Cambridge Journal of Economics*, **29**, 343–57.

Niosi, J., and T.G. Bas (2001), 'The competencies of regions: Canada's clusters in biotechnology', *Small Business Economics*, **17**, 31–42.

Niosi, J., and T.G. Bas (2004), 'Canadian biotechnology policy: designer incentives for a new technology', *Environment and Planning*, C, **22**(2), 233–48.

Niosi, J., and B. Bellon (1994), 'The global interdependence of national innovation systems: evidence, limits and implications', *Technology in Society*, **16**(2), 173–98.

Niosi, J., B. Bellon, P.P. Saviotti, and M. Crow (1993), 'National systems of innovation: in search of a workable concept', *Technology in Society*, **15**(2), 207–27.

Niosi, J., and M. Bourassa (2008), 'L'innovation dans les villes cana-diennes', in Institut de la Statistique du Québec: *Compendium 2008*, Québec City, 47–56.

Niosi, J., and S. Reid (2007), 'Biotechnology and nanotechnology: science-based industries as windows of opportunity for developing countries?' *World Development*, **36**(3), 426–38.

Niosi, J., and T. Tschang (2009), 'The strategies of Chinese and Indian software multinationals: implications for internationalisation theory', *Industrial and Corporate Change*, **18**(2), 269–94.

North, D. (1981), *Structure and change in economic history*, New York: Norton.

North, D. (1990), *Institutions, institutional change and economic perform-ance*, Cambridge: Cambridge University Press.

North, D. (1993), *The new institutional economics and development*, St Louis, MO: Washington University Working Paper.

North Carolina Board of Science and Technology (2000), *High-tech clus-ters in North Carolina*, Raleigh.

Noteboom, B. (1997), 'Path dependence of knowledge: implications for the theory of the firm', in L. Magnusson and J. Ottosson (eds), *Evolutionary economics and path dependence*, Cheltenham, UK, Edward Elgar Publishing, 57–78.

Nye, J.V. (1991), 'The myth of free trade Britain and fortress France: tariffs and trade in the 19th century', *Journal of Economic History*, **51**(1), 23–46.

Odagiri, H. (1999), 'University–industry collaboration in Japan: facts and interpretation', in L.M. Branscomb, F. Kodama, and R. Florida (eds), *Industrializing knowledge: university – industry linkages in Japan and the United States*, Boston, MA: MIT Press, 252–65.

Odagiri, H., and A. Goto (1996), *Technology and industrial development in Japan*, New York: Oxford University Press.

Okimoto, D. (1989), *Between MITI and the market: Japanese industrial policy for high technology*, Stanford, CA: Stanford University Press.

OECD (1997a), *International conference on policy evaluation in innovation and technology*, Paris.

OECD (1997b), *National innovation systems*, Paris.

OECD (1999a), *Boosting innovation: the cluster approach*, Paris, OECD Proceedings.

OECD (1999b), *Managing national innovation systems*, Paris.

OECD (2001), *Innovative clusters: drivers of national innovation systems*, Paris.

OECD (2002), *Science, technology and industry outlook*, Paris.

OECD (2006a), *Innovation in energy technology: comparing national systems at the sectoral level*, Paris.

OECD (2006b), *Innovation in pharmaceutical biotechnology: comparing national systems at the sectoral level*, Paris.

OECD (2006c), *Science, technology and industry outlook 2006*, Paris.

OECD (2007a), *Competitive regional clusters: national policy approaches*, Paris.

OECD (2007b), *Globalization and the regional economies*, Paris.

OECD (2007c), *Main science and technology indicators*, Paris.

OECD (2007d), *The regional dimension of innovation*, Paris, GOV/TDPC (2007) 20.

OECD (2007e), *STI outlook 2007*, Paris.

OECD (2008), *Main science and technology indicators*, Paris.

O'Rourke, K. (2000), 'Tariffs and growth in the late 19th century', *Economic Journal*, **110**, 456–83.

Osman-Gani, A. (2004), 'Human capital development in Singapore: an analysis of national policy perspectives', *Advances in Developing Human Resources*, **6**(3), 276–87.

Ozawa, T. (2001), *The 'hidden' side of the 'flying geese' catch-up model: Japan's dirigiste institutional setup and a deepening financial morass*, University of Colorado at Fort Collins, Department of Economics Discussion Paper.

Ozawa, T. (2002), 'Pax-Americana led macro-clustering and flying-geese style catch-up in East Asia: mechanisms of regionalized endogenous growth', University of Colorado at Fort Collins, Department of Economics Discussion Paper.

Papaconstantinou, G., and W. Polt (1997), 'Policy evaluation in innovation and technology: an overview', in OECD, *International conference on policy evaluation in innovation and technology*, Paris, Chapter 1.

Parayil, G. (2005), 'From "Silicon Island" to "Biopolis of Asia": innovation policy and shifting competitive strategy in Singapore', *California Management Review*, **47**(2), 50–73.

Patalinghug, E. (2000), 'Competition policy, technology policy and Philippine industrial competitiveness', *Social Science Diliman*, **1**(1), 31–59.

Patalinghug, E. (2003), *The Philippine national innovation system: structure and characteristics*, Makati City, Philippine Institute for Development Studies, Discussion Paper Series 2003–04.

Patel, P., and K. Pavitt (1994), 'National innovation systems: why they are important, and how they might be measured and compared', *Economics of Innovation and New Technology*, **3**(2), 77–95.

Pavcnik, N. (2002), 'Trade disputes in commercial aircraft', *World Economy*, **25**(5), 733–51.

Pavitt, K., and P. Patel (1999), 'Global corporations and national systems of innovation', in D. Archibugi, J. Howells, and J. Michie (eds), *Innovation policy in a global economy*, Cambridge: Cambridge University Press, pp. 94–119.

Peled, D. (2001), *Defense R&D and economic growth in Israel: a research agenda*, Haifa, Technion Institute of Technology, Samuel Neaman Institute for Advanced Research in Science and Technology.

Pellerin, C. (2007), 'U.S. Navy scientists share research benefits with the world', January 29. www.america.gov/st/washfile-english/2007/January

Pentikäinen, T. (2000), *Economic evaluation of the Finnish cluster programmes*, Working Paper 50/00, VTT, Group of Technology Studies, Espoo.

Perez, C., and L. Soete (1988), 'Catching up in technology: entry barriers and windows of opportunity', in G. Dosi, C. Freeman, G. Siverberg, and L. Soete (eds), *Technical change and economic theory*, London: Pinter, 458–79.

Perroux, F. (1970), 'Note on the concept of growth pole', in D. McKee, R. Dean, and D. Leathy (eds), *Regional economics: theory and practice*, New York: Free Press, 93–103.

Pianta, M., and G. Sirilli (1997), 'The use of innovation surveys for policy evaluation in Italy', in OECD, *International conference on policy evaluation in innovation and technology*, Paris, Chapter 19.

Pietrobelli, C., and R. Rabellotti (2004), *Upgrading clusters in Latin America: the role of policies*, Washington, DC: Inter-American Development Bank.

Piore, M., and C. Sabel (1984), *The second industrial divide: possibilities for prosperity*, New York: Basic Books.

Pisano, G. (2006), *Science business: the promise, the reality and the future of biotech*, Boston, MA: Harvard Business School Press.

Platt, D.C.M., and G. Di Tella (eds) (1985), *Argentina, Australia and Canada: studies in comparative development, 1870–1965*, Cambridge, MA: Cambridge University Press.

Porter, M. (1998), *On competition*, Cambridge, MA: Harvard Business School Press.

Porter, M. (2000), 'Location, clusters and company strategy', in G.L. Clark, M.P. Feldman, and M.S. Gertler (eds), *The Oxford handbook of economic geography*, New York: Oxford University Press, 253–74.

Porter, M., Monitor Group, on the Frontier and Council on Competitiveness (2001), *Clusters of innovation: regional foundations of U.S. competitiveness*, Washington, DC, Council on Competitiveness.

Porter, M., and H. Takeuchi (1999), 'Fixing what really ails Japan', *Foreign Affairs*, **78**(3), 66–79.

Prebisch, R. (1950a), *The economic development of Latin America and its principal problems*, New York: United Nations.

Prebisch, R. (1950b), *Theoretical and Practical Problems of Economic Growth, Mexico*, UNCTAD (United Nations Commerce, Trade and Development Organization).

Rasiah, R., X. Kong, and Y. Lin (2008), 'Semiconductors: explaining variations in catch up strategies in Malaysia, China and Taiwan', in F. Malerba and R. Nelson (eds), *Catching-up* (forthcoming).

Reinert, E. (2007), *How rich countries got rich and why poor countries stay poor*, New York, Public Affairs.

Research Triangle Region Task Force (2004), *Staying on top: a competitiveness plan for the Research Triangle Region*, Raleigh, North Carolina.

Richards, A. (1992), *Higher education in Egypt*, Washington, DC, World Bank Population and Human Resource Department Working Paper Series, WPS 862.

Roberts, B., and M.J. Enright (2004), 'Industry clusters in Australia: recent trends and prospects', *European Planning Studies*, **12**(1), 99–121.

Rodriguez, E. (1998), 'International migration and income distribution in the Philippines', *Economic Development and Cultural Change*, **46**, 329–50.

Rodriguez-Clare, A. (2001), 'Costa Rica's development strategy based on human capital and technology: how it got there, the impact of Intel and lessons for other countries', *Journal of Human Development*, **2**(2), 311–24.

Roeland, T., and P. den Hertog (1999), 'Cluster analysis and cluster-based policy making: the state of the art', in OECD, *Boosting innovation: the cluster approach*, Paris, OECD Proceedings, 413–525.

Romer, P. (1986), 'Increasing returns and long run growth', *Journal of Political Economy*, **94**(5), 1002–37.

Romer, P. (1990), 'Endogenous technological change', *Journal of Political Economy*, **98**(5), S71–S102.

Rosenberg, N. (1994), *Exploring the black box: technology, economics, and history*, Cambridge: Cambridge University Press.

Rosenberg, N. (2000), *Schumpeter and the endogeneity of technology*, London: Routledge.

Rouvinen, P. (2006), *Advantage Finland: past, present and future*, Presentation to the International Conference on Korea's Industry Vision 2020, Seoul.

Rumbley, L., I. Pacheco, and P.G. Altbach (2008), *International comparison of academic salaries*, Boston College, Center for International Higher Education.

Ruttan, V. (2001), *Technology, growth and development*, Oxford: Oxford University Press.

Sabatier, P. (ed.) (1999), *Theories of the policy process*, Boulder, CO: Westview Press.

Sadik, A.T., and A.A. Bobol (2001), 'Capital flows, FDI and technology spillovers: evidence from the Arab countries', *World Development*, **29**(12), 2111–25.

Sainsbury, Lord (2007), *The race to the top: a review of government's science and innovation policies*, Norwich: Her Majesty's Stationery Office.

Samuels, R.J. (1987), *The business of the Japanese State*, Ithaca, NY, Cornell University Press.

Santisteban, M.A. (2003), 'Las asociaciones cluster en la Comunidad autónoma del País Vasco (1986–2002), tradición, interacción y aprendizaje en la colaboración gobierno-industria,' *Economiaz*, 53.

Santisteban, M.A. (2006), 'Business systems and cluster policies in the Basque country and Catalonia (1990–2004)', *European Urban and Regional Studies*, **13**(1), 25–39.

Saviotti, P.P. (1996), *Technological evolution, variety and the economy*, Cheltenham, UK, Edward Elgar Publishing.

Saviotti, P.P. (1997), 'Innovation systems and evolutionary theories', in C. Edquist (ed.), *Systems of innovation*, London: Pinter, 180–99.

Saviotti, P.P., and A. Pyka (2004), 'Economic development by the creation of new sectors', *Journal of Evolutionary Economics*, **14**, 1–35.

Saxenian, A.L. (2004), 'Taiwan's Hsinchu region', in T. Bresnahan and A. Gambardella (eds), *Building high-tech clusters*, Cambridge: Cambridge University Press, 190–228.

Schellings, R., and F. Gault (2006), *Size and persistence of R&D performance in Canadian firms, 1994 to 2002*, Ottawa, Statistics Canada, Science, Innovation and Electronic Innovation Division, Cat. 88F0006XIE.

Schienstock, G. (2007), 'From path dependency to path creation: Finland on its way to the knowledge-based economy', *Current Sociology*, **55**(10), 92–109.

Schot, J., and F.W. Geels (2007), 'Niches in evolutionary theories of technical change: a critical survey of the theory', *Journal of Evolutionary Economics*, **17**(5), 605–22.

Schumpeter, J. (1934), *The theory of economic development* (1911), Cambridge, MA: Harvard University Press.

Schumpeter, J. (1950), *Capitalism, socialism and democracy* (1942), New York: Harper.

Shapira, P. (2001), 'U.S. manufacturing extension partnerships: technology policy reinvented?' *Research Policy*, **30**, 977–92.

Shevell, S. (2002), 'Law versus morality as regulators of conduct', *American Law and Economics Review*, **4**(2), 227–57.

Sigurdson, J. (2004), *Regional innovation systems in China*, Stockholm, European Institute of Japanese Studies, Working Paper No. 195.

Singapore (2007), *2006 education statistics digest*, Ministry of Education.

Smith, K. (1991), 'Innovation policy in an evolutionary context', in P.P. Saviotti and J.S. Metcalfe (eds), *Evolutionary theories of economic and technological change*, Chur, Switzerland: Harwood Academic Publishers, 256–75.

Solow, R. (1956), 'A contribution to the theory of economic growth', *Quarterly Journal of Economics*, **70**(1), 65–94.

Spitz, P.H. (1988), *Petrochemicals: the rise of an industry*, New York: Wiley.

Statistics Canada (2002), *Profile of spin-off firms in the biotechnology sector: results from biotechnology use and development survey – 1999*, Ottawa, Cat. 88F0006XIE02004.

Sterman, J. (2000), *Business dynamics, systems thinking and modeling for a complex world*, New York: McGraw-Hill.

Stiglitz, J. (1998), 'The private use of public interests', *Journal of Economic Perspectives*, **12**(2), 3–22.

Stiglitz, J. (2002), *Globalization and its discontents*, New York: Norton.

Tassey, G. (1991), 'The functions of technology infrastructure in a competitive economy', *Research Policy*, **20**, 345–61.

Tassey, G. (2001), 'R&D policy models and data needs', in M.P. Feldman and A.N. Link (eds), *Innovation policy in the knowledge-based economy*, Boston, MA: Kluwer, 37–72.

TEDCO (Technology Development Corporation) (2008), *Annual report*, Maryland.

Teixeira, P., and A. Amaral (2001), 'Private higher education and diversity: an exploratory survey', *Higher Education Quarterly*, **55**(4), 359–95.

Temple, J. (2001), 'Growth effects of education and social capital among OECD countries', *OECD Economic Studies*, **33**, 58–101.

Teubal, M. (1996), 'R&D and technology policy in NICs as learning processes', *World Development*, **24**(3), 449–60.

Teubal, M. (1997), 'A catalytic and evolutionary approach to horizontal technology policy', *Research Policy* **25**, 1161–88.

Teubal, M. (1998), 'Policies for promoting enterprise restructuring in national systems of innovation: triggering cumulative learning and generating system effects', Paris, OECD, *STI Review*, **22**, 134–70.

Teubal, M. (2002), 'What is the systems perspective on innovation and technology policy (ITP) and how can we apply it to developing and newly industrialized economies?', *Journal of Evolutionary Economics*, **12**, 233–57.

Texier, F. (2000), *Industrial diversification and innovation: an international study of the aerospace industry*, Cheltenham, UK, Edward Elgar Publishing.

Tödtling, F., and M. Trippl (2005), 'One size fits all? Towards a differentiated regional innovation policy', *Research Policy*, **34**, 1203–19.

Trajtenberg, M. (2001), 'R&D policy in Israel', in M.P. Feldman and A.N. Link (eds), *Innovation policy in the knowledge-based economy*, Boston, MA: Kluwer, 409–54.

Uenohara, M., T. Sugano, J.G. Linvill, and F.B. Weinstein (1984), 'Background', in D.I. Okimoto, T. Sugano, and F.B. Weinstein (eds), *Competitive edge: the semiconductor industry in the U.S. and Japan*, Stanford, CA: Stanford University Press, 9–34.

United Kingdom Department of Trade and Industry (1999a), *Biotechnology Clusters*, London.

United Kingdom Department of Trade and Industry (1999b), *Genome Valley*, London.

United Nations (2004), *Republic of Argentina public administration country profile*, UN Department of Economic and Social Affairs.

United Nations (2006), *Arab human development report*, New York.

United Nations Conference on Trade and Development (UNCTAD) (2007), *World investment report*, Vienna.

United Nations Educational, Scientific and Cultural Organization (UNESCO) (2005a), *Education in perspective 2005*, Paris.

UNESCO (2005b), *Education trends in perspective: analysis of the world education indicators*, Montreal, UNESCO Institute for Statistics.

UNIDO (2003), *Strategies for regional innovation systems: transfer and applications*, Vienna.

United States Department of Justice (2008), *Siemens AG and three subsidiaries plead guilty to Foreign Corrupt Practices Act violations and agree to pay $450 million in combined criminal fines*, Press release, December 15, 2008.

Valderrama-Ferrando, L. (2006), *Institutional inertia*, Washington, DC: International Monetary Fund Institute Working Paper.

Van de Loo, B. (2004), 'The failure of the Philippine presidential system', *Asia Europe Journal* 2, 257–69.

Van Leeuwen, B. (2007), 'Human capital and economic growth in India, Indonesia and Japan: a quantitative analysis, 1890–2000', PhD dissertation, University of Utrecht.

Vernon, R. (1966), 'International investment and international trade in the product cycle', *Quarterly Journal of Economics*, **80**(2), 190–207.

Wade, R. (1990), *Governing the market: economic theory and the role of government in South East Asian industrialization*, Princeton, NJ: Princeton University Press.

Wajda, J. (2007), 'Generosity of R&D', Presentation to the TIP Workshop on R&D Tax Treatment in OECD Countries: Comparisons and Evaluation, Paris.

Walter, R. (1969), 'The intellectual background of the 1918 university reform in Argentina', *Hispanic American Historical Review*, **49**(2), 233–53.

Walwyn, D. (2007), 'Finland and the mobile phone industry: a case study of the return on investment from government funded R&D', *Technovation*, **27**, 335–41.

Warda, J. (1999), *Measuring the attractiveness of R&D tax incentives: Canada and major industrial countries*, Ottawa, Statistics Canada, Science, Innovation and Electronic Information Division, Cat. 880006XPB No.10.

Weimer, D.L., and A.R. Vining (1992), *Policy analysis: concepts and practice*, 2nd ed., Englewood Cliffs, NJ, Prentice Hall.

Wells, L.T., Jr. (1983), *Third world multinationals*, Cambridge, MA: MIT Press.

Werke, C., and S. Athreye (2004), 'Marshall's disciples: knowledge and innovation driving regional economic development and growth', *Journal of Evolutionary Economics*, **14**, 505–23.

Williams, J.R. (1994), 'Strategy and the search for rents: the evolution of diversity among firms', in R.P. Rumelt, D. Schendel, and D.J. Teece (eds), *Fundamental issues in strategy*, Boston, MA, Harvard Business School Press, 229–46.

Williamson, O. (1985), *The economic institutions of capitalism*, New York: Free Press.

Witt, U. (ed.) (1993), *Evolutionary economics*, Cheltenham, UK, Edward Elgar Publishing.

Wong, P.K. (2003), 'From using to creating technology: the evolution of Singapore's national innovation system and the changing role of public policy', in S. Lall and S. Urata (eds), *Competitiveness: FDI and technological activity in East Asia*, Cheltenham, UK, Edward Elgar Publishing, pp. 191–238.

World Bank (2003), *Combating corruption in Indonesia: enhancing accountability for development*, New York: East Asia Poverty Reduction and Economic Management Unit.

Wössmann, L. (2002), 'Cross-country evidence on human capital and the level of economic development: the role of measurement issues in education', *Historical Social Research*, **27**(4), 47–76.

Wu, Y., D. Popp, and S. Bretschneider (2007), 'The effects of innovation policies on business R&D: a cross-national study', *Economics of Innovation and New Technology*, **16**(4), 237–53.

Yamawaki, H. (2001), *The evolution and structure of industrial clusters in Japan*, Washington, DC: World Bank Institute.

Zahra, S.A., and G. George (2002), 'Absorptive capacity: a review, reconceptualization, and extension', *Academy of Management Review*, **27**, 185–203.

Zerbe, R.O., and H.E. McCurdy (1999), 'The failure of market failure', *Journal of Policy Analysis and Management*, **18**(4), 558–78.

Zhu, P., W. Xu, and N. Lundin (2006), 'The impact of government's funding and tax incentives on industrial R&D investments – empirical evidences from industrial sectors in Shanghai', *China Economic Review*, **17**, 51–69.

Zucker, L., M. Darby, and M.B. Brewer (1998), 'Intellectual human capital and the birth of U.S. biotechnology enterprises', *American Economic Review*, **88**(1), 290–360.

Index

absorptive capacity vii, 1, 2, 72, 90–91, 189–90, 198, 205, 217

Argentina vi, viii 43, 50, 58, 62, 65, 67, 68, 70, 71, 77, 78–80, 86, 88, 91, 95, 97, 102, 118, 125, 127–8, 132–144, 148–52, 158, 163, 165, 208, 213, 218, 221

Arthur, W. B. vii, 10, 28, 32, 61, 200

Bas, T.G. 52 173

Basque region 29, 179, 184–6, 193, 199

Bellon, B. 26, 27

Bourassa, M. 167, 171, 190

Brazil 6, 7, 26, 32, 43, 50, 58, 65, 67–8, 70–71, 77–80, 95, 100, 104, 114, 126, 134, 140, 142–4, 151, 188, 157, 194–5, 208, 218

Canada vi, 3, 6, 13, 23, 25, 33, 35–7, 45, 46–53, 62, 64–5, 67, 70, 73, 75–7, 79, 80, 84, 86–7, 89, 93, 95–8, 103–110, 112, 114, 117–18, 122–3, 132–3, 138–9, 142–4, 151–2, 154–7, 166–7, 171, 173, 188, 190–94, 199, 200, 202, 206, 209, 213–18

China vi, 1, 6, 14, 16, 26, 53, 55, 58, 64–7, 70–71, 74, 88, 90, 95, 98, 102–104, 110, 114, 119, 124, 160, 168, 209, 210–2

Cohen, W. M. vii, 2, 65, 72, 90

complex systems 10–11, 15, 16, 19, 20–1, 24, 34–6, 40–3, 59, 62, 67, 124

David, P.A. vii, 9, 32, 61, 204, 206

Egypt 125–8, 132, 138–9, 141–2, 145–150

Finland 3, 24, 33, 45, 88–9, 93, 97–8, 100, 103–104, 112, 116–121,

122–3, 138–9, 142, 166, 179, 180, 191–3, 199, 202, 209, 214

flying geese model 55–6, 58–9, 65, 71, 89, 113, 121, 209

Freeman, C. vii, 22–4, 61, 74, 168, 170, 204

horizontal policies 12, 61, 72, 86–88, 89, 107, 91, 99, 100, 101, 102, 192, 216

human capital vi, vii, 2–3, 13, 15–6, 19, 37, 39–41, 52–3, 55, 57–8, 63, 71, 72–74, 81, 87–8, 90–2, 93–95, 98–9, 102, 105–106, 108–111, 113, 116, 121–3, 125, 127–132, 145, 154, 158–9, 166, 167–8, 170, 181, 188, 192, 194, 198, 202–3, 208, 210, 216, 218

import substitution model 35, 55, 56–60, 71, 113, 134, 135, 151

India 1, 6, 26, 53, 57, 65, 67, 74, 90, 95, 102–104, 114, 119, 124, 168, 195, 218

industrial policy 22, 46–59, 67, 144, 180

innovation systems 22–45, 72, 85, 92, 98, 101, 109, 116, 120–21, 123, 135, 137, 142, 150, 165, 167–8, 170–71, 188, 192, 203–4, 215

national innovation systems defined 23

regional innovation systems defined 28

sectoral innovation systems defined 30

institutions vi, vii, 1–21, 22, 23, 24–8, 30, 32, 35, 41–2, 44, 46, 48–9, 52, 54, 55, 57–60, 62, 63, 66, 71–3, 74–89, 90–2, 94, 98–101, 106, 109–10, 113, 115, 117–121, 123–5, 128–30, 132, 133–136, 140–2,